W9-DFH-728

THE ZANZIBAR REVOLUTION
AND ITS AFTERMATH

THE
ZANZIBAR
REVOLUTION
AND ITS
AFTERMATH

by
ANTHONY CLAYTON

ARCHON BOOKS
HAMDEN, CONNECTICUT

First published in 1981 in England by
C. Hurst & Co. (Publishers) Ltd, London
and in the USA as an Archon Book
an imprint of
The Shoe String Press Inc.
995 Sherman Avenue
Hamden, Connecticut 06514

ISBN 0-208-01925-1

Library of Congress Cataloging in Publication Data

Clayton, Anthony, 1928-
   Zanzibar, revolution and aftermath.

   Includes bibliographical references and index.
   1. Zanzibar—History—Revolution, 1964. 2. Zanzibar—
—History.   3. Karume, Abeid Amani, 1905-1971.   I. Title.
DT435.75.C58   1981   967.8′104   81-3486
ISBN 0-208-01925-1   AACR2

Printed in Great Britain

For Judith
and the Children

ACKNOWLEDGEMENTS

If no one had attempted to write an account of the Russian or Chinese Revolutions until all the documents were available and fieldwork on the ground permitted, the world would have had to wait a long time — perhaps it would still be waiting. I am only too well aware of the lacunae yet to be filled in the history of Zanzibar's Revolution. But this awareness leads me also to a sharpened sense of gratitude to the many people who have helped me, occasionally at interviews but more often by sitting down to write useful letters in answer to troublesome requests.

Space makes it impossible to list the very large number of such helpers, but almost all of them are named in the footnotes. Many letters contained apologies for failing memory followed by two or three sentences of detail concerning some event which were invaluable and for which I am very grateful. I feel, however, a particular debt of gratitude to those people who offered me expertise, sent me long and full accounts of events, or let me read their family or other correspondence of the times. These included Mr J. de V. Allen, Mrs Janet Adams, Mr W.R. Belcher, Colonel A.N. Bell, Mr. R.H.V. Biles, Mrs E. Brittain, Mrs Joyce Dickson, Brigadier P.S. Douglas, Mr B. Eccles, Ms S. Field, Professor T.M. Franck, Mr A.H. Hawker, Mr Justice G.J. Horsfall, Mr C. Knight, Mr A.C. Ledger, Dr E.B. Martin, Major-General R.S.N. Mans, Mr D. McQueen, Mr P.H. Piggott, Vice-Admiral Sir Arthur Power, Mr W.D. Scott, Mr M. Smithyman, Mr P.A. Trace, Mr G.E. Tidbury, Mr T. Waring, Captain F.H. Woolias and Professor F. Wilson. I also owe a great debt to a number of Zanzibaris, all of whom asked to remain anonymous, and to Dr Kamoo Patel who now lives in India.

It is a pleasure also to thank the Librarians, and their staffs, of the Royal Commonwealth Society, the School of Oriental and African Studies, the University of California at Los Angeles, and the Royal Military Academy Sandhurst for their help, and to record my debt to the Archives Section of the Trade Union Congress, the Commonwealth Parliamentary Association, the Freedom of Information Staff of the United States State Department, the International Division of the British Red Cross Society and the Economist Intelligence Unit.

Nearer home, two of my colleagues and one of my students were deprived of some academic calm while this book was being written. Dr W. Bowring assisted me with his greatly superior knowledge of

Swahili and Mr A.R. Ward filled gaps in my understanding of populism, while Mr R. Darnley showed me some useful material on Zanzibari refugees in Oman.

I am also grateful for the comments on the manuscript made by Dr Robert Buijtenhuijs of the Afrika-Studiecentrum, Leiden, and to Dr T.C. Niblock of the University of Exeter for permitting me to draw on material in his doctoral thesis.

Many kind people, then, helped me, but none of them should be blamed for the conclusions I have drawn from the material they provided.

In 1975 I completed a study of the Zanzibar General Strike of August-September 1948, and this was published by the Scandinvaian Institute of African Studies, Uppsala, as a *Research Report*; a shortened version appeared as an article in the *Journal of African History*. I am grateful to the Institute and the *Journal's* editors for permission to use this material again here.

Although they were not in any specific way concerned with this work, I would like also to express my gratitude to Professors Roland Oliver and Richard Gray and the staff of African historians at the School of Oriental and African Studies. They always welcome me at seminars at which I have learnt so much in terms of general understanding of African history.

I also owe an especial debt to Miss G.M. Alexander, who with her customary skill, speed and accuracy deciphered and typed my manuscript. The dedication of this work reflects my last, and most lasting debt.

CONTENTS

PLATES

MAPS

UNGUJA

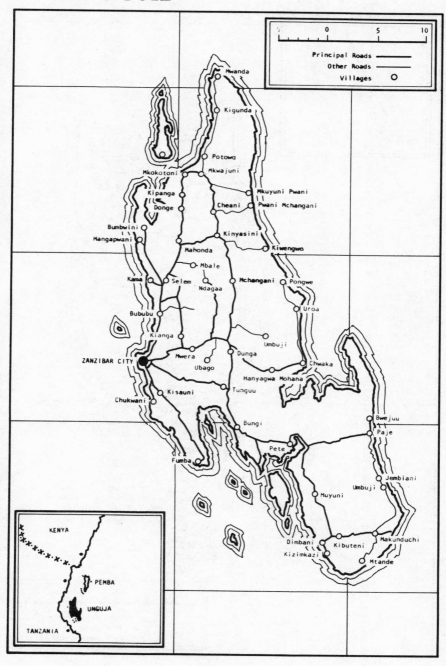

Principal Roads
Other Roads
Villages ○

Mwanda

Kigunda

Potowa
Mkokotoni   Mkwajuni
Kipanga
Donge   Cheani
                            Mkuyuni Pwani
                            Pwani Mchangani
Bumbwini
Mangapwani   Kinyasini
                                    Kiwengwa
            Mahonda
                Mbale
Kama   Selem   Mchangani   Pongwe
            Ndagaa
Bububu   Uroa
    Kianga
                            Umbuji
ZANZIBAR CITY   Mwera   Dunga   Chwaka
                Ubago
                Tunguu   Hanyagwa Mohana
        Kisauni
Chukwani
                        Bungi
                                        Bwejuu
                                        Paje
                            Pete
Fumba
                                        Jembiani
                                Umbuji
                        Muyuni
                Dimbani   Kibuteni   Makunduchi
                Kizimkazi
                                    Mtande

KENYA
PEMBA
UNGUJA
TANZANIA

PEMBA

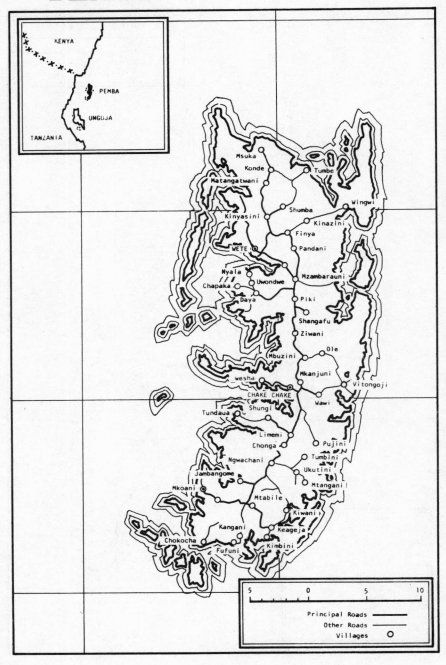

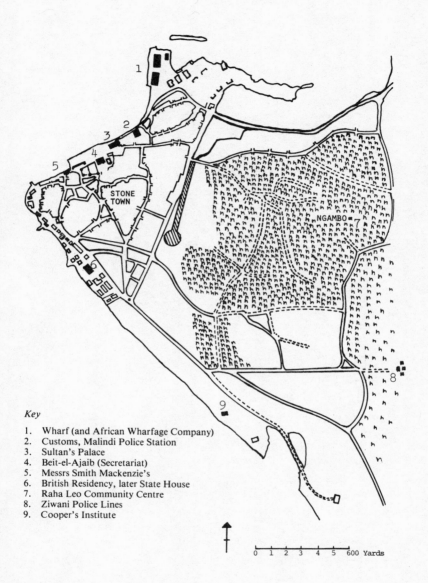

STONE TOWN

NGAMBO

Key

1. Wharf (and African Wharfage Company)
2. Customs, Malindi Police Station
3. Sultan's Palace
4. Beit-el-Ajaib (Secretariat)
5. Messrs Smith Mackenzie's
6. British Residency, later State House
7. Raha Leo Community Centre
8. Ziwani Police Lines
9. Cooper's Institute

0 1 2 3 4 5 600 Yards

ZANZIBAR CITY

INTRODUCTION

The January 1964 Revolution in Zanzibar is an event that has been surprisingly neglected by historians, appearing in many works only briefly as a violent preliminary to the formation of the United Republic of Tanzania and the development of Tanzanian Socialism. Only the causes of the Revolution have received some analysis in depth. The actual events in Zanzibar in the year 1964 and subsequently have not yet received the same attention, largely because of the impossibility of field research in the islands.

It is hoped that the present work will begin to fill this gap. Since it is based almost entirely on sources outside Zanzibar it must necessarily remain an incomplete account; on the other hand, it will at least place on record historical evidence from people present on the scene at the time which might otherwise be lost.

The Revolution, obviously, is significant viewed in Tanzanian terms, wherein it is perceived as the end of a period of an artificially imposed division between the islands and the mainland. But it is also an interesting and important event in several other contexts. Overall it highlighted one of Britain's failures in peaceful decolonisation. Some of the specific causes of that failure — commitment to the policy of indirect rule, the failure to recognise the significance of a large mainland migrant and partly settled labourer population, the inability of carefully drafted constitutions related to the distribution of Zanzibar's different communities and to the islands' political life to produce a government acceptable to a majority of the population, and the complete politicisation of the islands' communities to a level of pathological communal hatred — are of value in wider colonial and more general political studies. The Revolution itself was a notably bloody event, in bloodshed second only to Mau Mau in the period 1945–71 in East Africa. It was the product of a complex series of happenings which are themselves instructive, as are the actual processes of revolution at work in the streets, government offices and economic institutions. The bloodiness merits examination, since British colonial rule had not been harshly oppressive.

Zanzibar also briefly caught the attention of the world's major powers, their attitudes occasionally based on very misleading information or other diplomatic and political considerations, which in turn affected events in the islands. The Commonwealth was faced with a revolutionary and somewhat obscure régime expecting almost automatic recognition, an event for which there was no clear precedent although one was thereby created. The Union of Tanganyika and Zanzibar which followed the Revolution — in which Zanzibar retained, and still retains, a large measure of political and economic independence — is generally viewed as an interim arrangement until a more complete fusion can be effected. It is, however, more likely to be an early example of a new style of confederal or consociational arrangement that may emerge in states facing ethnic or regional secessionist demands. Tanzania was in its first decade an arrangement in which one region, Zanzibar, was much wealthier than the remaining areas, but there remained benefits in the Union for both parties which outweighed jealousies or resentments. In this sense the Revolution was a re-striking of the balance between the islands and the mainland; a dialogue, sometimes violent, that has long historical roots.

Lastly, the Revolution merits a place in any history of revolutions. Some revolutions merely replace one elite by another, others destroy economic structures and social systems, and still others not only re-stratify systems but also change the ethnic composition of a geographical area. Zanzibar's Revolution, despite the absence of any very clear or generally agreed ideas on what was to be introduced as an outcome, was one of this latter and in many ways most profound category of revolutions. The new balance struck between islands and mainland was one involving the expulsion of a large percentage of one major immigrant community, the Arabs, and the acceptance as permanent residents of a similarly large number of twentieth-century migrant African labourers from the mainland. But nevertheless, after a brief interlude in which it seemed a mainland assertion had ended the dialogue, it became clear that only those older-established mainland immigrants who accepted indigenous Zanzibar values and wishes for autonomy benefited or attained — and retained — office.

The dialogue between islands and mainland thus continued in a new form; it has not yet been replaced by either an administrative or an ideological absorption by the mainland. While Zanzibar retains its own sources of income, the dialogue seems likely to continue although its form is again, at the time of writing, in the process of change. And even if, as a precaution against any future loss of that income, Zanzibar merges more closely with the mainland, internal autonomy in many fields will undoubtedly be retained and the dialogue thus continued less conspicuously.

I. COLONIAL ZANZIBAR

The Pre-colonial Legacy and the Abolition of Slavery

Zanzibar belongs to two worlds; it is part of the African continent, but it has also, over centuries, been linked with Muslim politics of the Western Indian Ocean. On some occasions Zanzibar has been a gateway, on others a field of conflict. In a sense this dualism is symbolised by the different geographical origins of the two islands. Pemba was created by rift faulting, stretching up into Arabia, in the late Miocene age; while Unguja (Zanzibar Island)[1] became separated from the African mainland in the later Pliocene or Pleistocene ages, almost certainly by the submergence of an intervening track of low land. The waters between the two islands are very much deeper than the waters between Zanzibar and the mainland. These different origins produced two very different islands and societies with important local political consequences. However, the two small islands, with their teeming populations and plantation life only a bus journey or a walk from a township, stand in great contrast to the open expanses of the mainland.

The dualism is most marked in Zanzibar's indigenous population, a product of the great Bantu migrations on the one hand and successive Arab and other conquests on the other. The forebears of a present-day Zanzibari farmer in, say, the time of Augustan Rome, are likely to include both a peasant family in the area of the Cameroon Republic in West Africa, and a nomad family in the Arabian peninsula. Before the large-scale colonisation of Zanzibar begun by the Busaidi from Oman in the 1780s, there had been earlier Arab incursions both from Oman and elsewhere in Arabia. These had been absorbed, largely by intermarriage, and a local coastal culture had emerged based on Islam, the Swahili language (itself a product of this fusion, being a mixture of Bantu structures and many Arab words), and Indian Ocean trading links. This culture did not perceive the islands as two off-shore extensions of a vast African mainland but as something distinct and individual. In crudely physiological terms, the indigenous inhabitants of the two islands, too, are very often of a markedly lighter skin colour than Africans of the mainland.

1. To avoid confusion, and because it is so called by its inhabitants, the term Unguja will be used when reference is made to Zanzibar Island, as opposed to the Zanzibar Protectorate (of the two islands) or Zanzibar City.

1

British colonialism in Zanzibar rested politically (though not economically) on Arab sub-imperialism, which in turn stemmed from the Busaidi Omani Arab colonisation of the two islands, a process which began in the 1780s and continued till the middle of the nineteenth century. Slaves and cloves provided their motive. In 1840 Sultan Seyyid Said of Oman, the head of the Busaidi dynasty at the time, settled permanently in Zanzibar City; with him came officials and administrators, some of them Indian, to reinforce the land-expropriating Omani settlers and slave traders. The process of Arab colonisation was characterised by violence, often extreme, particularly in Unguja. Although some of the land seized was unoccupied, most of it appears to have been taken from the indigenous population by a mixture of physical occupation, intimidation and forced sales, with on occasions outright violence. The land taken was the best for clove-growing, the low hills that run a little way inland parallel to the western coast. There was in addition the violence of slave raiding and trading. Although this mostly took place on the mainland, the slave market in Zanzibar City, and the unloading, sale and subsequent despatch of gaunt, emaciated slaves into and out of reeking dhows all emphasised the atmosphere of violence — as did the sight, all too common in the mid-nineteenth century, of the corpses of dead slaves. Further, there were seasonal incursions of the Gulf Arabs, mainly from Muscat, who travelled to Zanzibar by dhow and for several months of the year lived as freebooters pillaging the land and its people at the point of the dagger. One of the most horrifying monuments to survive from the age of slavery is the group of slave pits at Mangapwani (trans. 'The Muscat men at the Coast') on the west coast of Unguja. In the early nineteenth century there were also minor feuds between different clans of Omani Arabs who forced the indigenous inhabitants into their private armies.

For the indigenous population the Arab colonisation of Unguja meant coerced labour, up-rooting, and a realisation that in their own island they were a subject race. The Arab administrators and plantation owners compelled indigenous men, reinforced by slaves from the mainland, to work, often in gangs, on ground clearance and the building of Zanzibar City, and in various forms of slavery or villeinage on their newly-acquired clove plantations. The total slave population in the mid-1890s amounted to some 40,000. The pressure of land alienation and labour obliged the true indigenous African peoples of Unguja to retreat to the large but less fertile and therefore less attractive coral areas of the island, the east and the north. The island's indigenous population was largely (but not entirely) composed of two ethnic groups, the Hadimu and the Tumbatu. These peoples had had a loose form of political organisation in the early part of the nineteenth century, more developed in the case of the Hadimu where a paramount ruler of part-Arab ancestry, the *Mwinye Mkuu*, presided over a number of local administrators (*sheha*) in whose selection the ruler had some say. The *Mwinye Mkuu*'s court was at Dunga. Initially the Arabs fought with this structure, exiling one ruler; they then used it as a means for extracting the land and labour they sought, but there was no room for two rulers on Unguja, and the paramountcy and Hadimu polity collapsed in the 1870s. The Tumbatu were less well organised and their resistance was even less effective. Both peoples were very different from the more homogenous ethnic groups of the mainland, their sense of unity was limited to vague (and often inaccurate) ideas of ancestry and an original home area, and each possessed certain distinct customs and linguistic usages; but these had evolved, as had the peoples themselves, from small groups that had together survived or adjusted to the successive waves of invaders. The groups were too small and the invaders too strong for any effective military organisation to have developed.

Much of Unguja is flat, or only very slightly hilly. Pemba, because of its different geological origin, has a number of higher hills and valleys and very much smaller areas of coral. This configuration makes it of very great economic importance, over 85 per cent of Zanzibar's cloves being grown there. Because of the difficulties of the terrain the Arab colonisation of Pemba took a different form from that of Unguja. The indigenous people were obliged to yield land to the Arabs, but thereafter the relationship was more amicable; although cases of torture and cruelty were noted, in Pemba they were exceptional. Indigenous labour used by the Arabs appears to have been rewarded, by either goods, pay or by the return of some land. The Arab plantations were smaller, and were often held alongside plantations still owned by indigenous people, some of the latter as well as the Arabs being sizeable slave-owners. Many plantations emerged on a half-and-half (*nusu-nusu*) pattern; ground was divided equally, the Arab provided clove seedlings and the local indigenous Mpemba cleared the terrain. Racial distinctions, so sharp in Unguja, soon became blurred in view of common economic interests, inter-marriage and concubinage. The island's traditional indigenous ethnic group, the Pemba, had even less cohesion than the Hadimu or Tumbatu, a feature again making a fusion and new loyalties easier.

Overall, to a very great extent in Unguja and even to some extent in Pemba, the pre-colonial legacy was one of a tradition of violence, covert if not overt. Among the indigenous peoples accounts of the past were passed on to the young by village raconteurs — and lost nothing in the telling. On their arrival, the British saw themselves as reformers and reconcilers, and in this they achieved for many years a substantial measure of success. But this success obscured from British eyes the passions of the past. To say that colonial Zanzibar possessed a sub-culture of violence among its indigenous inhabitants would be an exaggeration, but tensions from the past although temporarily submerged, were not forgotten and could surface suddenly in fierce quarrels or brawls. An observer as late as the early 1950s commented:

An official of the Clove Growers' Association whose duty it was to check and weigh bags brought in by Arab growers from their plantations told me how ugly situations could and did quite suddenly develop. A bag found short in weight, or faulty in some way and rejected, a small dispute about a matter of procedure, and there is growling. Soon clubs begin to be brandished and knives appear.[2]

The easy British belief of the 1920s, '30s and '40s that the past and its oppression had been forgotten was a dangerous complacency, as became clear in the later 1950s, and the pre-colonial legacy contributed to the pogrom character of the Revolution's bloodshed.

Britain's interest in Zanzibar stemmed from two major reasons, namely its strategic position in the Indian Ocean and the abolition of slavery. Britain's strategic concerns were constantly in the mind of London as a result of British interests in India, and fears over French activities in Réunion, the Comores and Madagascar, and later the German penetration of East Africa. But Britain was also heavily involved, throughout the nineteenth century, in attempting to end slave-trading and slavery itself. For this purpose the Sultans of Zanzibar were thought to be an agency that could be directed towards reform, and British consular officials applied strong and sustained pressure to reduce the trade and enslavement. After the closure of the slave market, Britain's interest turned to the status of the slaves within Zanzibar and the territories on the mainland claimed by the Sultans, a great weight of British public opinion demanding that Britain intervene to end slavery. This popular feeling in Britain coincided with British official anxiety over Germany's East African aims, and after the Anglo-German Convention of 1890 a formal protectorate was declared over Zanzibar in November of that year.

A variety of reasons led the British to use the Sultanate and the Arab oligarchy, wherever possible, as their agents in administration. One reason was a national predilection for monarchies and traditional institutions, a preference reinforced by experience of

2. F.D. Ommaney, *Isle of Cloves*, London, 1955, 120-1.

indirect rule in India. Another was some sense of guilt at Britain's inability to protect the Sultan's mainland interests, despite undertakings to do so. There was also a perception of possible repercussions in the Arab (Persian) Gulf and the Muslim world as a whole of any overthrow of the Sultanate. A final cogent reason was the cost of any alternative, notably more direct rule. So from 1890 to independence in 1963, under various constitutional and administrative procedures, the government of Zanzibar was carried on in the name of the Sultan. The Union Jack flew over the Residency and the Law Courts, but all other administrative offices and police stations flew the plain red flag of the Sultanate. The Sultan's Anthem was played before *God Save the King*. Most real power, however, lay in the hands of a senior British official, who from the time of the transfer of the Protectorate to the Colonial Office in 1914 was entitled the 'British Resident', and a small number of British colonial officials. While the appearance of British tutelage, protection and supervision over an Arab Sultanate was presented as a political policy, the British administration was also at times receptive to the considerable British and Indian trading and commercial interests that grew up in the Protectorate, particularly in and around Zanzibar City. Arab interests suffered in conflict with these wider British imperial and commercial concerns.

One of the first major measures of the British administration, the abolition of slavery, was an example of British response to these wider interests. As a result of persistent pressures from missionary and humanitarian interests, and frequent Westminster parliamentary debates and questions, a reluctant British Agent and Consul General, Arthur Hardinge, was directed to end slavery in 1897. Hardinge warned that Arab plantation owners would not survive the twin shock — the cost of the replacement of slave labour by wage labour and the loss of confidence arising from the destruction of a foundation of their social order. But on the insistence of Whitehall the measure was enacted. The main features of the legislation were that the legal status of slavery was no longer enforceable, slaves were to claim their freedom, and their former owners would receive compensation over a period of time. Freed slaves became liable for taxation — and prosecution for vagrancy if they were not gainfully employed. The consequences of the measure, particularly on Unguja, were to prove very important for the decades that followed. A general one needs mention here: in addition to the reasons for especial British concern for the Arab position in Zanzibar which have already been noted, feelings of apprehension and anxiety over abolition strengthened the British resolve to assist the Arabs retain political and economic ascendancy.

The Colonial Order

From abolition in 1897, a colonial order of political and economic institutions was developed under British supervision. This order gathered strength until the 1930s when, simultaneously, the first small cracks appeared: in politics the birth of an African nationalism and in the economy the consequences of the Depression and a change in the birth-rate of the indigenous Africans.

The hierarchy of government was dominated in practice by the British Resident. Under him British officials set the territory's finances in order and made a number of improvements in the efficiency of administration, the port, public health, agriculture and education. Economic activity was expanded, the export of cloves and later copra increased, and until the end of the 1920s Zanzibar profited from entrepot trade. From the *Beit-el-Ajaib*, the colonial secretariat, Zanzibar appeared to be making steady if unspectacular progress in the first thirty years of the century.

For most Zanzibaris the most significant figure in the Protectorate was not any British official but — after his accession in 1911 — the Sultan, Seyyid Khalifa bin Harub, who followed several rulers who were turbulent, short-lived or nonentities, and who was to rule until 1960. Khalifa has been largely ignored by historians as a British nominee of no particular relevance, but in a quiet and unostentatious way he was a most important figure. His ancestry and membership of the Busaidi dynasty made him, of course, popular with the Arabs; on the other hand, his partly African appearance[3], fluency in Swahili and concern for all his subjects gained him an affection and personal loyalty from Africans, both indigenous and mainlander. Another factor contributing to his popularity was his piety. He and his family belonged to the Ibadhi section of the Khawarij division of Islam, noted for their puritanism and dislike of public displays of wealth. Although Sultan Khalifa would often be taken for an evening drive in a large red car, before which his subjects touched their foreheads, laid their hands upon their chests or bowed — with genuine affection — his domestic life was of the simplest. So he was regarded as a figure who headed a culture at least part-African, in which the indigenous Zanzibari peoples and many Africans of the Kenya and Tanganyika coasts could feel a sense of participation and pride. His long reign, only disturbed in its last years by any serious violence which in his lifetime remained limited

3. The members of the House of Seyyid Said had not hesitated to use African concubines. These were in effect mostly no more than additional wives, who were well-treated, with their offspring enjoying equal status with the children of official wives.

in scale, accorded with general Muslim ideas of an order approved by Allah. Khalifa himself was seen to be treated with public deference and respect by the British officials who came increasingly to admire his courtesy, commonsense and blameless life. The British also saw what they wanted to see, a good monarch and a long reign of apparent peace. For his own part Khalifa kept himself well-informed of events in the islands[4] and was often able to alert the British administration to cases of abuse or discontent. Khalifa insisted at several points in his reign that Zanzibar must not be amalgamated with mainland territories (an idea favoured in Whitehall in the 1920s and early '30s). His insistence was based on his concern more for the protection of the Muslim religion and local culture than for the preservation of a privileged position by any race.

On these two major pillars, British administrative efficiency and a respected Sultanate, the political structure of the colonial order was therefore founded. The day-to-day life of administration, the appointment of junior officials and members of committees, school policy consultation and, later, appointment of members of the Legislature were all carried on by consultation with leading Arabs — to the Arabs' communal advantage. The African public had in consequence to deal in numerous ways and on frequent occasions with the administration's junior Arab officials. The British superiors of these officials deliberately delegated petty administration as part of the indirect rule policy, in contrast to the close interest in African society maintained by the administration of a directly administered colony such as Kenya. In particular most British officials felt that mainland migrant labour was only a temporary and not a permanent concern of the Zanzibar government — a Zanzibar version of the common British preference for Africans in traditional rather than urbanised societies.

The economic structure of colonial Zanzibar was based on British and Indian commerce and trade in Zanzibar City, on clove plantation owners — of whom many Unguja Arabs fell under the domination of Asian moneyleaders — and on the replacement of slave labour by the importation of mainland African labour in very considerable numbers — perhaps with hindsight the single most important feature of colonial Zanzibar — together with the ability of the Unguja indigenes to live without having to work on the labour market.

The Arab clove plantation-owners possessed estates of varying

---

4. It was said, and there seems no reason to doubt it, that one picturesque method of communication to the Sultan was the almost legendary one of singing under a palace window.

size; a small number of Asians also owned clove plantations. The large plantations on the west of Unguja were nearly all Arab-owned, while the smaller estates on the fringe of the clove area down the centre of the island generally remained in indigenous hands. The Arab-owned plantations had, however, largely fulfilled Hardinge's gloomy forecast at the time of abolition. The shock of abolition; the high wages which replacement labour required; poor management and husbandry standards; unwillingness to invest in improvement; an increasing tendency for owners to move into Zanzibar City (where life on Asian credit — often on severe terms — was thought more enjoyable), leaving their plantations to agents of varying levels of incompetence; crops leased to moneylenders; and lastly the use of unskilled, untrained labour poorly housed and sometimes poorly paid, who at times damaged trees at harvest time either by malice or ignorance, — all this amounted to a depressing picture. Some Arabs started to sell off part or all of their estates to indigenous Africans to pay off debts. The inheritance customs of the Arabs were based on Muslim law and required a division of estates between all male heirs (who could be numerous if a deceased landlord had had a number of wives or concubines). Female heirs also enjoyed certain rights which had to be respected. The prosperous trading years of the 1920s served only to delay and obscure the decline which had become a reality.

In Unguja the indigenous population, as has already been noted, had largely moved to the coral areas of the east, south and, in the case of the Tumbatu, the north where for a time they were able to preserve a considerable measure of economic independence. Several reasons contributed to this. It appears that the indigenous population total continued to decline in the first twenty-five years of the century. Tuberculosis was a major discernible reason, but with no doubt the impact of the Arab colonisation being equally important psychologically, though less easy to quantify. A second reason was that the African population of Zanzibar, indigenous and main-lander, paid no personal taxation; there was therefore no 'push factor' to coerce men out to work.[5] Lastly, indigenous communities were able to live at a standard they perceived as adequate. They occupied small but close-knit trading centre communities known as *miji* — aggregates of village clusters forming a small township, the land of which could not be sold to outsiders. The townships, often divided into moieties, would usually have a main street, stores, a mosque, houses and gardens, and a council of the more prominent

5. Colonial Zanzibar was financed principally by a clove export tax, though other forms of taxation were levied at different times.

citizens as an authority. Running across the townships were indigenous kinship groupings, *ukoo*, members of which might live near each other in one town but also possess family and commercial ties with others. Both the land arrangements and the social ones served to exclude outsiders.[6] The inhabitants of the *miji* were engaged in agriculture that was part-subsistence and part-commercial, the latter based on copra in the scattered areas where coconuts grew, but also including other fruits. They also engaged in fishing, and for a boat owner smuggling too was a lucrative pastime. Goods imported duty-free were taken by boat to the mainland where they undercut the same goods imported through a mainland port. 'Zanzibar uses in a year what it imports in a month' and 'The fishing boats set out at night loaded and return empty in the mornings' were two well-known colonial sayings. Other indigenes lived as small plantation owners in the centre of the island, also centred round small trading centres supplementing their home-grown food and clove sale incomes either with part-time work in the plantations, the rice-growing areas in the valleys and plains, or if they so wished in casual labour or petty trading in Zanzibar City. Of some significance for the future was the indigenous Africans' conservative concept of — within an ordered society — individually-owned plots of land for the growing of a variety of trees and fruits.

The last major constituent of the colonial order was the importation of mainland labour, the *wabara*. The significance of the mainlanders' role in the 1950s and in the Revolution requires that their place be given careful examination. They are an interesting social group. They fell into two broad categories, post-1900 immigrants on the one hand and ex-slaves or their descendants on the other. No figures for these categories exist, but a Survey made in 1948 made a division in the population tables between those born on the mainland and those born in the Protectorate, which is useful subject to the reservation that many of the children of earlier immigrants would have been recorded as Zanzibar-born mainlanders. The majority group were a variant of the colonial migrant labour system — recent or other twentieth-century immigrants who had come to Zanzibar to earn money to pay tax, purchase some preferred consumer goods or enlarge their families by the acquisition of an extra wife. This migration had begun early in the century; the Zanzibar and East African Protectorate (Kenya) authorities engaged in specific recruiting until the E.A.P.'s own labour difficulties ended this procedure, but the

6. For further details of these communities there is a useful account in John Middleton and Jane Campbell, *Zanzibar, Its Society and Politics*, London, 1965.

migration continued to be maintained by a steady stream of labour which arrived voluntarily. In the 1920s and '30s, the Zanzibar government operated a steamship which sailed weekly to and from Dar es Salaam with a very cheap deck passenger fare. The majority, however, travelled by dhow on cheaper and less formal arrangements. Mainland African labourers were virtually exempt from immigration control; in theory some control existed over men from Mozambique and Nyasaland (later Malawi), but this was rarely applied. No identity check existed until the 1950s, and anyone could enter under any name he wished. A vaccination certificate was required, but this could be obtained free, and if time was short, one could usually be borrowed. The need for the labour was made greater, up till *c*.1930, by the developing indigenous involvement with copra and consequent increased unwillingness to work as labour for the Arabs or anyone else. The system was facilitated by the fact that Swahili was spoken by the mainland peoples of the Kenya and Tanganyika coast, and migrant labourers from peoples further inland and in Nyasaland often had sufficient knowledge of the language to find unskilled work. Also, despite its past reputation, the prestige that was held by Zanzibar as the centre of Swahili cultural life was a real attraction.

The ex-slave category of mainlander did not in general possess the physique or strength necessary for sustained hard manual labour. Since the indigenes were reluctant to undertake plantation labour, there could be no reduction of immigration by means of a new young generation of Zanzibar-born labourers. Mainland labour, seen as migrant and temporary, was believed to be the only solution. The process of the recruitment of this labour in the 1920s was described by the Director of Agriculture in his report for 1924:

The Headmen of the Wanyamwezi were brought to my office and it was explained to them that the work they had to do in Zanzibar was very much less than they had been accustomed to do in their own country whereas the pay they received was very much higher. . . . The intention was that they should be better off here than at home because we wanted them to come here. . . .[7]

The wages certainly were among the highest paid anywhere in East and Central Africa, usually Shs 30 per month, far superior to the cash earning of a 'squatter' or resident labourer on a European-owned farm in Kenya at the time, who would be lucky to receive Shs 13 or 14.[8] The report later observed:

7. *Agriculture Department Report, 1924.*
8. A.G. Church, *East Africa: a New Dominion*, London, 1928, 168. Church was a member of the (British) East Africa Parliamentary Commission of 1924.

It is remarkable that the population of the Island Dominions of His Highness the Sultan amounts to about two hundred per square mile, and yet in spite of the fact that there is practically no industry outside agriculture, the country is to a large extent dependent upon imported labour.

The *District Administration Reports* record the following immigration figures:

	Mainlanders Entering	Leaving
1923	4,334	2,478
1924	4,233	1,740
1925	3,820	3,943
1926	5,392	2,813
1927	*No figures published*	
1928		
1929	448	1,025
1930	790	1,071
1931	2,368	965

Note: The issue of movement passes was stopped as an economy measure in 1932.

It seems reasonable to assume that this process had from the turn of the century increased the mainland population of Zanzibar by some 1,500–2,000 a year on average, perhaps more in the earlier years, as the First World War had ended the importation of rice from the Far East, and labour was needed to grow it in Zanzibar. Initially their tasks were limited to P.W.D. road gang work and plantation weeding, sometimes also cultivating work but with only the indigenous peoples retaining the interest in profiting from seasonal clove-picking. Later the mainlanders were able to participate in this also. Many mainlanders from coastal ethnic groups became boat crewmen. They generally arrived to work on contracts of 1–3 months; sometimes these contracts were renewed, and sometimes the labourer moved on to a new employer or became a squatter, the status of which is examined later. Although the government viewed them, in the words of reports of the time, as 'temporarily settled', many stayed for long periods and others for a year or two only. The increase tailed off at the end of the 1920s and was not to resume in any volume until the 1950s.

A large number of these mainlanders were animist or Christian; in the case of the Nyamwezi and the Nyasa, as many as one-third may have been Christian, but much smaller percentages are more likely for the Manyema, Yao and Matumbi. Others from the coastal areas of Kenya and Tanganyika were Muslim, notably the Zaramo who were almost entirely so. More precise proportions are difficult to estimate, one reason being that the mainlanders often temporarily professed a conversion (evident in the wearing of cloth caps by the men and *bui bui* by their wives) for their own advantage in seeking work, and while at work, in the islands.

A conversion either temporary or permanent had advantages of social status as well as those for work-seeking; wearing a *kanzu* a man identified himself with local society. The Moslem religion, too, accorded well with Bantu custom, with its respect for elders, its preference for community rather than the individual, and its liking for continuity. It imposed few restraints on private life.[9]

A census in 1948 suggests that the origins of the mainlanders (both categories) were as shown in the accompanying table.[10]

Ethnic group	Unguja	Pemba	Total
Tanganyika			
Nyamwezi	5,845	2,408	8,253
Zaramo	3,847	1,563	5,410
Makonde (incl. some from P.E.A.)	2,356	269	2,625
Dengereko	1,943	195	2,138
Maniema (incl. some from Congo)	1,899	303	2,202
Other	1,595	361	1,956
Nyasaland			
Nyasa	3,372	1,866	5,238
Yao	2,759	1,100	3,859
Mozambique			
Zigua	1,120	559	1,679
Kenya	173	134	307
Uganda	411	55	466
Other mainland tribes	12,084	5,060	17,134
Total	37,404	13,873	51,277

The reference in the table to other mainland groups included some of the second, minority category of mainlanders,[11] ex-slaves or their descendants, who were often reluctant to admit slave ancestry. On

9. An account of these processes at work in Dar es Salaam appears in J.A.K. Leslie, *A Survey of Dar es Salaam*, London, 1963, 11–12.
10. 1948 Census, quoted Middleton and Campbell, *op. cit.*, 21. The census totals were not taken at clove picking time when much higher figures would have appeared.
11. A Social Survey of Zanzibar 1948, 1962, 'Population' (I) notes that one-third of the male mainland Africans and one-fifth of the female were born outside the protectorate. In Zanzibar City 47% of the mainland population were immigrants, and in the rest of Unguja 32%. The Survey's projections estimated 14,400 immigrant mainlanders on Unguja out of a total of 18,000 immigrant mainlanders for both islands, and of these some 8,450 in the Unguja rural area and 5,960 immigrants in Zanzibar City.

their liberation they were landless; the close-knit indigenous communities prevented all but a handful of the freed slaves settling in the coral areas. Some tried out their fortunes as settlers on plots in the central area, and these found integration easier. The remainder, who were the majority of the ex-slaves, had remained with their masters in domestic service or with various forms of tenancy arrangements on the estates on the west side of the island. A few had gone to Zanzibar City. Those on the estates usually worked for a few days each week on their masters' land and clove trees in return for a small cash wage and a plot of their own, or for the right to grow their own cash crops under their masters' trees for their own use and for sale in Zanzibar City and elsewhere.

This relationship was known as 'squatting' but the term remained loose and undefined as was 'resident labourer' in Kenya; it covered a very wide variety of arrangements. Sometimes squatters were allowed to own fruit trees, the usual practice being the sharing of produce between farmer and squatter, but they were not allowed to grow cloves or coconut. These ex-slave squatters could, with permission from the plantation owners (this was usually given), pass on their rights to their descendants. The number of squatters was of course further increased by the newer arrivals from the mainland who preferred agriculture to work in the city. The 1924 census, for example, notes a higher proportion of the Nyamwezi group of peoples at work in weeding than in general labour of the road gang type, in contrast to the Zaramo, Nyasa and Yao, where the proportions were reversed. Many Mozambique Makonde became nightwatchmen on remote estates. Custom at the time permitted squatting, including hut-building and subsistence crop-growing on the land if there was room and the owner did not object; it further did not countenance evictions. One can therefore discern different types of squatter emerging. These have some relationship to their community of origin, although numerous exceptions must warn against too precise categorisation.[12] Many of the longer-established ex-slaves and their descendants saw themselves by the 1940s as Hadimu, either through beliefs about their ancestry or through marriage, and had been accepted as such. But some of the ex-slaves and almost all the twentieth-century immigrants still saw themselves

12. I am much indebted to Professor F.B. Wilson (lately Professor of Agriculture at the University of East Africa) and Mr G.E. Tidbury (Director, Commonwealth Bureau of Agriculture), both former Zanzibar Government Agriculture Department officers, and Mr T.C. Colchester and the Hon. A.P.H.T. Cumming-Bruce, both former Zanzibar administrative officers, for their advice to me on Zanzibar's agriculture.

as mainlanders. No statistical information is available, but it can be argued that the degree of economic integration of the ex-slave, and of the mainlander, is likely to have depended on length of stay, physical health and energy, and adherence to Islam, the religion of most estate owners who might be more generous to co-religionists. Many of the ex-slave squatters were a depressed community with little social cohesion and little energy; they squatted on old estates, lived in poorly-built huts and engaged in casual work while growing subsistence crops such as cassava, sweet potato and banana, with perhaps some rice. Additionally both men and women harvested cloves.

The twentieth-century immigrants often began simply as weeders on one of the better estates with a small plot for subsistence food-growing to supplement their meagre wages for the duration of their stay. A number returned to the mainland after eighteen months, but those that decided to remain used the asset of their superior physique, which made them popular with employers, to advance to improved terms which might provide rights to grow crops for sale but no rights to grow trees; in this category were also some of the more fortunate ex-slave mainlanders and a very few indigenous squatters. The complex Muslim land law arrangements allowed of situations in which one man might be in a position approximating to land ownership, with two, three or more others enjoying specific legal rights for cultivation or fruit-growing. The best-placed squatters were those with rights to grow both the actual fruit trees (orange, lime, mango, lemon, bread-fruit and pawpaw) together with cash crops; some mainlanders had advanced to this status, as again had a very small number of indigenes. Some mainlanders had been so successful in advancing themselves over the years that with the profits from their work they had purchased their own small plots of land. However, such men, who had advanced by hard work from the rough *makuti* shelter of a squatter weeder, on a remote estate managed by an agent on behalf of an impoverished absentee owner, to seeing themselves as permanent farmer residents could and did feel mounting resentment against Arab and indigenous exclusiveness. This in time led to overt contempt.

The clove estates on Pemba being smaller, the number of mainlanders was considerably lower — extra labour, in general, only being required at clove-picking times when large numbers of men arrived for a brief stay of two or three weeks only.[13] Indigenous clove plantation-owners, on both Unguja and Pemba, who grew most subsistence crops and lived less ostentatiously, were better able to

13. Census figures for mainlanders in respect of 1924, 1931 and 1948 are as follows (indigenous figures follow in brackets):

survive poor clove prices.

This triad of British and Indian commercial control, a flagging Arab plantation economy, and African indigenous peasants and mainland migrant labour, constituted the colonial order. It was an order that contained a number of distinctive features. The British administration, nourished on the Lord Lugard creed of Indirect Rule, never attempted to foresee the consequences of the changing social pattern. Not entirely without reason, the British believed Islam to be a unifying factor which could reconcile Arabs and indigenous Africans, but the mainlander was to be ignored. The British long-term aim for Zanzibar, never precisely set out, appeared to be something in the nature of a Gulf Sultanate. British officials were historically-minded; personal memoirs and official *Annual Reports* all showed a strong historical stance in favour of the House of Seyyid Said, devoting lengthy sections to the various Sultans. But this perspective became increasingly distorted. The exceptional beauty, romance and exoticism of Zanzibar also served to distract attention from its social problems. Although honest and reasonably efficient, the British administrators were often unimaginative; service in Zanzibar was in any case not attractive to the more ambitious colonial officials,[14] who quickly moved on elsewhere. Also, it was the style of British administration to prefer to see peoples in compartments. Asians were to be traders, Arabs junior officials and plantation owners, and Africans, indigenous or mainland, were to be labourers.

This style of labelling racial communities in social class terms was to provide fuel for subsequent unrest. Even in its heyday it served to strengthen an ill-founded social class structure, because the Arabs, who as landowners and junior administrative officials were supposed to be the chief beneficiaries, failed to meet British expectations — which was hardly surprisingly since on the land the plantations were debt-ridden, in trade the Asians were very much more

	Unguja	*Pemba*
1924	38,590 (68,383)	26,238 (50,977)
1931	44,492	*No figures available*
1948	37,404 (81,150)	13,873 (67,330)

A.H.J. Prins, in *The Swahili Speaking Peoples of Zanzibar and the East African Coast*, London, 1961, 19, speculates that the apparent fall in people of mainland origin in Pemba may be due to some measure of absorption and personal re-classification.

14. The post of Resident in Zanzibar was generally viewed as of 'failed Governor' status. Only two Residents ever received another appointment after Zanzibar.

capable, and in government the British retained senior posts. The classification was never formalised or rigid, but the few examples of social mobility served only to reinforce the British misconception that wider opportunities existed. Formal administrative and political debate in the period up to the outbreak of the Second World War was limited to administrative officers considering whether the government should attempt to preserve the Arab plantations, and if so how. The method selected in the 1930s took the form of official support for a largely Arab-dominated Clove Growers' Association, which included among its objectives a reduction in wages and some regulation of the market price of cloves (so many clove plantation owners had mortgaged their crops in advance that this latter aim was not achieved). Other measures designed to protect the Arab land-owners were controls on land sales to Asians, and various attempts to control Asian mortgages on Arab lands so as to force Asian creditors to pay more tax, and to impose a moratorium on Arab and indigenous debts to Asians. Such anti-Asian measures inevitably produced an Asian political riposte supported by the Government of India, and the policy had to be modified. All this, however, was essentially a conflict of interests between the different groups that controlled the economy. Neither the politics of the time nor the Legislative Council established in 1926 (which contained strong Arab Unofficial representation[15] but no African Unofficial Members, either mainland or indigenous) reflected the more fundamental fissures that had begun to appear in the colonial order in the 1930s. In the context of these fissures, colonial politics of the period were largely irrelevant.

Depression and the Birth of Nationalism

The first of the fissures in the colonial order was the stirring of a specific African nationalism. In 1934 an African Association for Immigrant Workers, later known simply as the African Association, was formed. Its immediate origins lay in football teams of young Africans that had begun to appear in the late 1920s;[16] in 1931 all con-

15. Colonial legislatures, before the introduction of full electoral systems, were divided into Official and Unofficial Benches. The Official Bench contained senior officials, also Government Nominated Members selected for expertness in a particular field but generally expected to support the government. The Unofficial Bench members were free to criticise any aspect of government policy.

16. See R.K. Mwanjisi, *Ndugu Abeid Amani Karume*, Zanzibar, 1967, 16 (Swahili text). The clubs bore such titles as Vuga Boys F.C., New Generation

verged to form an African Sports Club whose A team went on a tour to Tanganyika the same year. The Association protested against conditions of labour recruitment for Pemba, and began correspondence with the Tanganyika African Association; two joint meetings of members were held, one in Zanzibar and one in Dar es Salaam. The future post-Revolution leader, Abeid Amani Karume, first appears in this context.

Karume claimed to have been born on 4 August 1905 at Pongwe, some 14 miles from Zanzibar City. His father was a Nyasaland migrant agricultural worker and his mother came from Rwanda. Abeid was the eldest of a family of five, for whom he had to accept some responsibility as his father died when he was eight. He received some primary schooling, and then in 1918 went to Zanzibar City to earn a living. He became a sailor, at first on a coastal steamer that plied between Tanga and Mikindani; then he sailed on a larger British ship (so his biographer claims) to Europe, Canada, India, the Far East and Japan. His biographer adds that it was these travels that instructed him in the evils of capitalism and gave him the self-confidence to argue in debate. In 1938, after retiring finally from the sea, Karume used the status he had gained in the football clubs and the African Association to form a loose association of African boatmen to prevent an Asian motorboat fleet from forcing them out of business. In the war years he formed an African dancing club, using the popularised *taarab* music, originally Arab but now Swahili in culture. He perceived dancing as being as much political as social; he also became an official of the African Association. After the war Karume ran a syndicate of small boat owners which he was later to represent as a trade union and use as a base to defend the interests of Africans on Zanzibar City Council.[17]

The African Association, however, did not prove a very effective organisation; also, the distribution of the mainlanders, partly on the land and partly in Zanzibar City, and their many different original ethnic groups and languages militated against any effective organisation. There were no Zanzibar equivalents of the big ethnic associations to be found in Mombasa or Nairobi. Informal associations existed; the ex-slave mainlanders were often linked together in dance groups, and the twentieth-century immigrants were linked ethnically in loosely organised savings clubs, centred around a respected figure

---

F.C., New Kings F.C. and United Services F.C. Karume played for several of these teams. His biographer, in a section entitled 'Unity from Games', notes that the teams were seen by the African elders of the town as 'an arm of the elders who knew they had the same feelings'.

17. Mwanjisi, *op.cit.* 9–19.

of long residence who would arrange assistance from the club members in cases of sickness or death. Each member paid in a small amount per month and might take a small balance home when his turn came round. A largely Pemba-based 'Shirazi Association'[18] for indigenous Zanzibaris was formed in 1939, but it did not see itself in any way as a militant pressure group. Both the origin of this Association and the shape of the African Association until 1953 lay more in the government's need to have communal associations with whom to consult, itself a by-product of the typed, classified style of the British administration. Minor government officers were allowed to serve on the committees of both Associations, which again limited any tendency for sharp criticism of the colonial order. The two Associations did not work together and on occasions openly quarrelled. In 1947 the African Association in Zanzibar also severed its links with the mainland African Association whose politics were becoming too militant for the civil servant leaders of the former.

Thus the political fissures, although indicative of a profound trend, seemed on the surface to be slight. With the exception of the Depression of the 1930s, which was believed to be a passing phenomenon, and the continuing decline of the Arab plantations, it was equally hard to see in the economic fissures any potential future gravity. The Depression years saw a reduction of the clove prices by two-thirds or more (20–23 rupees per *frasila*[19] in 1928 to 7 or 6 rupees in the worst years); growing cloves was uneconomic and the Arab plight became more desperate. A contemporary estimate made out that some 25 per cent of the clove trees on Unguja were mortgaged to Asians; sometimes the Arab 'owner' had in fact 'sold' his estate and its crops to an Asian money-lender and lived and worked on the

18. Until 1939, most but not all of Zanzibar's indigenous peoples would have thought of themselves as belonging to one of the three peoples already noted — the Hadimu, Tumbatu or Pemba — or sometimes as a Swahili. As a reaction to the arrival of the mainlanders, the term 'Shirazi' started to be used by increasing numbers of indigenes, but again by no means all. 'Shirazi' reflects a claim that the indigenes originally came from a Middle Eastern civilisation and culture superior to that of the mainlanders. It can be said that all Shirazi would be indigenes, and, like almost all indigenes, Sunni Muslims. But not all indigenes, particularly before the 1950s, would choose to call themselves Shirazi.

A further factor is that before the 1950s an established status as an Arab was economically advantageous — particularly if some part — Arab ancestry could be advanced to support it. An apparently enormous increase in the Arab population in the first half of the century, indicated in the censuses of 1924, 1931 and 1948, can therefore be almost entirely ignored.

19. 64 *frasila* = 1 ton.

plantation as the nominal owner but in practice as the manager. It was against this background that the Arab-Asian political conflict noted earlier was fought.

The demand for immigrant workers fell. Much more seriously, both the numbers and perceived status of mainlanders, who had arrived as a 'labour aristocracy' and as such had settled temporarily, also began a slow process of decline, to become exacerbated in the years immediately after the Second World War. They were no longer a privileged category, paid well above other East African rates. This process is most conveniently summarised from the perspective of 1948, the year of the General Strike in Zanzibar City, one cause of which was a culmination of this process. Decline had not become acute in the years before the Second World War; it was limited to a beginning of doubt and uncertainty where previously among the more enterprising of the migrant mainlanders there had been confidence, security and a chance to prosper.

Also scarcely noticed at the time (where noticed, it was seen as a gain), the indigenous population almost certainly passed its lowest point somewhere in the late 1920s and began to rise.[20] At this stage the rise did not lead to anxiety over and competition for land, but again these were to appear shortly after the end of the war.

The matters formally discussed in political debate were irrelevant to these nascent African political and economic challenges. The administration was stagnant, content to let society crystallise into race, caste and class. One visiting British Indian Civil Service official, Sir Alan Pim, commented astringently on the Zanzibar administration as never having 'developed a consistent policy with reference either to the all-important question of land or to any other question of native development'.[21] Equally irrelevant to the real themes of conflict were the only examples of open violence and unrest in the years before 1939. Of the very few instances, two — which took the form of riots — involved the 'Manga' Arabs, the how crews and petty traders who still continued to arrive seasonally

20. R. Kuczynski, *Demographic Survey of the British Colonial Empire*, II, London, 1949, 684, quotes a despatch dated 10 June 1930 from the Resident noting the Director of Medical Services' view that 'a fairly large decrease in the resident population has now been turned into a slight increase'. No accurate figures exist, but this statement does appear to summarise the evidence available at the time. It also matches the pattern in Kenya.

21. *Report of the Commission appointed by the Secretary of State for the Colonies to consider and Report on the Financial Position of the Zanzibar Government in relation to its Economic Resources*, London, 1932, 21. Pim also commented on the general stagnation of the territory.

from Arabia, sometimes staying for a year or so. The first, a conflict between Manga and permanently settled Arabs over an issue of Arab custom, took place in 1928, and the second — following an attempt by the Agriculture Department to improve the quality of cloves and coconuts, the Manga grown quality being notably poor — in 1936. This violence was understandably seen as involving a community not permanently Zanzibari and one notoriously wild. Nor did the burglary crime rates in the period, often an important indicator, provide any particular cause for anxiety. The one outbreak of open unrest significant for the future but not leading to any bloodshed occurred in 1928 and early 1929, when disputes between ground landlords — Asian, Arab and occasionally indigenous — and house-owners (i.e. tenants who had built the huts) in the African areas of Zanzibar City resulted in disorders. The government arrested and deported the most violent elements, imposed a system of rent control, and believed the matter to have been settled. It remained the overall British view that the peace which had prevailed in Zanzibar since the turn of the century had come to stay.

II. THE FINAL COLONIAL YEARS

The Second World War proved unexpectedly to be a very prosperous time for Zanzibar, particularly after the Japanese conquest of the Netherlands East Indies. The latter stimulated even further the British demand for Zanzibar's copra which, together with cloves, fetched increasingly useful prices. The war and the return of prosperity produced a sense of purpose uniting all the islands' inhabitants, in particular ending much of the bitterness between Arabs and Asians. All the inhabitants of the islands benefited from the government's encouragement to grow more food. Many of the Arab plantations found themselves cleared of debt — which, a few years earlier, would have seemed inconceivable. The government found itself able to raise some direct personal income and profits taxation, the revenue from which was spent in some expansion of educational, medical and other social services.

The Post-War Scene

The British administration saw this as encouraging, and could see no reason why the conditions of the pre-1939 imperial heyday should not return. In the Indian Ocean Communism was perceived as the overriding threat to this outcome, particularly after the beginning of the Malayan insurgency; British reassertion therefore seemed very desirable. The significance of the growth of nationalism in West Africa was not recognized in East Africa, particularly in Zanzibar where the tried system of the British-supervised Sultan's law and order seemed in no need of change. Furthermore, the small size of the Protectorate, its apparent tranquillity and the dignity of the Sultan all led to an almost total absence of any metropolitan British interest in it, compared with the interest taken in bigger territories such as Kenya and Nigeria. The personal prestige of Khalifa seemed to the British also to be a guarantee for the Sultanate's future, as well as making any radical transformation of society appear both unnecessary and impracticable. There was universal popular rejoicing on the occasion of Khalifa's seventieth birthday in August 1949. Although the fact is not noted in his biography, even Abeid Karume was at this time proud to be an oarsman for the Sultan's ceremonial barge. Khalifa had achieved a natural personal legitimacy — partly as a consequence of his part-African ancestry, which likened him to the former *Mwinye Mkuu*, and partly as a personification of both

21

elements of Zanzibar culture, Africa and the Muslim Western Indian Ocean. The personal nature of this legitimacy was not perceived, nor was consideration given to its prospects of surviving combined challenges of racial nationalism and Khalifa's age and death.

Below Khalifa and an upper tier of senior British officials were a number of middle-rank Arab officials.[1] Men such as Yahya Alawi and Salim Barwani, the first Arab district commissioners, were of very high calibre and genuinely concerned for all the inhabitants of the islands; others were less able and impartial, and a few even professed an inability to speak any language other than Arabic, although all must in fact have been fluent in Swahili. Only at the very junior levels such as *sheha* (headman) were indigenous Africans to be found in the administration and in the other departments. In the police the great majority of non-commissioned officers and constables were mainlanders, whereas elsewhere mainlanders were only to be found in very small numbers and in very junior appointments in technical departments such as the Public Works Department (P.W.D.) and Public Health. The pre-war fissures of the early stirrings of nationalism, the presence of the mainlanders and the increase in the indigenous population were still not seen as serious. In fact, a series of crises was building up.

In the immediate post-war years the general arousal of nationalist and anti-colonial sentiments carried a particular local significance in Zanzibar, due to Arab resentment at British policies in Egypt and Palestine. As a reflex to the emergence of Zionism, an 'unfamiliar Arab arrogance' was discernible. Arab nationalism of course had roots reaching back to the establishment of British rule and the abolition of slavery, the latter being seen as having caused the decline of Arab agriculture. Young Arabs began to travel and study in Egypt when the war was over, and a Muslim day of shop-closure and strikes took place as early as 12 December 1947. Other forms of racial expression were bound to follow in a territory with so racial a hierarchical structure.[2] For example, many Zanzibar inhabitants, including both indigenous Africans and permanently domiciled Arabs, were from different points of view beginning to feel that

1. In 1947 'His Highness's Zanzibar Service' was created. One of its objectives was to train young Zanzibaris for more responsible posts after secondary and tertiary education. The large majority of appointments went to Arabs, and only to small numbers of Asians and of either group of Africans.
2. The Hon. A.P.H.T. Cumming-Bruce to the author, 20 June 1975: 'Just as it did more obviously at independence, this arrogance triggered off African self-consciousness; the term '*mwafrica*' was a new and unfamiliar one'.

wealth was being steadily drawn off either by British or by Indian commercial interests — to Arabia by the dhow trade or to the mainland through migrant labourers' wage packets escaping all taxation. As elsewhere in Africa, returning ex-servicemen were notably restive. The growing post-war use of the term 'Shirazi' — the assertion by indigenous Africans of their particularity — was an indication of this sentiment. This climate of opinion encouraged indifference to the predicament of mainlanders, and such indifference prompted the mainlander to see himself as the only true representative of African opinion.[3] Two further factors contributed to this growing racial consciousness and disquiet. One was the Zanzibar government's attempts — in accordance with overall British colonial policy at this time — to develop local government bodies, generally presided over by Arab notables. This was often highly unpopular among Africans,[4] as was the first appointment of an Arab officer as District Commissioner for Zanzibar City. Another cause of resentment was the report of a Colonial Office civil service salaries commission on public officials salaries in all four East African territories: this had reported in favour of racial salary scales disadvantageous to Africans.

The general overall economic climate of the early post-war years was also unfavourable. The clove harvest in 1947–8 was disastrous, with that of 1948–9 only a little better. To make matters worse an incurable disease, 'sudden death', attacked the clove bushes. In Zanzibar City the cost of living, in particular relating to foodstuffs and clothing for Africans, had continued to rise slowly, but wages had remained generally at the 1945 level. Although the government operated a number of price-control regulations, the scarcity of some goods, particularly imported foostuffs, led to a black market. Each of the two African communities, mainlander and indigenous, also found itself faced with particular problems. For the mainlanders — largely but not entirely a labouring population — the problems led to a General Strike in Zanzibar City in August-September 1948. In the case of the indigenous the problems underlay bitterness and tension over proposed land alientation for an extension to Zanzibar airport and also certain stock inoculation measures in the years 1949 to 1951.

3. *Annual Report, Zanzibar Protectorate, 1946*, Zanzibar and London.
4. D.B. Barber, Zanzibar Administration at the time, to the author, 24 May 1975. Barber commented that, as a district commissioner, he received numerous complaints from Africans on this subject.

The General Strike of 1948

By 1948 51,000 of the African population of the islands, which totalled just under 200,000, considered themselves as mainlanders. Of these 51,000, 37,404 lived on Unguja where they represented almost one-third of the African population. The Arab population at this time numbered 44,560, of whom 13,977 lived on Unguja; these totals include a number of people of mixed ancestry who in this period still perceived themselves as Arabs, or found it advantageous to do so. The Asian population was 15,892, of whom the large majority, 13,705, lived on Unguja. With smaller numbers of Comorians and Europeans the Protectorate's total population was registered as 264,162.[5]

Overall, despite exceptional success stories of squatters becoming small plot-owners, there existed little scope for mainlanders on the land, whether as a means of escape from the city or as a way of supporting demands for improved conditions in the city by providing a profitable alternative to employment there. An indication of the frustration was to be seen in March 1947 during a strike of resident labourers, who were on the whole mainland Nyamwezi, at the government's research station at Kizimbani. These labourers, by contemporary standards reasonably well-paid and living in a 'model village', backed their demands for higher wages with threats of intimidation.[6] Conditions in the city were also becoming more difficult for a variety of reasons. In a long-term perspective, Zanzibar had been a major entrepôt in the first decades of the century, but by the 1930s decline had begun, and the war years had seen the increased use and development of Dar es Salaam and Tanga. Conditions of work could and did improve on the mainland, but they remained static in Zanzibar. The advantages enjoyed by mainland labour on Unguja in relation to those of their kinsmen who remained on the mainland had begun to diminish in the 1930s, with the result that there was a slight decline in the number of mainlanders on the island, both in absolute terms and in proportion to the indigenous population. This is shown in the accompanying table (which refers to

5. These figures, and the analysis which follows, based on 'A Social Survey of Zanzibar' and *Notes on the Census of Zanzibar Protectorate, 1948*. The Social Survey was conducted in 1948-9 by Professor E. Batson of Cape Town University. Its twenty-one-volume manuscript report appeared in London and Cape Town in 1962, but material may have been available for official use much earlier.

6. One additional contributory frustration was, of course, the control over non-alienated land held by the close-knit indigenous communities.

Unguja only).[7] The decline in Zanzibar's overall position was
reflected in the wage rates which mainlanders earned in Zanzibar
City; these fell in relation to the opportunities on the mainland or in
their home areas, although rising slightly in absolute terms. In 1930
an unskilled P.W.D. labourer could earn Shs 30 (in rupees) per
month in Zanzibar but only Shs 22 in Dar es Salaam. In 1939 the difference was still several shillings, but by January 1948 monthly-paid
labour in Zanzibar was being engaged at Shs 32/50, while the Dar es
Salaam rate was Shs 30-32, and daily-paid casual labour was earning
slightly more in Dar es Salaam.[8] Furthermore, migrants tended to
have to spend longer working in Zanzibar if their income was to
exceed the costs of the journey. These factors also served to reduce
the support or subsidy which a labourer's own stake in his community's peasant economy could provide for him — the small
parcels of food or cheap-rate fuel or charcoal supplied by kinsmen
which occur among mainland urban workers. Thus the mainlander
tended to fall to the bottom of the social ladder in Unguja. Among
manual labourers, domestic servants and landless squatters the
mainlanders formed the largest proportion.[9] In addition, mainlanders were not directly represented in the Legislative Council. A
Hadimu, Ameir Tajo, was the first African to be added to its Unofficial Benches in 1945. A second indigene, Ali Sharif Musa from
Pemba, joined him in 1947.

7.

Unguja Island

	1924	1931	1948
Indigenous	68,384	n.a.	81,150
Mainlander	38,590	44,492	37,404

This table is based upon *Report of the Native Census, 1924,* and *Notes on the
Census of the Zanzibar Protectorate, 1948* (both published in Zanzibar); and
J.E. Goldthorpe and F.B. Wilson, *Tribal Maps of East Africa and Zanzibar*,
Kampala, 1960, which provide 1931 census figures. Both sets of figures
represent totals collected outside the clove-picking season.

8. These wage rates are taken from the Zanzibar and Tanganyika Annual
Colony Reports. Zanzibar's attraction lay in its local freedom from direct
taxation, linked to the fact that many mainland Tanganyikan district officials (but not all) would not tax a man who had been away at work. For a contemporary comment on a similar decline in the fortunes of coast labour in
Kenya see A. Clayton and D.C. Savage, *Government and Labour in Kenya
1895-1963*, London, 1975, 271-2.

9. The Social Survey's tables on 'Social Class' (IV), 'Occupations' (V),
Numbers in Households (VII), 'Personal Socio-Economic Rating' (XII),
'Wage Earners' (XIII), 'International Occupational Classification' (XIV),
'Nature of Employer' (XVII) and 'Plantation Ownership' (XV) all indicate
that the mainlanders' position was at the bottom of the scale.

Nearly 25,000 mainlanders lived and worked in or near Zanzibar City. Within the City itself, just under one-third of the total population of 9,850 were mainland Africans born outside the Protectorate.[10] They worked in domestic service, in the port, for the P.W.D. and the Public Health Department, and other urban activities. In general they formed the bulk of employed labour at bare subsistence wage levels, in contrast to the informal sector of indigenous petty traders, *hoteli* owners and other minor independent and more lucrative — and less physically exhausting — activities; although there were some indigenous Africans in manual labour, the numbers of those were not great.

Zanzibar City was in practice two towns.[11] 'Stone Town' consisted of tall stone houses, a handsome main street and waterfront, and a number of picturesque narrow streets and alleys. The Sultan's palace, the *Beit-el-Ajaib*, the Residency, the two cathedrals and the main public buildings all lay in Stone Town. Across a creek formerly used for drainage lay the Ng'ambo (lit. 'the other side'), the largely African township of Zanzibar City. The contrast could not have been more marked. Just under 15,000 Africans together with some of the poorer Arabs lived in Ng'ambo, with a further 10,000 in nearby commuter suburban settlements at Bububu, Kimera, Mbweni and Mombasa.

They mostly lived in small square or rectangular mud houses, with roofs of flattened kerosene tins or thatch made from coconut palms. The few better houses had cement floors and plastered walls with a privy and cesspit; the great majority were much rougher, barely rainproof and with no sanitary arrangements. The 1948 Annual Report admitted that Ng'ambo contained 'some of the worst features of native slums', with 'serious congestion and lack of adequate sewerage, drainage and ventilation'.[12] Such huts could be built easily and cheaply (£50-60), and many were owned by both mainlanders and indigenous Africans. They did not, however, own the site, which was usually the property of an Arab or Indian to whom rent had to be paid; the average rent for one small room — Shs 4/50-5 per month — led inevitably to over-crowding. Considerable sums of British Colonial Development and Welfare Act money had been granted for improvements in the City's urban housing and social services, but by 1948 the work had made little progress; most of the inhabitants of the area had benefited only marginally, if at all.

Dock workers' strikes on the mainland in Mombasa and Dar es

10. Social Survey, 'Population' (I).
11. See map at the front of this volume.
12. *Annual Report, Zanzibar Protectorate, 1948,* Zanzibar and London.

Salaam had brought spectacular gains to the strikers. In Mombasa, a major strike in January 1947 led to an increase from Shs 2/50 to Shs 3/25 per day for stevedores and from Shs 2 to Shs 2/75 per day for shore labour. At Dar es Salaam, an equally effective strike in July had increased casual labourers' wages from Shs 2/30 to as much as Shs 3/80 per day.[13] In the first months of 1948 it would have appeared to workers in the port that Zanzibar's economic circumstances were improving. Clove and copra exports were both increasing and the port was busier since it was being used as unloading station for the Tanganyika groundnuts project.[14] Also, duties on the mainland had recently been increased, and many consumer goods were unloaded for sale in Zanzibar but smuggled quickly to the mainland. This sign of a slight improvement may well have precipitated the action which followed.

At Zanzibar port, the African Wharfage Company (Zanzibar) held a total monopoly of cargo-handling. This Company was wholly owned by a parent Mombasa African Wharfage Company (owned in turn by the British India and Union Castle Steamship lines), and it was staffed by officials of Messrs Smith Mackenzie, the important export-import trading firm. The movement of goods to or from the quayside to the merchants' godowns and warehouses was in the hands of porters: some had very short distances to move goods, others — some 800 *hamali* carters paid on piece rates — pulled hand carts through the streets. From 1945 onwards, and under the paternal tutelage of the District Commissioner, they had organised themselves into a loose Association which owned some carts, and which from 1946 onwards formed the employees' side of a committee which determined rates of remuneration. The African Wharfage Company, after the Dar es Salaam award, began negotiations in its Works Council with representatives of its work force. These representatives were selected informally by their fellows, the Company reserving a right to veto any nomination of which it disapproved. There was no trade union. As a result of these negotiations the stevedores and quay workers entered into monthly terms of service on six-month contracts designed to create a professional, permanent labour force, which provided for a monthly wage paid in half-monthly instalments of Shs 45, rising by annual increments

13. Clayton and Savage, *op.cit.*, J. Iliffe, 'A History of the Dockworkers of Dar es Salaam', *Tanzania Notes and Records*, No. 71 (1970), 119–48, gives details of these awards.

14. Cumming-Bruce to the author, 20 June 1975. Cumming-Bruce and others have suggested that the huge sums of money being spent on a project believed by Africans to be doomed from the start must in itself have spurred on a demand for higher wages.

of Shs 1 to Shs 55, one free meal a day, overtime payment of 25 cents per hour for more than nine hours' work, and sickness benefits.

One immediate cause of the strike which followed so quickly, and which so surprised both the government and the Company, was no doubt a suspicious reaction to this paternal, coercive approach. There were, however, other immediate waterfront causes: Zanzibar had acquired a reputation for unloading ships diverted during the Dar es Salaam strike,[15] and behind the events that ensued there appears to have been some measure of organisation connected with the mainland and probably connected also with the Dar es Salaam strike.[16] The only identifiable leader of the Zanzibar strike appears to have been a Tanganyika Dengereko named Abbas Othman, who some three weeks before the strike had been engaged as a labourer with the African Wharfage Company under the name of 'Jomo Kenyatta'[17]; it may be conjectured that he travelled to Zanzibar to organise a strike. But the strike was characterised far more by a sudden clear demonstration of unity, albeit inarticulate in its written or verbal expressions, rather than by any charismatic strike leadership. Indeed, in this respect, it resembled the Copperbelt strike in 1935 and the Mombasa general strike in 1939.

After various vague rumours of a strike (and after the half-month pay day), the Company on 18 August received a demand, in the form of an unsigned and somewhat unclear letter, apparently claiming a monthly wage of Shs 60 and other improved conditions.[18] This claim was not unreasonable in the light of the Dar es Salaam settlement,

15. D. McQueen, Branch Manager of Smith Mackenzie Ltd, in Zanzibar at the time, to the author, May 1975 (interview).

16. In reconstructing the events of the strike, I have used the British Resident's address to the Zanzibar Legislative Council (*Proceedings of Zanzibar Legislative Council, 6 Sept. 1948*), Colonel A. Bell to the author, 19 September 1975, and the *Zanzibar Annual Report, 1948*, as a basis for the sequence of events. Colonel Bell's letter enclosed extracts from a report written by him to the Inspector-General of Colonial Police forces at the Colonial Office, 31 January 1952, and extracts from his own diary.

17. McQueen to the author, confirmed by Y. Alawi, District Commissioner Zanzibar Urban at the time, to the author, 10 July 1975; E. Stiven, interview March 1976; and Captain J.B. Robertson to the author 10 August 1975. Robertson wondered whether Abbas Othman had been only a 'front man'.

18. The *Zanzibar Voice*, 22, 29 August 1947, notes the claim, warning that the Company's monopoly position could, and perhaps had, led to its identification with the government. The Company's labour force did not contain a preponderance of any mainland ethnic group; the fact that it represented so great a mixture perhaps made it the more militant.

but the manner of its submission — so soon after the July agreement, in the form of a demand which was not presented through the Works Council, and was backed by threats of a strike within two days if the demands were not met — was unacceptable to the Company.

Two days following the ultimatum were spent in efforts to avoid a strike; all these efforts failed, and on 20 August the strike began. As on the mainland, it was at first orderly, although pickets carried sticks and there were reports, never substantiated, that some other members of the Company's staff had been intimidated. The first attempts to involve other labour — that of the Shell Company, the P.W.D. and the Clove Growers Association — were also made at a meeting arranged by the Company employees, but such attempts, coming at the end of a month with pay day approaching, lacked appeal. Nevertheless, by 22 August three ships had already sailed away without unloading and all further attempts to persuade the men to return to work had failed.

On 25 August the government, becoming more alarmed by the threats of intimidation, issued a warning by loudspeaker vans, alleging that intimidation might be used to spread the strike and again urged a return to work. But its case was weakened by its own decision — in the light of the findings of a cost-of-living enquiry — to increase the wages of its own labour force by between Shs 1/30 to Shs 1/40 per day (including cost of living allowance) to Shs 2/80, retroactively to 27 July.

The situation continued to get worse. On 26 August an Italian liner arrived at Zanzibar with a crew of 201 and some 700 passengers, among whom were altogether thirty-two suspected cases of typhoid. Striking dockworkers tried to prevent urgently needed water supplies from reaching the ship, and emergency measures had to be taken by the police and the harbour authority. The Company made various unsuccessful initiatives and wage offers to match the government rates, but all in vain. An indication of the increasingly tense atmosphere occurred on the evening of 28 August. When the alarm siren at the Ziwani police barracks sounded for a routine practice, a large crowd, many of whom were armed with sticks, poured out of Ng'ambo and parts of Stone Town, rushing towards the dock gates and shouting a rumour of clashes with the police. The payment of the August wage packet to monthly paid labour in the city also made it more likely that the strike would spread.

All these events together led the Resident, Sir Vincent Glenday, to decide that the strike could no longer be left alone for time to heal. The economy of the territory was severely affected, and in some areas food shortages became acute. Glenday directed that all weapons, defined in wide terms to include clubs and bludgeons as well as all kinds of firearms and swords, should be delivered to the Central Police Station — a measure which posed difficulties of interpretation as many East African coastal peoples often carried light walking sticks. He followed this by issuing rules on 1 September which forbade all meetings without police permission.

Glenday also decided that fresh labour must be found to handle ships and supplies of foodstuffs. In the small town of Mkokotoni the *mudir* (a junior administrative official) was directed to recruit Tumbatu men, who were to be brought to the Customs Gate in lorries just before 0700 hours on 2 September.[19] The labour so recruited absconded in fear over their likely reception, but the administration and police in the City were not informed of this desertion, and a substantial force of police was sent to the Customs Gate to escort them in. These were greeted by a hostile crowd of strikers, early risers having noticed the arrival of the police guards. The buses were attacked with sticks and stones. The police secured their entry to the dock through the Customs Gate and arrested two men for carrying sticks. News of this spread like wildfire, and the crowd outside the Customs Gate quickly increased to about 1,500; the police were quite unable to disarm them although reinforcements were sent. At the same time throughout the city the large majority of Africans working for government or for other employers joined the strike, either in sympathy or under threats of violence to themselves or their families.[20] In particular, Africans working for white employers in government, commerce or domestic service were expected to strike, and with indigenous as well as mainland strikers, the strike became an all-African urban protest.

While the strike was spreading, the situation at the Customs Gate worsened, the crowd becoming ever larger and more abusive. Parley with the District Commissioner and town *mudir* both failed. The Town Magistrate was then summoned to read the Riot Proclamation ordering the strikers to disperse, again with no effect; the crowd, armed with bludgeons, crowbars and matchets, threw stones and demanded the release of the men arrested. The Magistrate did,

19. Bell to the author, 19 and 27 September 1975, and Seyyid Saud Busaidi, town *mudir* at the time, to the author, July 1975.

20. Ph. Pullicino, a senior colonial officer in the secretariat, to the author, 10 June 1975; 'Soon office messengers were called on by the strikers to stop work, and the stoppage rapidly spread to domestic servants. . . . Later a gang or gangs of men went from house to house to ensure that *all* servants were out. . . .' The compact area of Ng'ambo made the rapid passing of the strike call and the summoning of a crowd very easy, a point made in the *Tanganyika Standard*, 18 September 1948.

however, manage to ascertain that the crowd would not resort to violence if the two arrested men were released. He reported this to Bell, the Commissioner of Police, adding that the police officer at the Gate wished to open fire. He told Bell that he thought that shooting of this type would be totally unjustified and that he would reiterate this at any subsequent enquiry. Bell decided that the arrest of the two men had been unjustified as the sticks they were carrying had been light ones, but that their arrest had created a situation even more tense than that which might have arisen if the Tumbatu labour had arrived. While he was so engaged, the mood of the crowd — now nearly 5,000 — became so ugly that the police at the Gate decided that they were in danger of being rushed and fired a tear-gas bomb. This proved almost totally ineffective as some ex-servicemen in the crowd immediately covered the bomb with sand, which in turn further encouraged the crowd to attack.

Bell decided that there was only one course of action open to him which would avoid bloodshed, namely the release of the two men. He accordingly recommended this action; Glenday at first disapproved, but then gave way. Bell then took the men back to the crowd and, amid cheers, released them. The crisis passed. The crowd broke up into smaller groups and paraded through the streets of the town calling for all Africans to cease work. Traders kept their stores closed and shuttered.

The government was now thoroughly alarmed, and accepted the Tanganyika government's offer of police reinforcements. An emergency meeting of the Legislative Council was called for 6 September, the Sultan issued a personal message appealing for a return to work and law and order, and the Senior Commissioner and the Information Officer toured the area in loudspeaker vehicles, trying to induce workers to be less militant. A 'Labour Conciliation Committee', in effect a temporary Minimum Wage Board,[21] was appointed under the chairmanship of the Chief Justice, and representations were made to it in the course of the next few days from people who appeared on behalf of the town's working population, including two trade unions, the *hamalis*' Association and the European Servants' Union.

The strikers in their turn began attempts to divert food supplies from the city, and on 3 September a further rowdy demonstration against the police took place outside their Ziwani barracks. This was dispersed, but threats of further action led the Resident to ask for a small military detachment from the mainland, and to rush an

---

21. The Committee operated by recommendations rather than awards, but the recommendations were immediately accepted.

Emergency Powers Decree through the Legislative Council. These measures gave the government wide powers over food and essential services and prevented further demonstrations. The Resident also appointed a Price Control Committee to examine various price control measures for goods needed by the town labour force.

Despite all these efforts, few Africans returned to work, and the strike continued until 10 September. Persuasion, both militant and peaceful, of workpeople either to remain in or join in the strike continued. One victim was Glenday himself; he was playing a round of golf on 6 September with a senior Secretariat official and two other Europeans when they all lost the services of their caddies.[22] More serious was the deteriorating situation in Zanzibar City, with food shortages and garbage remaining uncollected. In efforts to protect their own interests, various organisations, such as the Arab Association and the Indian National Congress, tried in vain to mediate.

At a formal level the Conciliation Committee continued its hearings, although it was not to complete its work until after the strike was over. At a more direct level, secret negotiations were taking place in which the President of the African Association, Herbert Barnabas,[23] a Christian Tanganyikan mainlander who was a sanitary inspector in the Public Health Department, acted as the link man. Barnabas was in touch with the strike leaders through the Health Department sweepers who were on strike, and with Pakenham, the British Senior Commissioner. The town *mudir*, Seyyid Saud Busaidi, was used at some risk to himself by Pakenham to carry messages by night to Barnabas's house because the strike leaders were either unwilling to see Pakenham in his office or afraid to be seen doing so. At the Wharfage Company the detail of events is equally obscure, but their employees had had no pay since mid-August and many were short of money. Their men returned to work on Saturday 11 September, following an offer made to them by the Company of new terms — a reversion to casual labour terms with a rate of 25 cents per hour for a nine-hour day (i.e. some Shs 2/25 a day, or Shs 56 for a twenty-five-day month), one free meal a day, and overtime at a rate of 30 cents an hour;[24] these new terms had been

22. J.J. Adie, the secretariat official, to the author, 28 March, and Bell to the author, 19 September 1975.

23. Barnabas was not a militant figure, but a quiet and deeply religious man of peace-loving temperament. He remained in Zanzibar until after the revolution, which he soon found discouraging, and retired to the mainland where he died in 1965. Bishop Neil Russell to the author, 1 August, 1975; Mrs V. Davies to the author, 14 September 1975.

24. *Zanzibar Labour Report, 1948.* Robertson to the author, 10 August 1975, believes the strikers' major error was not to have arranged that the

offered to representatives of the Company's workforce in writing the previous day. The Company's manager did not believe that they had returned to work because of improved conditions, but because 'Jomo Kenyatta' had called a meeting of strikers and read them a letter purporting to come from the Company, promising the original increase if they reported for work on the Saturday morning. Abbas Othman did not remain in the Company's service; early that morning he was seen on the deck of a launch bound for Dar es Salaam. This version of events adds that he had collected a 'strike fund', allegedly to assist the workers while on strike, and had departed with it. The Company telephoned Dar es Salaam, where — again according to this narrative — he was arrested.[25] The other city workers, who had been drifting back in increasing numbers as the week progressed and intimidation was no longer feared, were also all at work by 13 September. A small group who attempted to spread the strike to Pemba was peremptorily ordered off the island by the District Commissioner.[26]

There was a certain selectivity in the calling out of domestic servants employed in houses. Almost all Europeans, including the Resident, lost their servants. But the Sultan's staff were specifically not called out, nor did the servants of a few leading Arab families participate in the strike; some of these latter were loyal to a patriarchal relationship, while others may have feared counter-threats from the worse Arab employers. Another noteworthy occurrence at the same time as the strike — caused exclusively through rising prices — was a mass meeting of African women, both indigenous and mainlander and several thousand strong, who decided not to purchase imported *khangas* (cloths which formed dresses) for three months, as a protest against the prices charged in Asian stores. The protest seems to have been effective at first; it was reinforced by pickets, and at least one case was noted of a woman who purchased a *khanga* being persuaded to hand it back.[27]

A significant feature of the whole strike was the way in which it

strike was simultaneous in port and city.

25. McQueen to the author, May 1975. Robertson to the author, 10 August 1975, states that at the time he also heard of Abbas Othman's departure and subsequent arrest. He judged that the fund could not have amounted to more than a few hundred shillings and that the labour force bore him no illwill.

26. K.G.S. Smith, Zanzibar Administration at the time, to the author, 27 April 1975.

27. The *Tanganyika Standard*, 25 September 1948. The report noted that the meeting took place and the boycott began while the strike was in progress.

was reported by the press. The *Tanganyika Standard*, the most important local paper and part of the East African Standard group of newspapers, deliberately played it down.[28] Despite its gravity and the disruption it caused, the strike never appeared on a major news page and no reference to it being primarily one of mainlanders appeared at any time; again neither Abbas Othman's name nor that of any of its other leaders was mentioned, nor was there any reference to Othman's subsequent fate. Even the report of the Italian liner's visit played down the impact of the strikers' intervention. All this served to obstruct any appreciation of the issues.

With the return of the labour force to work, various improvements were made in the City's working conditions. With effect from 1 December the Company increased labourers' rates to Shs 1 in respect of the first two hours of work and 25 cents per hour for the remainder of a nine-hour day, giving a total earning for a normal full day of Shs 2/75. Employees in other occupations received similar wage increases in the months which followed. The State of Emergency was ended on 23 September and a Port Labour Advisory Committee was appointed to advise the government on labour conditions in the port. With this, the government's former laissez-faire attitude to port employment was ended.

This event has been described in some detail because of its special significance. It was a general strike caused by industrial grievances, and as such was a continuation, using much the same methods, of those which took place in Mombasa and Dar es Salaam in 1947. But Zanzibar's strike was more than a local industrial flare-up. Its distinctive feature was the very high proportion of the City's workforce from ethnic groups of the mainland and outside the Protectorate who took part. When the strike spread from the docks to all Africans, particularly those in government service or British commercial or private employment in the city, it created for the first time a sense of unity, however transitory, among the Africans. This unity became more political than industrial, the politics being those of mainland protest, African and anti-foreign — anti-British as much as anti-Arab. The colonial government understood the significance of the industrial discontent, but saw the demonstration and the mainlanders' role in creating an African solidarity as only an 'unfortunate feature' in an industrial fracas of no deep-rooted

---

28. A.B., a British business man resident in Zanzibar at the time, to the author, 14 July 1975. A.B. was connected with the East African Standard Group. The postponement of a much publicised ceremonial visit of the Royal Navy's Indian Ocean flagship was presented as a news item unrelated to the strike.

structural significance.[29] Its significance as the first major African move in Zanzibar's historic dialogue since the Arab colonisation was not perceived at all.

With hindsight, too, we may see it as comparable to the St Petersburg riots of 1905 — it too being the harbinger of a Revolution to follow. And both in 1948 and in 1964, events were directed by a group of mainlanders, the chief figure being one who had arrived in Zanzibar, using one assumed title, to create trouble, and subsequently returning to the mainland in obscurity.

Kiembe Samaki, July 1951

Also important, though perhaps less significant for the future, was the next African move — this time of indigenous peasants. This move was a protest centred around two specific issues, land alienation and the inoculation of cattle against anthrax. However, beneath it lay a similar African basic uncertainty — in the case of the indigenes, over their land and their future status at a time of population increase. Their indigenous population on Unguja rose (as already noted) from 68,384 in 1924 to 81,150 in 1948, but the arrival of the mainlanders, almost all only too anxious to become landowners if possible, created additional uncertainties.

Although in the economic and social structure of the territory the mainlanders lay at the bottom of the table, the position of the indigenes was only slightly better.[30] A consistent pattern emerges from the 1948 Social Survey, in particular the tables relating to social class and plantation ownership on Unguja:

29. The *Zanzibar Labour Report, 1948*, belatedly admitted: 'A particularly unfortunate feature of the strike was the clearly evinced inspiration by agitators not normally resident in the protectorate. . . . It was apparent that a number of African workers came out on strike for no better reason than a mistaken sense of loyalty to their own race. . .'

30. Social Survey IV, XV. Batson's survey used the administrative division of Island into the two districts of Zanzibar Urban (Stone Town and Ng'ambo) and Zanzibar Rural; this latter unfortunately includes the commuting suburbs with purely agricultural areas. The different surveys were also taken on different days and weeks during the survey period, there are in consequence differing total numbers. The basis of the survey was that of households selected as a series of probability samples designed to yield estimates with a tolerance not greater than 5% of the population. Batson claimed that the accuracy was even greater, to within 2%, and his tables correct to the last two digits at least, but certain discrepancies and anomalies cast doubt on this claim.

SOCIAL CLASS, ADULT MALE AFRICANS

	Zanzibar Mainlander	Urban Indigenous	Zanzibar Mainlander	Rural Indigenous
1. Upper level occupation	20	30		
2. Upper-middle level occupation	50	200		
3. Middle level occupation	570	400	1,000	2,200
4. Lower-middle level occupation	4,010	1,580	11,000	32,400
5. Lower level occupation	1,570	550	1,000	300

PLANTATION OWNERSHIP, ADULT MALE AFRICANS

	Zanzibar Mainlander	Urban Indigenous	Zanzibar Mainlander	Rural Indigenous
Very large	-	-	-	-
Large	-	10	-	-
Medium	30	20	100	300
Small	90	30	700	1,200
Very small	140	30	700	4,300
None	6,630	2,220	8,600	1,720

As the majority of the large Arab plantation owners were on Unguja, while the indigenous large and medium plantations were on Pemba, these totals for Unguja are the more striking and significant for the future. In one respect, that of education, the indigenes were even worse placed than the mainlanders, owing to the concentrations of the latter near the towns. The Social Survey notes that only 2.9 per cent of pupils in the Standards XI and XII of the school system were indigenes compared with 32.1 per cent Arabs and 16.4 per cent mainlander.[31]

An event in Western Unguja was symptomatic of the unease.[32] South of Zanzibar City lies the airfield. From 1940 onwards the government was anxious to expand it and to build houses for airport employees. The land, however, included some of the best cattle-grazing soil in the Protectorate, over which indigenous communities had grazed cattle for as long as anyone could remember. The government took land for the airport extension in small areas at a time in an attempt to avoid too much disruption of life, but the succession of demands had the effect of heightening uncertainty, to which in the late 1940s was added a religious factor when an area of land on which a village mosque stood was required. Crisis was reached in the

31. Social Survey 'Educational Achievement' (X).
32. For an eye-witness account of this event see Ommaney, *op. cit.*, v, and M.F. Lofchie, *Zanzibar: Background to Revolution*, London, 1965, 147–51.

Kiembe Samaki area in July 1951 when, in addition to intense resentment and suspicion aroused by the land issue, the government, alarmed by an outbreak of anthrax, decided to embark on a compulsory cattle innoculation programme. In the eyes of East Africans, cattle innoculation had an evil reputation, because a scheme to protect the cattle of Kenya's Maasai against rinderpest by means of innoculation had not long before killed thousands of head of cattle on account of a defective serum. Although the purpose of the scheme was explained to the inhabitants of Kiembe Samaki, the atmosphere was charged with suspicion. The villagers believed the whole scheme was designed to kill off cattle, and a number refused to produce their animals when ordered to do so. These recusants, some nineteen of them, were prosecuted. When the prosecution was taking place in the local courthouse, a large crowd, estimated at some 500, assembled, among whom could be seen a small core of activists not from the area, inflaming opinion still further. A local religious figure appeared on the roof of the courthouse and proclaimed a *Jihad* or holy war. The excited crowd began beating the shins of the barefooted police constables, which was redoubled when sixteen of the defendants emerged to be hustled into police lorries for transportation to the nearby prison, having received a sentence of six weeks' hard labour. The crowd intercepted one lorry and released the majority of the prisoners.[33] The second lorry reached the prison, and when the British police officer dismounted to open the doors, he was accidentally left outside as the lorry entered. The almost hysterical crowd advanced upon him, a knife was produced to cries of 'kill him', and the police guard (composed of a handful of bandsmen) opened fire killing three outright and injuring two more who later died, together with a small number of demonstrators who were injured but not seriously. Rioting continued for the rest of the day in the Kiembe Samaki area, and for forty-eight hours the atmosphere in all Western Unguja and Zanzibar City remained tense — police reserves were called out, drums beat in Ng'ambo and there was talk of another strike. The Kiembe Samaki confrontations can be compared with their counterpart on the mainland, the Meru land case, for importance in the arousal of popular nationalism.

Communal Politics and Communal Hatred, 1952–1963

The eight years 1952–60 saw the transformation of Zanzibar from a territory where different communities had lived, albeit compartmentalised and labelled, in reasonable amity with each other and had

33. These obligingly reported to the prison on the following day.

acquiesced in certain economic relationships among themselves, even while not fully agreeing to them, to a land of almost pathological communal suspicion.[34] This suspicion in turn produced the politics of hatred and the destruction of economic relationships; what in the past had enriched Zanzibar now tore it apart. From 1950 to 1955 the luxury of communal politics could be enjoyed against the background of large clove harvests, in their turn necessitating a fresh incursion of mainlanders. These mainlanders brought with them the awakening nationalism of Kenya and Tanganyika; though most only saw their stay in Zanzibar as temporary, the Sultan's law and order seemed to be both more glaringly unjust and easier to agitate against than British rule on the mainland. They were in contact in particular with the Hadimu, rather less with other indigenes. In the later 1950s, as a result in many ways of the success of the earlier years, clove prices fell; prosperity declined and the wished-for expansion of social services was not realised; there was some unemployment, and for the first time in Zanzibar's history crime, particularly burglary, increased.

The Arabs were the first to move to a militant nationalist position. The first Arab challenge was based on the Arab Association, in particular its Vice President Saif Hamoud, an Omani radical, and Ahmed Lemke, a Zanzibari who had been imprisoned for subversion by the British in Egypt. Lemke formed a body called the Zanzibar National Union, a cultural organisation with marked political undertones. It was intended that it should be non-racial, but inevitably the preponderance was Arab; it sought to marshal general support from all races for a radical anti-colonial and pan-Muslim movement. The government forbade its officials from being members, and among those who had to give up their posts was Aboud Jumbe. Demands were made of the British administration, overtly for a broadening of the franchise to include a number of Africans, but a major though covert objective was the gaining of control before African nationalism was aroused and organised. When these demands were refused, an Arab boycott of the Legislative Council was organised in 1954, and lasted until 1956. The British attempted to resist this challenge initially by use of more

34. This period is dealt with in great detail in Lofchie, *op.cit.*, Parts II and III, and this section draws in part on Lofchie's work. It is however this author's opinion that Lofchie presents the Zanzibar Nationalist Party, and in particular its leader, Muhsin, in too favourable a light and is at times somewhat too severe on the British administration; in the final years the two last British Residents, Sir Henry Potter and Sir George Mooring, made strenuous efforts to try and reconcile the different communities.

moderate Arab opinion, then by a show of force in which almost all the Arab Association's executive committee, moderate and militant alike, were arrested; they were convicted collectively on a charge of sedition and fined. With these political moves the British also reformed the constitution, plans for which had been under debate since the late 1940s and by which it was hoped that a non-communal form of political life might emerge, within which an African curb on extreme Arab militancy would develop.

The Arab reply to these British policies took two forms. A small fringe group took to violence. The one member of the Arab Association executive committee who had not been arrested, Ali Sultan Mugheiry, a Member of Legislative Council, defied the boycott and returned to the council chamber.[35] He was murdered by one Mohamed Hamoud Barwani, whose family is to appear again later, as his son was to murder Karume. Hamoud was sentenced to death but the sentence was commuted to ten years' imprisonment. He was generally believed to have had influential Arab backers, some of whom emerged as members of the new Zanzibar Nationalist Party (Z.N.P.) formed a month later in December 1955.

Links have been traced between the founders of the Z.N.P. and an association formed earlier at Kiembe Samaki, which numbered at least one of the defendants in the 1951 prosecution of farmers who refused to produce their cattle for innoculation among its members.[36] This was probably true, but the membership of several leading Arabs who later joined this Association greatly altered its character.[37] Although starting with a good claim to be non-racial, the party developed an increasingly Arab style rather than an indigenous one, although to the end it retained an indigenous African membership in certain rural areas and on Pemba. It could and did claim to be non-racist and Muslim, and was prepared to support pan-African aims in East Africa. These claims had some validity in the middle and late 1950s but by the early 1960s the party's practices in power more and more reflected the support given it by the leading Arab families and landowners. From the start the Z.N.P. was against mainlanders, whom it regarded as nothing more than

35. Mugheiry had apologised to Sir John Rankine, the Resident. Mugheiry, a man of moderation, was widely suspected of informing the government about the activities of the more extreme members of the Arab Association.

36. Lofchie, *op.cit.*, 147–54.

37. This Association was called the 'National Party of the subjects of the Sultan'. *Hizbu l'Watan l'Riaia Sultan.* The name 'Hizbu' was certainly commonly used later to describe the Z.N.P., much as 'Tory' is used to describe the British Conservatives — the origin being forgotten.

'temporarily settled' in the way the colonial officials had done in earlier decades. The party's leading figure was Ali Muhsin Barwani, a member of a leading Zanzibari Arab landowning family (though not without some indigenous ancestry also), a Makerere graduate, radical nationalist and proselytising Muslim, and a friend and admirer of President Nasser.

Although the Z.N.P. always took care to have indigenes as its president and vice president, and in its policies to call for a Muslim multi-racial state to replace British rule, by the early 1960s its leaders in their rhetoric were placing increasing emphasis on Arab leadership. The fact of solid Arab support for the party, the extreme anti-European and anti-African utterances of Muhsin, and the unguarded anti-African utterances of the other Arab leaders were all to prove its undoing. Africans with a sense of nationalism sharpened by developments on the East African mainland came to suspect the Z.N.P. of being a party representing wealthier urban and rural Arab landlords only. The appeal of Islam and the momentum it had generated from being the first and most efficient nationalist party still, however, retained for it some African support even as late as 1963.

Early African reactions to the Arab nationalists were ones of apprehension over their own future role and their educational backwardness. There were also sharply differing African views on the claims of the mainlanders to be full participants in Zanzibar's political life, an issue complicated by the British concept of the mainlanders being treated as a separate group, and the very different life-styles and interests of the two African communities. The indigenes of Pemba had little or no quarrel with the Arabs, and the Tumbatu had no serious issues in dispute with them, but many Hadimu could see common ground with the mainlanders. However the very militancy of the mainlanders added some indigenous support, in all areas, to the Z.N.P. This militancy was of course often a reaction to the consistent anti-mainlander attitude of the Z.N.P. and the developing trends in that party's style. Any leadership that could span the islands' differing African communities would therefore be difficult to arrange, the difficulty being enhanced by the generally weak and mediocre quality of those who did emerge. A major impediment was the government's ruling that public servants who wished to enter politics must resign; the few educated Africans were almost all public servants with careers and pensions at risk, and few were prepared to make the sacrifice. African awareness of this weakness led many to prefer — at this stage — continued British tutelage. Julius Nyerere and T.A.N.U. officials from the mainland tried to reconcile difficulties, but without success.

Constitutional reforms introduced by the British in 1956, leading to elections in 1957, provided a ground for political battles — which in turn immediately took the territory a further step down the slope of communal bitterness. On a qualitative franchise, some 40,000 voters being eligible, an election for six constituencies[38] was fought. It created passionate interest and produced a high turn-out of voters. The Z.N.P. campaigned for an Islamic Zanzibari patriotism, implicitly anti-mainlander, their opponents arguing that the Arabs were alien and non-African. The pressures of the campaign led to the formation on Unguja of a loose common African front, the Afro-Shirazi Union (A.S.U.). This was of immense significance for the future, the Union being led by Abeid Karume, who had succeeded Barnabas as President of the African Association in 1953. Karume's supporters from the African Association included a trained teacher, Kassim Hanga, and from the Shirazi Association an Agriculture Department field officer, Othman Sharif, both later to be important members of the Revolutionary Council. Ameri Tajo and Thabit Kombo were other well-known Unguja Shirazi political figures. Underlying this Unguja alliance was the growing identity of interests and aims between the Hadimu and the mainlanders, the pattern of 1948. On Pemba, Muhammad Shamte Hamadi, a former education officer and leader of the Shirazi Association, and Ali Sharif Musa stood with Shirazi Association support, and both won. The Shirazi Association on Pemba had felt itself so far apart from the mainlanders that it would not subscribe to the A.S.U. front of Unguja. The A.S.U. swept the board everywhere on Unguja except in Stone Town where an Asian was elected. In Ng'ambo Karume overwhelmed Muhsin as the former made a great appeal with the rough working-man style of his oratory.

The result brought no ease. On the political front the two Unguja Associations merged, but the Pemba Shirazis refused to do so; they did however allow the Pemba victors, Shamte and Ali Musa, to link with the alliance. This link endured only till 1959, when Pemba's moderation and unease at the worsening tensions found clear expression in the formation by Shamte and Ali Sharif, with some Tumbatu Unguja support, of a new party, the Zanzibar and Pemba People's

---

38. Zanzibar North (mostly indigenous but some Arab and mainlander), Zanzibar South (indigenous and some mainlanders), Pemba North and Pemba South (mixed indigenous and Arab, the former in the majority), Stone Town and Ng'ambo. The franchise required voters to be subjects of the Sultan, which in practice excluded some but not all of the mainlanders. The government still retained a majority in the Legislature through the continued use of nominated members.

Party (Z.P.P.P.).[39] This in turn led the A.S.U. to style itself A.S.P. (Afro-Shirazi Party). All parties alleged bribery, corruption and non-fulfilment of political promises made in 1957, and all government efforts to reconcile and ease the bitterness proved futile.

More threatening for the future, however, was the overspill of the communal tensions from the purely political to the economic life of Zanzibar, at a time of declining general economic fortunes. Arab plantation owners evicted mainlander squatters; in their turn some Arabs, especially the Manga, found themselves threatened with violance and withdrew to the City. African labour, indigenous and mainland, began to boycott Arab and Asian stores, particularly again those of the Manga. On the estates squatters planted bananas (which damaged clove bushes) and, asserting the A.S.P. cry of 'The soil is ours, the trees are theirs', neglected weeding and harvesting. The Z.N.P. attempted, with the support of some Tumbatu, to sponsor an agricultural workers union. The A.S.P. in turn tried to break a shipowner's association consisting largely of Z.N.P. supporters by fomenting unrest among the mainlander and Hadimu seamen, to which the Z.N.P. replied by employing Tumbatu and alleging that the A.S.P. were seeking cheap labour. The trade union movement split into two. A Z.N.P.-supported Federation of Progressive Trade Unions (F.P.T.U.) attracted four unions totalling approximately 1,200 members and the support of a further four, adding some 500 more. A much larger A.S.P.-supported Zanzibar and Pemba Federation of Labour attracted nine unions whose membership added up to just over 3,000; it had the support of two other unions, with some 1,200 members. The Z.P.F.L's. secretary-general, Hassan Nassor Moyo, was a member of the A.S.P's. national executive and generally moderate, but a number of younger Z.P.F.L.-affiliated union officials were sent to Communist countries at this time for political instruction. Previously the Arab officials of the government had enjoyed some reputation for impartiality, but they were now systematically portrayed by the A.S.P. as the executive arms of the Arabs and the Z.N.P. Racist songs of abuse

39. The detail of the political story behind this move is complex; its only relevance is as evidence of the mounting passions and tensions. In essence, it concerned the Z.N.P. allegation that the A.S.U. was indifferent to early independence; the bitterness this aroused led to intervention by political leaders from Tanganyika and Nyasaland and a 'Freedom Committee' was created as a patched-up reconciliation. Some mainlander A.S.U. militants supported by Karume began to demand an immediate African-led independence, this was too much for the Pemba Shirazi.

were sung;[40] politics pervaded everything from sport to social occasions and even Muslim worship. Ghana, China and Radio Cairo supported the Z.N.P. while Nyerere in Tanganyika supported the A.S.P. As a final blow to social unity, Zanzibar's last remaining unifying factor disappeared when Khalifa, the keystone to the whole Sultanate system, died in 1960.[41] His successor, Sultan Seyyid Abdulla, was old and infirm and furthermore was reputed (probably correctly) to have declared his support for the Z.N.P. Certainly on visits to rural areas in 1959 Abdulla was greeted with Z.N.P. demonstrations and party songs, which inevitably aroused A.S.P. resentment. With Khalifa's death many felt free to behave in a way they would not have done in his lifetime. The British *Colonial Annual Report* for 1959–60 wrote gloomily:

The period was one of intense political activity. The Islands were covered with political emblems, the cock, the well and the fish. Electioneering speeches were the order of the day. There were endless newspaper articles and processions. The political struggle occupied the minds of the people of Zanzibar to the exclusion of everything else. Both men and women took a full part in these activities. If a meeting was to be held in the rural areas, a few hours before Zanzibar town resembled the marshalling area for an army. Lorries and cars were going in all directions, often with flags and singing supporters. Some convoys took an hour to pass.

The last three years of colonial rule, 1960–3, saw only the deepening of communal politics and bitterness into overt racial hatred, evinced in two elections in 1961, a London constitutional conference in 1962, and a further election in 1963. After much debate, which itself aroused bitterness, the British government in 1960 provided Zanzibar with a new constitution, the chief features of which were to be a large elected majority of twenty-two seats in the Legislature, the enfranchisement of women, and a ministerial system by which the leader of the winning party was to become Chief Minister. Under these arrangements the first 1961 election was held in January, but the result was a disastrous tie. The A.S.P. won ten seats (eight on Unguja and two on Pemba), the Z.N.P. won nine seats (five on Unguja, of which three were in Zanzibar City one each in an Arab

40. Notably abusive were the songs of the Youths Own Organisation, the youth wing of the Z.N.P., disowned in this respect by Muhsin but doing irreparable harm to his cause.

41. It is noticeable that the A.S.P. only became openly republican after Khalifa's death. Mwanjisi, *op.cit.*, 29–50, claims that Khalifa had secretly favoured the Z.N.P. but he gives no evidence to support this and his assertion leaves an impression of wishing to discredit the institution of the Sultanate.

plantation area and a Tumbatu area, and four on Pemba), and the Z.P.P.P. three (all on Pemba, of which one, Chake Chake, was won by a single vote). The Z.P.P.P. then divided on the action to be taken, two supporting the Z.N.P. and one the A.S.P.[42], giving both sides eleven.

Full introduction of the constitution was delayed as no ministerial system could be introduced, and fresh elections were arranged for June after the hurried creation of a new seat in Pemba to avoid another stalemate. The campaign for this election was held in an electric atmosphere, and rioting and violence broke out on election day. The A.S.P. charged the Z.N.P. with being anti-African (in particular against an East African Federation of which there was much talk at the time) and pro-Communist. Its meetings and rallies displayed portraits of Kenyatta and Nyerere with T.A.N.U. flags. The party in particular attacked the Manga Arabs, who they claimed were to be a Z.N.P. militia. The Z.N.P. campaigned for national and Muslim unity against British and extreme African attempts to divide. The Z.P.P.P. claimed to represent true indigenous interests. The youth wings of the two major parties fought physical battles during the campaign. Frequently the rhetoric was that of hysteria. Arabs made accusations that Zanzibar was to be ruled by a Christian district commissioner sent from Nairobi or Dar es Salaam and the population diluted by mass migration, and old African memories of slavery, castration of men, disembowelling of pregnant women, and women sweeping floors with bare breasts were all recounted by 'survivors'. British troops, mostly of the Brigade of Guards, were flown in from Kenya after the declaration of an emergency. Sixty-eight people were killed — all except three being Arabs and most of these the vulnerable Manga — and over 350 more were injured. The troops had to remain for more than eighteen months.

The Z.N.P. and Z.P.P.P., the latter after some internal division, fought the campaign in a loose anti-A.S.P. alliance and gained ten and three seats respectively, while the A.S.P. retained its ten. The winning alliance was invited to form the administration, selecting as their leader the less controversial Shamte rather than Muhsin of the Z.N.P. But a number of important Pemba indigenes, including Othman Sharif, remained in opposition despite their fears of the mainlanders. Their main reason for so doing was a belief that bribery had taken place, but another was a more local Pemba one, namely that Shamte came from Chake Chake while Othman and Ali Sharif were from Wete. The Z.N.P. provided all the ministers

42. This ZPPP member was Ali Sharif who had always had reservations about the ZNP.

other than Shamte. This election (and that of 1963) indicated the weaknesses of the 'first-past-the-post' election arrangements. The A.S.P., who had in fact obtained over 1,000 more votes than the other two parties combined, made political capital with accusations of British-Arab gerrymandering;[43] they refused to enter any form of national coalition or power-sharing without full parity of ministers and the promise of new elections after a re-drawing of constituencies. A Constitutional Conference, held in London in March 1962 to consider the final moves towards independence, accepted the A.S.P's. insistence on new elections but rejected demands for independence in 1962. The Colonial Secretary, Maudling, repeatedly warned the Z.N.P. leaders of the dangers of ignoring African aspirations.

Two events which followed in the intervening period before the July 1963 election were to have considerable bearing on the Revolution. The first of these was a minor split in the Z.N.P. A leading and very radically oriented member of the Z.N.P., Abdulrahman Muhammad Babu, became dissatisfied with Muhsin's leadership of the Z.N.P. and began to propagate a Marxist revolutionary programme.[44] For 'Babu', who was of mixed Arab-Comorian ancestry, Marx was much more important than Islam; within these perspectives, Muhsin and the Arab Z.N.P. leadership were monarchical, racialist and linked to the upper class of Arabs. Babu, born in 1924, had studied at Makerere and in London, apparently without great success; in London he had been an active member of the Movement for Colonial Freedom. He had then worked for the Clove Growers' Association in Zanzibar, which he followed with a spell in a bank in

43. There is little real evidence to support this. Numerous elections elsewhere have produced majorities of votes for one party or front and an actual win for another party or group; it is never possible to produce constituencies of identical size. In this election all the constituencies except three comprised a population which ranged from 12,750 to 15,700, averaging some 4,300 eligible to vote in each. Of the three small constituencies one was a particular area of Pemba and of no especial political significance, the other two were in the Stone Town of Zanzibar City, with populations of 8,381 and 9,978 respectively. The reader must decide for himself whether the delineation of these two latter constituencies was a response to real special circumstances or manipulation. But even if they had been fused into one, the result would not have differed. Also, the generally even appearance of the constituency boundaries does not suggest attempts to include or exclude any particular local communities.

44. As General Secretary of the Z.N.P. he organised and edited a daily broadsheet *Zanews* which proclaimed that it was an agent for the New China News Agency. At this time the Z.N.P. was in receipt of a number of scholarships for study in Communist countries.

West London before being recalled by the Z.N.P. to help restore the party after the 1957 defeat. He developed his own contacts with China and Cuba, and arranged for the despatch to Cuba of a number of young Zanzibaris for a course of training in both revolutionary ideology and its practice; in this it is possible to see the first significant Cuban involvement with modern Africa. In 1962 Babu instigated the burning of the British Information Office and other acts of sabotage in protest against Britain's refusal to grant immediate independence, for which he was arrested on a charge of sedition and sentenced to fifteen months in prison. Babu strenuously denied the charge and his followers alleged that the arrest followed an arrangement made by the Z.N.P. leadership, Shamte and the British Resident to remove Babu from the political scene. On his release he was given a tremendous public welcome arranged by the Z.N.P. youth wing, a few of whom had recently returned from China; and immediately before the July 1963 elections he broke with the Z.N.P. to form his own Nasserist *Umma* (Masses) Party,[45] appealing to lower middle-class and bourgeois Arab nationalism in opposition to the monarchy and leading families. The Z.N.P. leadership reacted sharply; Babu was criticised for adventurism, personal ambition and Marxism and many who had cheered him on his release from goal now barricaded his house. The second event, a week before the election was the death of the Sultan, Seyyid Abdulla and the succession of his son Seyyid Jamshid, aged thirty-three. Jamshid's political ideals were an ill-integrated mixture of reverence for his grandfather Khalifa and a known strong personal sympathy for the views of Muhsin and the Z.N.P. His mother, Tafu, was said by British officials to have exerted a particularly unfortunate influence on him. He lacked experience and at times common sense; he could show charm, but was also proud. He had little liking for the British, which apparently stemmed from an unhappy period serving as a midshipman in a British warship. In his grandfather's lifetime he had once threatened a traffic policeman with a stick, an incident much discussed by Africans. His own personal interests were hunting and sailing, he surrounded himself with an entourage of Arabs and Muslim Asians, and he seemed to have little interest in his African subjects and to support few of their activities. His

---

45. There were various issues that caused the final breach. Some Z.N.P. leaders accused Babu of misusing party funds. Babu himself wanted the Z.N.P. to offer African candidates in the City constituencies and Arab ones in the rural areas, to prove the party was truly non-racial. The party leadership saw this as an attempt by Babu to secure safe seats for his own followers. *Umma* offered no candidates in the election.

personality was not one which could provide a focus for a renewed loyalty to the monarchy. Jamshid had few illusions concerning his position, and he made preparations to leave in the event of an A.S.P. victory.

The British continued to make many efforts to lessen the tension in Zanzibar, efforts which even included a visit from Duncan Sandys, the Commonwealth and Colonial Secretary. But the two groupings could never agree on conditions for co-operation, and Sandys ordered the new elections for thirty-one seats on a universal franchise. This campaign was fought with less violence than that of June 1961; however, the racial harangues and arguments became even more divisive with repetition. The Z.N.P. campaign drew heavily on themes centring around the defence of the Faith and the Sultanate. Although it paid lip-service to equal opportunities on the land and in the public service and to the ideal of pan-Africanism in foreign affairs, the subjects it chose to stress — a local variant of the law and order theme — reflected the direction in which the party had moved and was still moving. The A.S.P. sometimes paid token respect to the Sultanate and Islam, but it was also at times overtly republican. It campaigned for specific land redistribution measures and advantages for Africans in education and the public service to correct past under-privilege. Each accused the other of hypocrisy, and appealed heavily to the emotions, the Z.N.P. with quotations from the Koran and the A.S.P. with horrifying tales of past slavery. The result was yet more unsatisfactory than that of July 1961. The Z.N.P. won twelve seats, six in each island; the Z.P.P.P. won six seats, all on Pemba; and the A.S.P. won thirteen seats, eleven on Unguja (out of the island's total of seventeen) but only two on Pemba, in impoverished areas of poor soil. But the voting percentage produced an entirely different showing. The A.S.P. gained 54.3 per cent of the votes (63.2 per cent on Unguja and 44.4 per cent on Pemba), while the Z.N.P.-Z.P.P.P. alliance gained only 45.7 per cent of the votes (36.8 per cent of Unguja and 55.6 per cent on Pemba). The A.S.P. immediately repeated its charge of gerrymandering.[46] However, the major cause of this electoral freak was the distribution of Unguja's population, which threw up huge — and wasted — A.S.P. majorities in eight safe areas, but allowed Z.N.P. members to scrape home with much smaller majorities in all their seats[47] except for the two in Stone Town which, inevitably, they won

46. Once again, however, apart from two Stone Town constituencies in Zanzibar City, the constituencies were all of approximately equal size, and if the two Stone Town Constituencies had been merged the overall result would not have been affected by the loss of one Z.N.P. seat.

47. The traditional structure of the indigenous township system on

easily. There were also much more pertinent reasons for the failure of the A.S.P. to capture the non-Hadimu constituencies on Unguja. One was its poor organisation and deployment of electoral effort, caused by poor leadership[48] in face of a sitting government with a powerful political machine and money, jobs, scholarships and social service assets to distribute. Another was the wider Shirazi Muslim appeal — Islam and Sultan — which still attracted indigenes and even some mainlanders to the Z.P.P.P. on Pemba, and was not entirely without appeal towards the Z.N.P. on Unguja, particularly again in Tumbatu areas.[49] Muslim Asians tended to support the Z.N.P., while some Hindus supported the A.S.P.

Fortified by its victory, the Z.N.P.-Z.P.P.P. coalition now turned against any form of conciliation, Shamte even demanding that A.S.P. members of the legislature should leave the party and join the Z.P.P.P. if they wished to be considered for office, a final bar to any last-minute national coalition before independence on 9 December. The last British Resident, Sir George Mooring, warned Whitehall that the territory was not in a fit state for self-government[50] but in these years of the 'Wind of Change', British policy was for rapid decolonisation. Another who expressed his apprehension to the British government was Julius Nyerere.

In this period, 1952–60, it can be said that the British administration saw the cracks in Zanzibar society and attempted, belatedly and at first not entirely wholeheartedly, to bridge the widening gap by wider representation of all communities in the legislatture. Britain's appreciation of the true situation in Zanzibar was delayed by her difficulties in the Middle East; she wanted no further pretexts for anti-British feeling among Arabs. But the major reasons for the British failure in Zanzibar were partly the pre-colonial legacy, and the depth of local ethnic and class divisions, and partly the very nature of British rule, which had for so long compartmentalised the

occasions worked to Z.N.P. advantage, both through patronage and support of one moiety against another.
48. Lofchie, op.cit., 231–5, comments on the still-persisting gap between indigenous and mainlanders, personal and political faction squabbling and bickering between party and Z.P.F.L. officials. The A.S.P., too, persisted in needlessly concentrating effort where they were secure.
49. A certain number of establishment property-owning indigenous supported the Z.N.P., further many of its Arab leaders had obvious part-African ancestry. Both factors assisted the party.
50. Lady Mooring to the author, 8 January 1977. Mooring also warned of the military weakness of Zanzibar in the event of unrest.

communities, sharpening Zanzibar's historic dialogue rather than reducing it. The 1963 election, and to a great extent earlier elections too, had turned on the whole question of the territory's identity. Lastly, in any assessment confined strictly to the quality of British colonial rule, the British were extraordinarily unlucky. The 1963 election should have produced a small A.S.P. victory, and the British were justified in anticipating a result less fatally divisive. But the poverty of the A.S.P.s' organisation had not been anticipated; the leadership of Othman Sharif was seen by many on Unguja as vacillating and equivocal. But a significant sign of the times was the A.S.P.s' increase in votes on Pemba. In June 1961 the party had polled 15,741 votes out of 43,678 or 30.6 per cent, in July 1963 it polled 33,853 out of 77,841 or 44.4 per cent.[51] The Z.P.P.P. was beginning to decline, and if the A.S.P. had been content to wait, electoral victory would undoubtedly have fallen to it before long. But after 1961 and 1963, many indigenes and all mainlanders had lost confidence in the ballot box — and further believed that the Z.N.P.-dominated government would never permit another free election. The independence conferred by Britian was seen as unreal, and needing to be overthrown. It was *uhuru wa uarabu tu*, independence for Arabs only.

51. Some evidence does, however, suggest that bribery may have played a part in this gain, but bribing of voters was not a practice confined to the A.S.P.

III. PROFILE OF A REVOLUTION

John Okello

In 1959, a little less than four years before independence, the mainlander labourer community in Zanzibar was joined by a Ugandan whose name was later to achieve a brief world fame as the Revolution's leader, John Okello.[1] Okello was born in 1937 in a Lango (North Uganda) village, and because his parents died when he was still a boy, his schooling was limited to an unfinished Church Missionary Society school primary course at Aloi. He went to work in a number of occupations, first in Uganda and later in Kenya. According to his own version, he first worked for an Asian employer in Soroti as a domestic servant; then he moved as a clerk to a cotton ginnery where he organised a strike. He then returned to Soroti as a small peddler, moving again to Mbale in 1953 to train with an Asian tailor. He claims that the Asian gave him no training, so he left to be a builder's foreman first in Uganda and then in Kisumu, Kenya. He next moved to Nairobi working successively in building, as a gardener and as a clerk. In Nairobi he was a supporter of C. Argwings-Kodhek's Nairobi African District Congress, the most militant nationalist party permitted at the time. He was then sent to prison for a sexual offence, which he was to repeat later in his life; his sexual frustrations and their effect on his political ambitions appear

---

1. There is the widest variety of theories from which to select an account of the Revolution and Okello's part in it. These range from Okello's own version, in which he maintains that the Revolution was his, to the 'Official Version' (which appeared in *The Nationalist*, 12 January 1965, and is conveniently published as an appendix in Okello's book, *Revolution in Zanzibar*, Nairobi, 1967, 209-22) in which Okello is not mentioned at all. Another theory holds that the real leader was killed at the outset of the Revolution and that Okello assumed his role (one variant of this theory being he assumed the name Okello as well). This writer, after careful study and consideration, believes that the general interpretation of the Revolution set out by Keith Kyle in two articles in the *Spectator* of 7 February 1964 (entitled 'Gideon's Voices') and 14 February 1964 (entitled 'How it happened') is in general correct; these articles, written by an observer on the spot, confirm Okello's role. The writer also believes that the similarity in style of the broadcasts made during the Revolution and the narrative in Okello's autobiography establish beyond any question not only his identity but also his dominant role in the early stages of the Revolution.

to bear comparison with those of Adolf Hitler. On his release in 1957 he first worked in a Machakos butchery, and then moved to Mombasa where he was unable to find work. He travelled next to Takaungu where he was addressed by the Kenya coast Arabs in the traditional term of '*mtumwa*' or slave. There followed minor jobs on the Kenya coast as a quarry lorry-loader, a petty trader and a stone-mason. At this stage he began to dream and he moved to Pemba in a journey reminiscent of St Paul's voyage to Malta, in which a storm arose but calm returned after prayer. In the course of these varied occupations he claims to have persistently led unrest and demands for improved wages and conditions of employment. He certainly also acquired a dislike for colonial rule and a hatred for aliens, particularly Asians and Arabs. In June 1959, armed with these ideas and prejudices, he began work as à labourer on a Pemba Arab plantation. His political interests quickly transferred themselves to Zanzibar affairs, and he joined the local branch of the Z.N.P., the party of which he was later to be the scourge.

After the 1964 Revolution, Okello wrote his autobiography while in prison in Kenya.[2] This book, although perhaps tidied up by some kindly editing, is nevertheless a major document of the Zanzibar Revolution. It is, first, a fascinating self-revelation of a figure born for controversy and violence; secondly, Okello's account is equally revealing in its omissions; and thirdly, it is full of useful clues for the unravelling and detection of something of what actually happened. Lastly, it has a strange prophetic quality: Okello claims that he knew from before the Revolution that he would not make any lasting personal gain or political career from it, and that he would be repudiated by those he had helped. Here, although he is writing of himself, it is possible to sense that he was also writing of his section of the community, the most recently arrived mainlanders — those of the 1950s — who were to make the Revolution largely for the benefit of others.

Okello records that his best school subject was religion, and this certainly accords well with his character. He increasingly saw himself as appointed by God — a God of Old Testament Christianity, also a God of the Africans who had nothing whatever to do with Islam — to lead a revolution purely of African liberation.[3] This

2. Okello, *op.cit.* Much of the biographical material in this section is based on this work.

3. In his work Okello wrote in summary 'God alone knew and still knows what is happening with me. He is my Teacher. My power in regard to the Revolution was as a Messenger of God. . . .' Again, a comparison with Hitler's March 1936 statement 'I go the way that Providence dictates with the assurance of a sleep-walker' seems relevant.

God spoke to Okello in prophetic dreams. In the first of these he was warned to be ready to combat danger on an island, and in the second a voice directed him: 'God has given you power to redeem prisoners and slaves.' Two factors — periodic ill-health with disturbed mental balance, and worship with a Quaker community on Pemba — strengthened his vision of himself as a man of destiny. He claims to have been baptised 'Gideon' in 1937: this name reinforced his self-perception as a chosen figure ordained to smite and strike down his Godless opponents.

At the end of 1959 he ceased working as a labourer and started a small masonry business in Vitongozi, a poor area on Pemba's east coast; he instructed a number of young Kenyans in his craft and in politics. In the following year he transferred his political support from the Z.N.P. to the A.S.P., the latter being an African party. He became secretary of the party's youth wing for the island.

A curious gap then appears in the narrative. Okello writes of this period that he became injured while helping a woman in labour and was sick for some eighteen months. He also states that he made friends among Tanganyikans and Kenyans in the local police. It has been persistently rumoured that Okello was a Pemba policeman himself at this time — which his later knowledge of police armouries and procedures seems to bear out. The present writer would assert only that, whether in Pemba or earlier elsewhere, Okello must have worn Her Majesty's uniform — police or military. A glance at photographs of him on the day after the Revolution shows a man in a well-ironed shirt, with stocking tops turned neatly over and the wool pattern arranged straight down the leg, with shoes well-polished and a peaked cap worn at a slightly jaunty tilt to emphasise self-confidence. His book, too, when describing the various 'battles' of the Revolution concludes each description with the note on 'own casualties' and 'enemy casualties', familiar to anyone who has ever followed British Army report procedures.

Early in 1963 Okello moved to Unguja. He describes this move in a characteristic passage that well conveys his burning sense of God-appointed mission:

About this time I decided to go to Unguja to see what the situation was there. No revolution could succeed in Pemba alone unless Unguja also fell. I was inspired by the following words from the epistle of St. James, Chapter IV and V:

'Go now, you rich men, weep and howl for your miseries that shall come upon you. Your riches are corrupted, and your garments are moth-eaten. Your gold and silver is cankered, and the rust of them shall be a witness against you, and shall eat your flesh as if it were fire. You have heaped treasure for the last days. Behold the hire of the labourers who have reaped down your fields: . . . the cries of them which have reaped are entered into the ears of the Lord of Sabbath [*sic*]. You have lived in pleasure on the earth and been wanton: You have nourished your hearts as in a day of slaughter. You have condemned and killed the just. . . . You lust and have not; you kill and desire to have and cannot obtain; you fight and war, yet you have not. You ask, and receive not, because you ask amiss, that you may consume it upon your lusts. *You adulterers and adulteresses, know you not that the friendship of the imperialist is an enemy to your countrymen? Whoever befriends the imperialist is an enemy of the people.* . . . Be patient, therefore, brethren, until the coming of the Lord. Behold the husbandman waits for the precious fruit of the earth, and has long patience for it, until he receives the early and latter rain. Be you also patient, establish your hearts; for the coming of the Lord of the Sabbath is near. . . .[4]

On Unguja, Okello says he gave more and more of his time to preparations for revolution, and after the result of the 1963 election he said that he 'renounced all personal pleasures and enjoyment. . . . I dedicated myself wholly to the Revolution.'[5] He developed — or maintained — contacts with the police, notably with Constable Absalom Amoi Ingen, a Mluhya from Kenya[6] later to figure as the 'Deputy Field Marshal', and Corporal Joseph Mugambwa, a Giriama also from Kenya. He built up a knowledge of places, particularly those important in any bid for power, and of people especially those who co-operated with the government and might be informers.

In another remarkable passage Okello conveys the atmosphere of the times very clearly. He describes Arabs, from the context almost certainly Manga, speaking to Africans:

'Whether you like it or not', they would say, 'you niggers and black slaves will remain forever under the flag of our Holy Sultan. You black men are devils and you have no place here on earth. Anyone who offends the Holy Government of the Sultan must know that his place in the grave is ready . . . do not dream that this is the government of Nyerere, Obote or that 'Mau Mau' creature called Jomo Kenyatta. You killed our holy brothers in June 1961 thinking that you would win; but the time is near when we shall deal with you as we please.[7]

During this time on Unguja, according to his narrative, Okello became Assistant General Secretary of the Zanzibar and Pemba

---

4. Okello, *op.cit.*, 87. The footnote in Okello's book here reads 'This is my own reading of this passage. (J.O.)' and the italics are Okello's.

5. *Ibid.*, 95.

6. Ingen appears to have pronounced his name 'Engine'; many European residents in Zanzibar have told me of events in which 'Engine' featured. He was a much more human figure than Okello, not without a sense of humour.

7. Okello, *op.cit.*, 95.

Paint Workers Union, which he claims to have united with the Construction and Building Workers Union. He used his union activities to further revolutionary militancy, and upon this power-base he claims that he formed a close partnership[8] with Seif Bakari, a young indigene who some evidence suggests had recently returned from Cuba[9] and who was President of the A.S.P. Youth League (A.S.P.Y.L.). Bakari was undoubtedly one member of a small 'Committee of Fourteen' of A.S.P. indigenous revolutionaries, a committee which included a number later to figure prominently.[10] Okello states that the committee worked without Karume's knowledge, fearing a leak of the conspiracy. In the light of subsequent events this seems probable, although post-revolution official accounts claim that the 'Fourteen' were entrusted by Karume with the organisation of a revolution as early as August 1963. The 'Fourteen' probably saw Okello as a useful organiser and hired gunman whom it would be easy to control. It is also possible that what the 'Fourteen' had in mind was a campaign of sabotage — attacks on government offices, fuel installations and transport — rather than the violent overthrow of the government, all in an attempt to change the government's policies rather than to overthrow it in a specific revolution. If this was the case, the militancy of the mainlanders and of some of the *Umma* party members, all uniting under Okello's leadership, was by no means to be satisfied with so limited a range of action.

Okello claims that, drawing on support from mainland labour, the Z.P.F.L. trade union branches and the A.S.P.Y.L, he toured the island between October and December 1963 and addressed meetings. He succeeded in overcoming African fears occasioned by their lack of weapons, telling them how to make side arms; he also raised money to be spent on transport, drugs, matchets, axes and crowbars.[11] At these meetings he found volunteers for his plans, and

8. Okello's book provides texts of letters; Okello was in prison in Mombasa when he wrote the book and the texts are not likely to be accurate. But the essential features of the alliance seem confirmed by the subsequent events.

9. This fact is not noted in Okello's book; the British source of this report is confidental to the author.

10. The Official Version notes the other key members as Yusuf Himid, Said Abdulla Natepe, Ramadhan Haji, Said Bavuai, Said wa Shoto, Muhammed Abdullah, Pili Khamis, Hamisi Darwesh, Khamis Hemed, Hafiz Suleiman and Hamid Ameir. Some of these were officials of other trade unions. All were indigenous except Muhammed Abdullah who was probably a Tanganyikan.

11. Okello describes in great detail a meeting in north Unjuga on 18

at the end of his tour he chose from among them 'the hard core of my soldiers, making sure that most of them came from outside the Island: of 330 recruits only thirty were indigenous Zanzibaris.' He lists his lieutenants as Ramadhan Haji, an indigene who had been dismissed from the police; Abdulla Mfarinyaki, a Tanganyika Ngoni carpenter with military experience from the Second World War; Mzee Kenya, a former Tanganyika Police bugler; Said Idi Bavuai, an indigenous A.S.P.Y.L. member; Matias Simba (the name adopted by Corporal Joseph Mugambwa); Mzee Mohammed, another former soldier and almost certainly a Tanganyikan; and Amoi Ingen. He also issued orders. Some of these enjoined abstinence from alcoholic drink, sex and all cold food, in particular fish-heads or left-overs, and forbade the borrowing of clothes from other men; the rest of the orders more realistically required self-discipline and restraint in behaviour so as not to attract attention. His lieutenants were directed to recruit other fit and reliable men to be selected for the revolutionary force. In November and December Okello set up smaller councils of war with his principal lieutenants to draw up plans, and in December he began the 'registration' of those recruited by his lieutenants. Those he selected were called Freedom Fighters and, according to Okello, took an oath to fight to any conclusion. The form of the oath, Okello claims, occurred to him after a dream in which God commanded him to collect a particular stone coloured black, white and red from a particular location, and then to crush the stone so that grains from each colour could be inserted with water into a bottle and be preserved. The oath, again on a divine directive in a second dream, required the Freedom Fighters to kill a black cat and a black dog, mix their blood and brains in a pot and add some of the mixture from Okello's bottle, after which the Fighters were to jump three times across the mixture, which was to be spread on their line of advance. The concoction represented the revolution — the stone (black) was Africans under foreign domination, the blood the Africans dead in the days of slavery and 'imperialist' blood shortly to be shed, and the brains (white) the bravery of Africans about to be displayed. The remains of the original stone was to be Okello's own mark of divinely-appointed authority and courage. Whether this oath was even taken is uncertain, since no record to that effect exists. Okello also claims that he issued very careful orders that the lives of the young, the old and

October, one near Zanzibar City on 26 October, and one in the south two days later. Writing as he was, in prison and without notes, the value of these lengthy descriptions of the numbers present and matters raised lies simply in the clues to his support. Okello, *op.cit.*, 104–15.

The Revolutionaries of Zanzibar I: John Okello with associates and members of the Committee of Fourteen. *Left to right, standing*: Muhammed Abdulla, Abdulla Mfarinyaki, Khamis Darwesh. Said idi Bavuai, Abdullah Said Natepe, Hamid Ameir, Hafidh Suleiman, Pili Khamis, Said wa Shoto. *Seated*: Ramadhan Haji, John Okello, Seif Bakari.

pregnant women were all to be spared, although they were to be detained. All Arab men between eighteen and fifty-five were to be killed, in particular the Sultan and three particularly abusive Z.N.P. ministers. Attacks on Europeans were forbidden.

As in his accounts of his October meetings, Okello provides much detail and precise figures of the 'registration' of his volunteers. These need not be taken seriously, but the heavy weighting of mainlanders in the figures he offers is significant.[12] The men he selected were generally from strong A.S.P. areas which served to provide overall security; they could be relied upon not to betray any organisation or such rudimentary military training and preparations as were made. He said he was under great pressure to launch his revolution on the day of independence, using the celebrations as a screen to cover movement of personnel, but he forbade this (on God's advice, he said) because Zanzibar had so many foreign visitors, and because his preparations were not quite complete. Perhaps the presence of two British infantry companies and a naval detachment, all in Zanzibar for ceremonial purposes but nevertheless fully armed, was his real reason.

Following events to be noted later, Okello received a most effective reinforcement in December in the form of a group of dismissed Zanzibar policemen, all mainlanders whose services had been abruptly terminated by the Z.N.P.-dominated government; the authorities had been unwise enough not even to pay for their return home. These men knew the security system and the locations of armouries and magazines. Okello claims that forty-two ex-policemen joined him at this time.[13] On 4 January he held a command council at Kibozi, an African area, at which he directed his lieutenants to order his followers out ostensibly for an A.S.P. fête, their weapons concealed but wearing a piece of yellow cloth on their left

12. Okello's figures (Okello, *op.cit.*, 131) are as follows:

	Indigenous	Mainlander	Total			
North Unguja	113	600	713	out of	2,400	volunteers
Central Unguja	10	500	510	" "	1,010	"
South Unguja	150	650	800	" "	1,800	"
Zanzibar City	25	245	270	" "	4,000	"

Okello claims the mainlanders came from Kenya, Uganda, Tanganyika, Congo (Zaire), Zimbabwe, Malawi and Mozambique. From the rural areas, just under half were nominated for combat in Zanzibar City, reinforcing the City contingent.

13. He states there were respectively 27 from Kenya, 4 from Tanganyika, 3 from Uganda, 2 from Malawi, 3 from Rhodesia, and one from Mozambique, together with two Zanzibaris.

arm, on 11 January. At this time, Okello says, he began to style himself the 'Field Marshal'; this, in his eyes, was not simply a superior military rank superior to that of the 'generals' and 'colonels' he had appointed, but was also a job description based on the rank's original European meaning: the officer who marshalled the field of battle. In the Revolution Okello was often to say: 'Karume is President of the Government, I am the Field Marshal.'

Formal Independence

The major event of the period from July 1963 to the Revolution in January 1964 was the formal transfer of sovereignty on 10 December 1963. The period does, however, form a whole, with independence merely serving to emphasise rather than change the direction of events. Before these events are considered, the contribution of geography and the environment to the gathering storm should be mentioned. Zanzibar City lies on a peninsula on the western coast of Unguja; the centre of government, secretariat and Sultan's Palace lay in Stone Town, on the seaward side of this perimeter. Around Zanzibar City, cutting it off from all land access, lay Ng'ambo, beyond which were the commuter suburbs, all solidly A.S.P. Support for the government lay mostly in Pemba, with some measure of support also in North-West Unguja. Pemba's separation from Unguja by water was to prove crucial. In addition Mtoni and Ziwani, two of the major district police stations (with the force's armouries) for Zanzibar City, and the territory's radio station were all in Ng'ambo as if ready to be captured or besieged. The stage could hardly have been better prepared.

Election success, the Sultan's over-confidence and the apparent prospect of a long and unchallengeable period in office led the coalition ministers into a series of ill-judged and rash policies, especially unfortunate in the economic circumstances of 1963. For these circumstances the government was not to blame, since they were a local form of the familiar Third World 'one crop' situation. Clove prices had fallen badly as Indonesia and India, the major clove purchasers, were both suffering from a shortage of foreign exchange and, in Indonesia's case, from internal unrest as well.[14] Other territories, notably Madagascar and Indonesia itself, were producing cloves in competition. Clove purchasers had not in 1963 learnt to appreciate the superiority of Zanzibar's cloves for one major use, the flavouring of tobacco. The result, however, was a fall in both

14. Indonesia's purchases had fallen from approximately £1m. to approximately £150,000 in 1963.

purchase prices and wage rates in Zanzibar; this had in turn led to budget deficits,[15] which the coalition government proposed to meet by reductions in social services, specifically expenditure on schools and medical facilities, also on some housing and welfare projects. The shortage of money led to the slowing down or cessation of a number of private enterprises and other government development work, which in turn created unemployment, almost for the first time in colonial Zanzibar. The reductions in services fell chiefly on the African areas, adding fuel to the resentment and bitterness. The coalition government's plans for agricultural land, produced at this juncture, were also singularly inept. A Land Bank was proposed, through which a large sum of money donated by the British government as an independence gift was to be made available for loans to farmers to improve their farms; the loans were to be given on the security of existing farm land. This inevitably favoured the big land-owners to the disadvantage of the small peasants and those living on communal land. The A.S.P. leaders asked for a reform of land ownership, but when they opposed the measure in the legislature they did so in vain, the government taking no note of their arguments. This failure of the A.S.P. to achieve anything in so crucial a matter as land disillusioned more A.S.P. members as to the value of parliamentary opposition. A further cause of profound resentment was the difficulty which indigenous Africans, even sometimes those with good academic qualifications, had in obtaining promotion, or even appointment, in the government service.

In this climate Babu's *Umma* Party made some headway, in particular among young Arabs of middle-class origin attracted to Arab Socialist political ideals and revolutionary anti-Western Marxism. Babu also gained a following in the youth wing of the Z.N.P. and the Z.N.P.-linked F.P.T.U. unions (see above, p. 42). Khamis Abdulla Ameir, Secretary of the 250-strong Maritime and Allied Workers Union, was a significant figure in this development. Babu further began to make some impression on the more radical leaders of the A.S.P., notably the party's Deputy General Secretary, the Soviet-educated Kassim Hanga,[16] who was the member of the

15. In 1957–8, cloves were fetching some £37–£42 per 100 lb., and in some cases up to £45; by 1963 £6 10s. The British government provided certain grants-in-aid to help ease the situation, but these could not cover the whole shortfall. The budget deficit was £450,000 on a budget of £3,247,000.

16. Abdulla Kassim Hanga was born in 1932. He had studied at the Zanzibar Teachers Training College where he was the first Chairman of the Students' Union. He then moved on to London, whence he hoped to go to the University of Illinois to study Economics, for which purpose a scholar-

legislature for Kikwajuni. Hanga's Marxist views generally followed those closely of Moscow, which was unusual among African political leaders in the early 1960s. A small formal Communist party was formed at this time but it made no impact in spite of the large quantities of Communist literature which were on sale in Zanzibar City and the offer of visits to the Soviet Union and to China,[17] whose interest in Zanzibar had been aroused by the events of 1961. A Chinese trade union official, Kao Lang, developed contacts with Zanzibar's unions through the New China News Agency. One of the influential trade union leaders who visited Peking as a result of these contacts was Khamis Masoud, who was both Secretary of the Pemba P.W.D. Workers Union and Deputy Secretary of the A.S.P.-linked Z.P.F.L., and who became a supporter of Babu. The measure of *Umma*'s direct appeal to the general public though is hard to assess.[18] Babu's organisational ability, together with support from the All Zanzibar Journalists Organisation (A.Z.J.O.) whose members, including several who had hitherto been A.S.P. members, vigorously abused the government in the local press, gave the appearance of a movement rapidly gaining mass support. But the

ship had been arranged. The U.S. government however refused him a visa, almost certainly on the advice of the British colonial authorities. This left him with a strong sense of injury and led him to Moscow for his further Economics studies. There he married a Soviet citizen, who appears to have been an American-born Communist who had assumed Soviet nationality. They later separated. The rigidity of Kassim Hanga's views made political dealing and negotiation with him exceedingly difficult; for example, although an A.S.P. delegate at the 1962 London constitutional conference, his only contributions were of political rhetoric.

17. 'There is a flourishing little Communist bookstall, well equipped with the stock works of Marx, Lenin and Mao Tse-tung. Politicians, teachers and trade unionists go off at regular intervals on cultural tours to meet their Russian or Chinese counterparts', as J. Ridley wrote in an article entitled 'Black Cloud over Zanzibar' in the *Daily Telegraph* of 24 July 1963. One method used by the Chinese to attract a following was always to answer any postal enquiry about Chinese Communism with pamphlets and letters.

18. In R. Rotberg and A.A. Mazrui, *Protest and Power in Black Africa*, New York, 1970, VII, 924-68, Lofchie estimates the support to be considerable. Several British observers in Zanzibar at the time, however, held the view that outside the trade union movement *Umma*'s appeal was very limited. The large proportion of *Umma*'s leaders who were Arab or part-Arab undoubtedly impeded its appeal to the African population: Muhammed Foum, like Babu, was a Comorian, and Ali Mahfoudh and Salim Rashid were Arabs; all had recently returned from Cuba. Only the very small Pemba branch of *Umma* contained a significant percentage of Africans.

meetings held in the capital did not draw large crowds. Certainly outside Zanzibar City the vast majority of the African population, mainlander and Shirazi, remained loyal to the A.S.P., though some, particularly in the small Pemba branch, were attracted by *Umma*. But to Africans generally the theme of Babu's rhetoric, that the Z.N.P. leadership of landlords and merchants was only concerned to maintain social divisions, appeared as no more than a quarrel between two Arab groups.

The British Resident, Sir George Mooring, made a final attempt to find a parliamentary solution to the situation by trying to persuade the government ministers on the one hand and some of the more moderate leaders of the A.S.P. on the other to broaden the basis of the governing coalition. This was not an improper procedure in any parliamentary system of government, though perhaps politically incautious.[19] In this case many A.S.P. leaders resented what they saw as an attempt to divide them, and the already acute tensions and rifts between them worsened. Karume's replacement of the quiet and courteous Othman Sharif by himself as Leader of the Opposition was a sign of these rifts.

Preparations for the independence celebrations, and the celebrations themselves, proved as divisive as other measures by the government, almost as if it wanted to taunt the opposition to exasperation, and then proclaim victory by a show of strength and superiority. Inexperience can to some degree explain its behaviour, but racial arrogance and contempt for Africans were larger ingredients. On the podium for the handover of power[20] with the Duke of Edinburgh were the Sultan and his ministers, all in Arab dress; no African was in any conspicuous position. Whereas Stone Town was well decorated with illuminations in the streets, Ng'ambo's coloured celebration lights were distributed with much greater distances between them[21] and there were no signs of celebration among the inhabitants.

The celebrations however provided cover for other activities. Drilling of men, ostensibly for independence day parades, was

19. The attempt was bitterly attacked as deliberately divisive in the post-revolution 'Official Version' of events, where it was referred to as 'the August Plot'.

20. The official Zanzibar term preferred at the time was the 'resumption of sovereignty'.

21. P. Piggott, in the Zanzibar Education Department at the time, to the author, 16 November 1976. Piggot also recalled the construction of a metalled road through the Creek area of Ng'ambo for the use of a Z.N.P. minister whose house was nearby. The African houses in the area had only mud tracks.

reported in many areas;[22] these were undoubtedly the followers of Okello, or in some cases adherents of other conspiracies. The Z.N.P. Youth Wing, by now more loyal to Babu than to the government, drilled in the gardens of houses on the airport road. The government was already losing control of events while the revolutionaries used official preoccupation with the celebrations to press ahead with their own preparations, which even included attempts to recruit adolescent schoolboys.[23] Others moved about posing as market traders. The government had unwisely, and against British official advice, allowed its supporters to wear a political uniform at rallies and marches. The A.S.P. followed suit.

Independence saw a change in the government[24] and the assumption by the Sultan of the style 'His Majesty'. With independence the British Resident, Mooring, and the Chief Secretary, Robertson, departed.[25] The attainment of sovereignty by Zanzibar included full Commonwealth membership as its smallest state, and led soon afterwards to full United Nations membership as well. The actual moment of independence was midnight on 9–10 December. On the morning of the 10th, Sultan Jamshid formally opened the National Assembly. On both occasions the Sultan and Shamte together promised government policies aimed at the removal of causes of

22. For example, Piggott to the author: 'Numerous incidents of young men drilling in quiet, and not so quiet, spots were well known in Ng'ambo and elsewhere in Zanzibar Town.' The A.S.P. followers drilled near the burial grounds on the Makunduchi road. Mrs V. Davies to the author, 2 March 1977.

23. Piggott to the author: 'During the last six months or so before Independence, there were considerable attempts to subvert the boarders at my school. Cars would drive through the grounds at dusk and drop off left-wing propaganda near the domitory block.' The senior British department officials were unable to convince the coalition ministers of the seriousness of the situation.

24. This final pre-Revolution government was composed as follows: Prime Minister M. Shamte Hamadi (Z.P.P.P.); External Affairs, A. Muhsin (Z.N.P.); Finance and Development, Juma Aley (Z.N.P.); Home and Legal Affairs, Salim Kombo Saleh (Z.P.P.P.); Health and Welfare, Abdulrahman Edarus el Balaawy (Z.N.P.) who also held the portfolio of Communications and Works; Education and Information, Maulidi Mshangama (Z.N.P.); Agriculture, Abadhar Juma Khatib (Z.P.P.P.); Minister without Portfolio Ibuni Saleh (Z.N.P.).

25. A number of the Arab elders openly wept as they bade Mooring farewell (Mrs J. Dickson, Mooring's Private Secretary, to the author, 3 February 1964). The Sultan was expected to attend the farewell but did not in fact appear, no reason was ever given.

discontent, communal and economic. In the course of his speech to the Assembly Jamshid said:

We can properly be guided in our affairs by the words of the Koran, 'Be not like those who are divided among themselves and fall into disputations — after receiving clear signs. For them is a dreadful penalty.'

For Jamshid and his government the penalty was less than six weeks distant, and in these last weeks the style and demeanour of the Z.N.P.-dominated government reached its final level of ineptitude and insensitivity. Ali Muhsin, the External Affairs Minister, paid two well-publicised visits to Cairo, which appeared to many Africans to indicate the nature of his policies and priorities more clearly than his professions of non-racial aims. The other strong Z.N.P. personality in the government, the Finance Minister Juma Aley, was openly partisan despite a good education and considerable personal charm. He spoke of Karume contemptuously as 'the boatman' and let it be known that he believed all Africans to be illiterate and incapable of exercising authority and power. A new decoration, the Order of Istiqlal (the Arabs' word for independence), was distributed mainly to Arabs, though Karume and the A.S.P. General Secretary received Commander and Officer titles respectively.

At independence the Zanzibar government still depended heavily on the assistance of British officials. Although the major provincial administration posts, Senior Commissioner and district commissioners, were in Arab hands, most of the Permanent Secretaries were British, as were all heads of major departments, including the Chief Justice, the Attorney General, Commissioners of Police and Prisons, the Comptroller of Customs, and the Port Officer. Most senior scientific or technical appointments, with a number of lower-level posts in the medical, education and works fields, were also still held by British officials. It was planned to replace quickly the Permanent Secretary to the Prime Minister, M.V. Smithyman, by an Egyptian official, but little urgency was seen in respect of other changes except in the police force; there, in addition to some retirements of British officers, other changes were made for the reason already noted, that of distrust of the mainlanders who formed a major part of the force at inspector and N.C.O. level.

Thus the Zanzibar Police had lost many of its most experienced British officers, including one or two in the Special Branch, in December 1963 and early January 1964.[26] Arabs promoted in their

26. K. Kyle, the *Spectator*, 14 February 1964, states that twenty out of twenty-six British police officers left in this period.

place were neither competent nor sufficiently trained. As already noted, the Shamte government did not trust, sometimes with good reason, a number of the mainland African inspectors and N.C.O.s and abruptly dismissed them; to crown this unwise act, as we have already seen, the government refused to pay their travel expenses back to the mainland, so leaving at large a body of embittered men with a specialist knowledge of the police armoury system to be recruited by revolutionaries. By the end of the year the force was demoralised, too small and ill-trained to contain a revolution, and with most of its sources for intelligence no longer operating.[27] The police knew that several plans for revolution were afoot, and at least one remaining Special Branch officer knew of Okello's preparations (though not of Okello himself), but to the harassed police head-quarters this was seen as just one more rumour.[28] Lastly, some of the remaining junior officers, not all of them African, had some sympathy and links with the A.S.P.; several of these must have known what was afoot but they were not likely to pass this infor-mation on to Arab superior officers, or even British officers in the service of an Arab-dominated government. In the Revolution a number of serving African police, including at least one inspector, actually fought for the revolutionaries from the outset. Others either made some small show of resistance or none at all — and then joined the new regime.[29] Zanzibar's police reflected the divisions of its society.

The Shamte government had refused any form of military co-operation agreement with Britain, an arrangement which might have produced a small British garrison to maintain stability. Instead it

27. Until the ministerial rushuffle at independence, the Minister respon-sible for the Police was Ali Muhsin, a major reason why information ceased to be forthcoming.

28. M.V. Smithyman, Permanent Secretary to the Prime Minister, in a letter to the author, 16 June 1977, wrote that as a member of the Zanzibar Government's Security Committee he would have known if anyone had been aware of Okello's preparations. After the Revolution, Smithyman met one of the remaining British officers of the Special Branch, who never mentioned to him any prior knowledge of Okello.

29. After the Revolution the Revolutionary Council quickly appointed four superintendents (Ramadhan Khatibu, Ramadhan Haji, J. Peter, R. Mulieli), one deputy superintendent (Nasser Abdulla) and six assistant superintendents (C.d'Goa, D. Kazungu, A. Kadenge, T. Mbau, A. Yustino, J. Omega), with E. Kisassi as Commissioner and B.L. Raymond as Deputy Commissioner. All of these were serving inspectors, assistant inspectors or N.C.O.s prior to the Revolution. Kisassi, a Tanganyikan by birth, was the senior African officer.

talked of negotiating such an agreement with the United Arab Republic at some unspecified time in the future; there was no sense of urgency. No army existed, but following the events of 1961 a gendarmerie-type Police Mobile Force (P.M.F.) had been established with headquarters and armoury at Mtoni. In 1963 great efforts were made to recruit Arabs for this force, which was commanded by a British officer of the police. The Shamte government had appointed another Briton as this officer's successor, with instructions to him to think in terms of tripling the P.M.F., to make it the nucleus of a small army to be officered by Egyptians.[30] Also in 1963 all weapons held at the smaller police stations on both islands were withdrawn and concentrated in the two armouries, Ziwani and Mtoni, near Zanzibar City, a move that proved unwise since it reduced to impotence areas loyal to the government. By January 1964 the P.M.F. had attained a total of some 150 trained men and thirty recruits. But its morale was a microcosm of that of the whole force. Discipline was openly restive, and the camp canteen was boycotted as a result of political agitation.

On January 2 the tensions within the A.S.P. came to a head, with the resignations from the party of Othman Sharif, Hasnu Makame, Idris Wakyl and Saleh Saadalla. These four were moderate men of good education, and although the reason for their resignation is not known for certain, it is probable that they left the party because the rest of its leadership was moving towards a decision favouring early revolutionary action. Sharif, certainly, was totally dissatisfied with Karume's leadership. He argued that Karume was not a true Zanzibari — once again a matter of identification, and a view reflecting Sharif's Pemba origin. On Unguja Karume was of course a much more representative figure, being a descendant of early twentieth-century mainland immigrants; these pre-1950 mainland immigrants were a major element in his power base. These sharp, at times bitter, divisions in the party leadership appear to have had the effect of making those in favour of revolution more militant rather than more cautious; suspicion was growing that although the decline of the Z.P.P.P. on Pemba might be to the A.S.P's advantage, that advantage would favour the non-Hadimu indigenes and Pemba moderates within the party at the expense of the Unguja Hadimu and mainlanders. Certainly this suspicion motivated the rest of the largely Unguja A.S.P. executive when it met and reaffirmed its

30. The British P.M.F. commander, Waring, pointed out the political implications of so powerful a force and added that Africans might object to serving under Egyptians.

confidence in Karume and the party's general secretary, Thabit Kombo.

During the first week of 1964, the government proscribed the *Umma* party, a reaction of alarm to the spate of propaganda being issued by its journalist and other supporters. The party office was raided and files and vehicles were confiscated. The raid, by two lorry-loads of men from the P.M.F., was carried out in mid-afternoon to make a specially public show of force. Babu's house was searched. Initially no arrests were made, but Babu and others were refused passports. The proscription was justified by allegations of breaches of the Registration of Societies ordinance. Babu himself departed secretly by canoe for Dar es Salaam, while a warrant for his arrest was being prepared. The significance of this event lay in its indication of the direction from which the government perceived its major threat at the time, a perception based on the reactions of the members of the Z.N.P. who had remained loyal. For Okello this affair proved a useful distraction.[31] *Umma*'s proscription had consequences for the A.S.P., since it had been hinted that it too would be proscribed when the legislature debated the Land Bank and loans arrangements. The fear that their party would be the next candidate for proscription strengthened the resolve of some A.S.P. leaders to revolt, with a sense of urgency. In fact it seems unlikely the government was seriously thinking of proscribing the A.S.P. at the time. Babu's party was proscribed because of its Communist links, which the government saw as something to be taken seriously.[32] The government's prejudices and arrogance led it to despise the A.S.P.; it saw the differences between Karume and Othman Sharif as amounting to a deep-rooted feud between the indigenes and the mainlanders which weakened the party to its advantage, and believed that Karume could be managed by flattering him as Leader of His Majesty's Loyal Opposition, while it totally ignored the most

31. K. Kyle, the *Spectator*, 7 February 1964, wrote: 'In a sense Babu was a splendid decoy — though I doubt whether this was his conscious role. He was a conspicuous figure whose activities in permeating trade unions and organising propagandist (and potentially revolutionary) cells throughout Zanzibar Island were eminently visible to the previous government's intelligence service. John Okello, whom the government had never heard of before, was by contrast not noticed.'

32. Another consequence of the proscription of *Umma* was that the government began to delay preparations to exchange diplomatic missions with the Soviet Union and China, in the words attributed to one Zanzibar External Affairs official 'for at least a little while until he [Muhsin] has cleaned up their boys here' F. Picard, U.S. Chargé d'Affaires, to the State Department, 6 January 1964.

dangerous of the A.S.P. militants, Kassim Hanga.[33] Of Okello it had of course never even heard. A final, religious factor contributing to Arab complacency was the period of feasting immediately before Ramadan.

A catalyst for the violence to follow was a widespread belief that the government was secretly arming the bitterly disliked Manga Arabs in order to have a force on which it could rely to rescue it in case violence should cut it off in Zanzibar City, or to use for the suppression of the A.S.P. The rumour was almost certainly untrue as the government did not have the weapons to issue even if it had wished to do so.[34] But many Manga Arabs possessed their own sporting weapons which they were apt to carry with them at times of tension; this, coupled with the A.S.P.'s past allegations that the Manga were a Z.N.P. militia, no doubt served to disseminate the story. Okello makes more specific claims for Arab designs; he alleges that there were plans for the mass repatriation of mainlanders and the reduction of others to slavery, the encouragement of immigration from Oman, and the banning of all African organisations. His wild talk of longer-term aims to kill African babies, breed a new lighter-skinned race and then re-occupy Mombasa well illustrates the passions that were bubbling to the surface.

So in the heat of the warm weather season on Unguja in January 1964, everyone was tense, waiting for something to happen. The atmosphere of uncertainty and impending violence was not confined to Zanzibar. Kenya had just become independent after a decade of turbulent politics, culminating in three years of bitter controversy between political parties based largely upon rival ethnic groupings. British press reports suggested that Kenya was on the verge of collapsing into anarchy, and there was little confidence in Kenyatta's ability to contain his most militant supporters. Press photographs of 'Mau Mau' freedom fighters receiving an official welcome and rewards appeared, and the crisis on Kenya's border with Somalia, together with occasional attacks on Europeans and cattle thefts, were all reported. In Tanganyika Nyerere had returned to power as

33. The 'Official Version' claims that after the Revolution a list of 120 names of leading A.S.P. members and trade union leaders to be arrested was found at Ziwani. This list was not published, and the statement needs to be taken with caution. If the list did exist, it could well have been only a 'contingency plan' list.

34. J.M. Sullivan, Commissioner of Police at the time, to the author, 14 December 1976, and Smithyman to the author, 17 June 1977. A rumour current at the time suggested that one or two members of the government were attempting to purchase weapons, possibly for later issue to the Manga.

President of the Republic after a sabbatical year. But the rivalry between him and the ambitious and militant Oscar Kambona, then his Minister of Defence, was already developing, and observers in Dar es Salaam were predicting an open clash. Uganda had just deported a number of Britons for indulging in racial abuse. The events of 1960–3 in the Congo (now Zaire) were fresh in everyone's mind. 'It will be another Congo' was said by many colonial officials departing from East Africa. One, perhaps two, of the A.S.P. leaders appeared to have some inkling of the storm about to burst in Zanzibar. Karume himself heard rumours, and — for reasons which may be guessed but which can never now be confirmed or denied — was at first not unwilling to let the event take its course in the belief that if successful Okello would need his authority. But it appears that Karume came increasingly to see revolution as premature and to doubt its chances of success. He certainly visited one British police officer privately to say that disturbances would occur over the week-end of the 11–12 January and that he was not responsible for them.[35] This led the government to secure its armouries on the night of 11–12th with an extra guard, mount road blocks, and call out a handful of European residents who were reserve police officers. The P.M.F. was kept in barracks by its commander on his own initiative.

More easily explained is the behaviour of Othman Sharif. On the night of 10–11 January he sought an urgent meeting with Shamte to try and persuade him to abandon the Z.N.P. alliance and leave the way free for a Z.P.P.P.-A.S.P. coalition government.[36] At this extremity he was prepared to forget his past differences with Shamte. He may also have seen himself as the most likely leader for such an alliance, one in which the non-revolutionary A.S.P. members, including those who had recently resigned, might hold the political balance if they entered an alliance with the Z.P.P.P. All his

35. Smithyman to the author, 16 June 1977, notes Karume's apprehensions and actions. He suggests they were a consequence of the 1961 events for which Karume feared he might be held responsible and imprisoned. The Commissioner of Police saw Karume's warning as only yet one more move in a war of nerves. Several officials of the U.S. mission in Zanzibar were aware of trouble planned for the night of 11 January. Kyle, *Spectator*, 14 February 1964, and W.R.M. Belcher, a Zanzibar resident who lived next door to a U.S. diplomat, to the author, 24 November 1976.

36. B. Eccles, a former Zanzibar government administration officer then serving on the staff of the British High Commission in Zanzibar, to the author, interview, 1 December 1976. Kyle, telephone conversation to the author, 2 December 1976, added that he too knew of this meeting.

inclinations — due to personal temperament, education professional training, and, most important of all, due to being from
Pemba — led him to reject a revolution which to him was an alien
one. Shamte however either refused or claimed that such a change
was not possible. The last chance of averting revolution was lost.

The Revolution and its First Days

Zanzibar's Revolution was a complex series of events and it will be
simplest for a reader to follow the details if an account of these is
preceded by a short outline summary.

Essentially, the Revolution was completed within three hours, and
was the work of John Okello. However at least one other grouping
of people, and possibly two or more, were preparing revolution and
on finding the Revolution actually happening around, hastily joined
in. Their contribution made little difference to the course of the
fighting, since victory had already gone to Okello. However it did
entitle their leaders, some of whom either were in or had hurriedly
departed for Dar es Salaam, to claim the right to participate in the
post-Revolution arrangements. In one of these groupings the major
figure was Kassim Hanga and in another Babu.

Kassim Hanga had much in common both in temperament and in
political ideology with Tanganyika's Oscar Kambona. Also, the two
men had been personal friends, sharing a room when they were
students in London. If Kassim Hanga's plans had been successful he
would have emerged as the real leader in Zanzibar, with Karume in
some figurehead role. This ambition was known to Okello who saw
Karume, in his capacity as leader of the A.S.P., as the legitimate
chief of any post-revolution government; Okello viewed Kassim
Hanga as an ambitious usurper, too closely linked to Tanganyikan
politics, while Okello himself preferred a Kenya connection.
Kassim Hanga was in fact on Okello's list of people to be killed and
in the Revolution Okello broadcast demands for him to present
himself.[37] Kassim Hanga may have been aware of his danger, or
possibly he was confused to discover a revolution in progress that
was not his own. For whatever reason, he reacted to the Revolution
by departing hurriedly to Dar es Salaam for talks with Kambona.[38] It
seems probable that the plan of Kassim Hanga and Kambona was

37. T. Waring, formerly of the Zanzibar Police, to the author, telephone
conversation, March 1977.
38. After the Revolution, Kassim Hanga refused to give any reason for his
flight, simply saying he was 'on a mission'. Kyle, *Spectator*, 14 February
1964.

for a week-end of violence a week later on 18–19 January, taking the simultaneous form of an army mutiny in Tanganyika and a revolution in Zanzibar. President Nyerere may have known something of the proposals to assist Kassim Hanga, but he knew nothing of the army unrest. Kambona was well aware of the plans for the army mutiny, and he expected to profit politically from the disturbances that would occur. He had been formally warned of the unrest within Tanganyikan units by British officers still serving with them, but he had taken no action to enquire into the reasons for the discontent or to seek its redress, planning to throw the blame for trouble, when it broke out, on to the British officers. Also, for purposes not entirely clear but possibly including help for Kassim Hanga, Kambona had earmarked a consignment of arms and ammunition from Algeria which arrived in Dar es Salaam on 3 January 1964 and were unloaded under special arrangements.[39] The weapons were mostly obsolete Second World War North Africa campaign pieces, British, Italian and German and without spare parts, together with some explosive. They had apparently been ordered by the Tanganyika Government, ostensibly to assist Frelimo in Mozambique, and the Algerians had charged a heavy price. The consignment was unloaded by soldiers under African officers only, and stored under guard. The unfamiliar appearance of the weapons, however, necessitated British expert advice. Certain boxes were marked with a black cross, and perhaps these were intended for Kassim Hanga. The weapons, however, never reached Zanzibar, events having moved too fast.

Babu, who arrived in Dar es Salaam on 8 January, had had little or no time after his flight from Zanzibar for any detailed preparations. He did, however, have one asset, namely a group of young Zanzibaris trained in revolution in Cuba under arrangements made between him and the influential black Cuban ambassador in Dar es Salaam, Pablo Ribalta. This group had recently returned to East Africa, and its members were observed in Dar es Salaam early in 1964; their Cuban revolutionary-style attire and Castro beards, together with their salute of '*Venceremos*' (We will conquer), made them conspicuous. It is more significant that later, after their return to Zanzibar, this salute was the cause of the persistent belief that there were Cubans present in Unguja, a belief which was to have important diplomatic repercussions. Their presence in Dar es Salaam had caused anxiety among Kambona's followers, and a

39. In the end, most of these weapons were taken out to sea and sunk by British Royal Marines, who had been called in to Dar es Salaam at the request of the Tanganyika Government to restore order. (*Source*: British officers serving in Tanganyika at the time to the author, 1976.)

meeting to consider some role for them was held at Bagamoyo on the
night of 9 January. But the confusion of revolutionary groups and
plans was so great that although some form of co-ordination was
said to have been attempted by means of a letter from A.S.P. militants on the mainland to others on the island, carried by a member of
the crew of the government steamer *Salama*, no real co-ordination
was achieved, and the return of these revolutionaries to Zanzibar on
the night before the Revolution was coincidental. Nevertheless they
promptly joined in. They were transported in a boat belonging to a
firm called Ocean Products operated by two Israeli brothers-in-law,
named Feinsilber and Abramovich[40] (as Israelis they had a dislike for
an Arab government which might well have closed their business
down had it lasted, and they had been friendly with both Babu and
some of the A.S.P. leaders for some time).[41]

Okello's Revolution falls conveniently into two stages, one principally of seizure of power on the night of Saturday 11 January, and
one of Terror.[42] The seizure of power was camouflaged by publicity
for the large A.S.P. fête and dance at the Raha Leo Community
Centre in Ng'ambo.[43] Despite the road blocks, a large number of
people arrived at the function, armed — seemingly in accord with
Okello's prior instructions — with a variety of weapons: spears,

40. Smithyman to the author, 16 June 1977, records a conversation
between his wife and Abramovich in Dar es Salaam after the Revolution, in
which Abramovich openly admitted this journey. T. Waring to the author,
21 March 1977, recalled seeing a strange boat off the coast near Zanzibar at
that time.

41. It should be recalled that at this time Israel was pursuing a forward
policy in Africa, offering aid, training and education facilities in a number of
fields in the hope of creating a group of nations friendly to herself 'behind'
the Arab states. It is reasonable to note the possibility that Feinsilber and
Abramovich may have been in some relationship with the Israeli government. W.M.L. Hall to the author, 1 November 1976, and R.H.V. Biles,
Sullivan's predecessor as Commissioner of Police, Zanzibar, to the author,
13 November 1976, note the friendship of the brothers-in-law with Zanzibari
political figures. A. Badawy to the author, 9 November 1976, noted that
Babu lived near the firm's houses.

42. The narrative of the seizure of power which follows is largely based on
Okello, *op.cit.*, 140–6; excerpts from Okello's writings and broadcasts are
also taken from these pages.

43. The 'Official Version' notes Karume and other A.S.P. leaders as being
present on this occasion. Some of the other leaders may have been, but
Karume himself certainly was not. Other social events which distracted
attention were a small police officers' party and the absence of the Permanent Secretary for Home Affairs (whose Ministry included Security)
yachting.

sticks, tyre-levers, hammers, matchets, even knives and bows and arrows. Some had taken drugs as a stimulant. At Mwembe Okello, with his principal fellow-conspirators Haji, Mfarinyaki, Mzee Mohamed, Matias Simba, Seif Bakari and Said Bavuai, issued his final orders to a force of some 800. He ordered Haji and one group to take Mtoni; Mzee Mohamed and a second group, the '2 Battalion' consisting of about 100 men, to take the nearby broadcasting station; Mfarinyaki with a group known as '4 Battalion' to take the Ziwani police headquarters lines and later the customs, airport and hospital, and lastly Simba with Mzee Kenya to take the Mazizini prison and the post office, using a '3 Battalion' of some 150. Ingen was to deal with transport and water supplies. Just after midnight the groups set off, Okello and Ingen accompanying Mfarinyaki, and began their attacks.

The Ziwani police building was fairly new, with an armoury on the ground floor and barracks upstairs; a few huts were sited nearby and the whole was surrounded by a barbed wire fence. The attack began with the cutting of the wire, at which point many of the attackers took fright, but a cadre of thirty or forty persevered and attempted to rush the building. A sentry killed two of the attackers and wounded one more before they were overwhelmed. Okello and 'Albert, a Kenyan' killed a second sentry. Okello's narrative of the next events runs as follows:

Front doors had been opened, but by this time the government police, who had been upstairs sleeping began to rush towards the stairs. Some forty of them were under attack by my men, who used mainly bows and arrows and stones to hold the men upstairs while we broke into the armoury. The rifle which I had taken from the sentry had three shots in it — this was the first 'modern' weapon in our Revolution, but it was the most important one for it gave us an advantage for a few minutes.

In the wild confusion the government forces began to ring sirens and blow trumpets and to throw tear gas down on us. We smothered the tear gas bombs with our shirts momentarily, and I cut the wire to the siren. With the rifle, I shot the trumpeter out of his place at the top of the stairs and his trumpet fell and clattered on the floor. Using axes, hammers and other house-breaking implements, our men had smashed open the doors of the armoury. About half of the government police had been killed or wounded and the remainder had surrendered even before we began to distribute the weapons and ammunition. My men had been prepared to use pistols and simple rifles; the commanding officers, most of them with police or military experience, gave instructions on loading and using Bren and Sten guns and other automatic weapons. Brigadier Amoi Ingen and myself were using both Bren and Sten guns, and we took up central positions on either side of the building to prepare for a counter-attack from the Sultan's small group of para-military forces, a unit created after the 1961 riots.

By the time the government troops arrived, around 4.30 a.m., the 200 men who had scattered at the initial assault had joined us and been deployed throughout the building and the compound, well-armed and supplied with plenty of ammunition. We fought the Sultan's troops, who had only conventional rifles, for about an hour, firing relentlessly upon them from all angles, until the entire area was in flames. At this stage it was mostly a matter of superior fire power, coupled with our well-enforced position in the police building itself. By 5.30 a.m., most of the government forces had been killed or had run off; we sent out small units to hunt for remaining troops and posted guards at the armoury and barracks doors, and generally occupied the building under massive armed security precautions. We also hoisted the flags of the Revolutionary Army and of the Field Marshal over the building.

The counter-attack by the P.M.F. was not mounted with any determination, although Okello's account credits it with more resolution than other accounts which suggest that at the first shots the P.M.F. detachment simply ran away.

Okello claimed that Ziwani was the first key-point to fall, but it is probable that Mtoni with its raw recruits fell even more quickly: its perimeter had not been protected with a barbed-wire fence, and policemen were cut off almost at the outset from their officers. With Mtoni's fall the revolutionaries captured some 200 rifles, twenty-five sub-machine carbines, two Bren light machine-guns and a number of pistols, with ammunition; also grenades and tear-gas canisters. One of the senior African officers at Mtoni, Inspector Anton, had been in league with the revolutionaries. Haji was slightly wounded in the attack, but he nevertheless sent a message of success to Okello who, according to his account, moved through cheering crowds to visit this second prize before making his headquarters at the broadcasting station where a B.B.C. engineer on loan had been forced at gunpoint to operate the transmitter. The quick capture of the station by Mzee Mohamed's group was of enormous significance. The revolutionaries could now broadcast, while the government was reduced to the use of the telephone only. Okello then began, at about 7 a.m., the first of his notorious broadcasts.[44] These served to terrify many Arabs whom Okello was not at that moment in a position to capture. At the outset he simply described himself as 'Field Marshal of the Freedom Fighters', the anonymity of the broadcasts and Okello's

44. Okello, *op.cit.*, 143. This technique of sapping an opponent's strength by taunting broadcasts and cowing opposition by terror was first used in the Spanish Civil War by General Quiepo de Llano on Radio Seville; no other Civil War or revolutionary example between then and 1964 seems to be on record, and the idea could well have been Okello's own. *The Times*, 14 January 1964, notes that Okello simply described himself as the Field Marshal of the Freedom Fighters.

strong mainland accent adding to their dread nature. Later in the day he used his own name. His book provides an example of his style at this point:

Wake up you imperialists, there is no longer an imperialist government on this island. This is now the government of the freedom fighters. Wake up you black men, let everyone of you take a gun and ammunition and start to fight against any remnants of imperialism.

Okello adds that he ordered Aboud Jumbe to broadcast in his support, gave an ultimatum to the Commissioner of Prisons to surrender at Mazizini, and ordered any resistance to be overcome by shooting. After broadcasting Okello moved on to the Mazizini prison with a group armed with captured rifles and supervised an attack launched at approximately 10 a.m., which resulted in the capture of the complex of buildings, some of which were burnt in the process, within thirty minutes. Neither the attack nor the defence appears to have been very resolute. The prison defenders had a machine-gun but one observer commented that in his opinion it was firing high, probably deliberately.[45] At this point Okello received a report that the Manga Arabs had begun to kill Africans in the rural areas and he divided those of his forces which he could effectively command, some to depart to fight the Manga and others to beseige the last remaining police post, Malindi, at the entrance of Stone Town.

Some of Okello's followers, and more particularly many other would-be revolutionaries who were joining in, had by this time begun to pillage the Asian and Arab bazaars in the Darajani area, the area of Stone Town nearest Ng'ambo. Because of this and the fear of a Manga counter-attack, as well as the difficulty of fighting in a built-up area, the mob of armed Africans had not yet made any large-scale entry into Stone Town. In certain areas there was mindless shooting by small groups, and a number of Goan children were massacred on their way to an early church service.[46] Europeans had however only been mildly stoned rather than attacked. This pause in momentum enabled the Sultan and his family to carry out at 7 a.m. a prepared plan for a hurried departure to the government steamer *Salama* anchored in the harbour. The plan provided for whichever government steamer was in port at the time to move away from the quay at the first signs of trouble. On this occasion the *Salama* was unprepared, and it required help from the engineer of a

45. Noted in Waring to the author, 21 March 1977.
46. E. Norman to the author, 17 January 1977. Norman himself saw the corpses.

French ship calling at Zanzibar to move the vessel. The Sultan and his entourage arrived in a heavily-guarded convoy of three cars. British officials advised government ministers also to embark in the *Salama*, so they would thus leave the revolutionaries with no formal renunciation of power, and they could continue government from Pemba where they would have been well received. The ministers however refused, and it would seem that some preferred to try and negotiate with the rebels from where they were, while others feared to leave their hiding place. Several were seeking refuge in the British High Commission; Muhsin and Juma Aley visited the last major uncaptured police station, Malindi, in a state of shock. Also, at some point in the early morning Karume was woken at his home at Miembelado by a group of Okello's men and taken by dhow to Dar es Salaam. The reasons for his removal appears to have been concern for his safety in case of the revolution failing or a chance local Arab reprisal, and so that he could be a focus for further revolution, again in the event of failure. Karume now found himself in Dar es Salaam as confused over events as Kassim Hanga and Babu who were already there. Othman Sharif was similarly handled. He was woken by two men, one with a gun and one with a bow and arrow, told he must remain incommunicado for several hours, and ordered to advise the revolutionaries where the radio engineers lived.[47] Other A.S.P. leaders were placed under 'revolutionary protection'.

At the first outbreak of firing, Smithyman, the Permanent Secretary in the Prime Minister's office, attempted from the *Beit-el-Ajaib* to find out what was happening. He also notified the next senior British official of the Zanzibar government, H. Hawker, the Permanent Secretary for Finance, who in turn warned T. Crosthwait, the British High Commissioner and thus the senior British diplomatic representative. Although the broadcasting station was quickly captured the telephone system remained in operation throughout the Revolution — as, until the afternoon of 12 January, did the airport wireless communication system. Almost certainly via the airport, the outside world was informed and the provision of some help was arranged, in particular the despatch to Zanzibar of a small Royal Navy surveying ship, the *Owen*, which arrived to the great relief of the British community late in the evening of the 12th. Major political considerations, to be noted later, precluded the despatch of any substantial force, although there were two battalions in Kenya which could have been moved, and R.A.F. transport aircraft were available. Smithyman found the *Beit-el-Ajaib* untenable after 8 a.m. and departed to swim to safety aboard *Salama*, having

47. Kyle, *Spectator*, 14 February 1964.

handed over authority to Hawker who was in touch with the Sultan's ministers.[48] Of these, Shamte twice telegraphed President Nyerere on the morning of 12 January, first asking for the help of a police unit which Nyerere refused, saying that Tanganyika could not interfere in a Zanzibar internal affair, and later asking for a Tanganyikan minister to come to Zanzibar and act as a channel of communication with the rebels, which Nyerere also refused.[49] He also requested British help.

After the slight lull in the late morning, the pace of events quickened again in the afternoon, the Malindi police station being the decisive point. Two major road entrances to Zanzibar City existed, one from the south which the revolutionaries were entering in small groups in the morning, and one from the north; the latter was controlled at an important road intersection near the Customs Gate by the Malindi police station.[50] Here Sullivan, the British Commissioner of the Zanzibar Police, together with a small number of European reserve officers armed with hurriedly requisitioned sporting guns, and some seventy-five loyal African police N.C.Os. and men were still in control, and able to communicate by telephone with Hawker, with the British military commander in Kenya, and with other East African police forces. Malindi received a series of desultory and unsustained attacks. The post-revolution 'Official Version' of events approved by Karume, some Arab writers and Okello attempted subsequently to dramatise Malindi as the scene of a 'last stand'. In fact, not a window of the station was broken. The insurgents attacked in small groups which were easily dispersed; one group possessed a machine-gun with a distinctive slow rate of fire but it hit no one. Some Manga Arabs attempted to seek refuge in the police station in the late afternoon. The revolutionaries used a Police Special Branch officer who had sided with them to try and tempt Sullivan to march out and re-occupy Ziwani, which they said was unoccupied, but the trap was perceived. In the course of one of the

48. Hawker also arranged for the return of the larger of the government's steamers, the *Seyyid Khalifa*, from Tanga. She arrived in Zanzibar in the late afternoon, when the Sultan and his entourage transferred to her.

49. H. Hawker, Diary (an unpublished typed ms.). Hawker was told of these communications by R. Miller, head of the U.N. mission in Tanganyika. Miller was himself asked by Nyerere if he were willing to go to Zanzibar to mediate, but felt that as a Technical Assistance Officer he had no authority for such action. Other developments and reactions in Tanganyika are noted later.

50. The author is greatly indebted to T. Waring of the Zanzibar Police for a very full eye-witness account of the events at Malindi. Letter, 21 March 1977.

attacks Seif Bakari and another revolutionary leader were captured by the police. They were questioned about the events and answered that the rising was one of Afro-Shirazis, organised by Babu who had crossed over from the mainland secretly by canoe. This entirely false story, probably told as the one which British officials were most likely to believe, furthered the misconceptions about Communist involvement.[51] Sullivan, after discussion with Hawker, released them with a message to their leaders, then still unknown, seeking discussions and negotiations. But Okello was in no mood for saying anything other than that Europeans would not be molested, in itself a statement calculated to strengthen British caution; his broadcasts at this juncture consisted of threats to massacre the Malindi garrison and orders to the Sultan to commit suicide. When, therefore, Shamte changed his mind and requested an escort to the *Salama* he was advised by Hawker that not only was there no escort available but that he should resign to save life and property.[52] Shortly afterwards, on being promised safe conduct for himself and his colleagues (a promise not to be honoured), Shamte formally resigned.

The attacks on Malindi, watched by a large crowd of people, lasted until mid-afternoon. Then, apprehensive of the political and military consequences of a confused night fight, running out of ammunition, and after a fruitless attempt to negotiate a ceasefire with Raha Leo by telephone, Sullivan marched his men, white and black, in a body down to the quay. From there they were ferried to the *Salama*[53] and mostly later transferred to the *Seyyid Khalifa* in which they sailed to Dar es Salaam.[54] With the political system collapsing, casualties being reported at other stations, and having a number of unreliable African staff, Sullivan had little choice. The estimate of police casualties made at the time was 300; the actual figure was probably less since many desertions may have been counted as casualties. Elsewhere the most effective resistance had been at a City police station commanded by an Arab officer, Sketi,

51. Kyle, *Spectator*, 14 February 1964. Babu was in Dar es Salaam at that time.

52. Hawker pointed out that even before the Revolution his was a government elected by a minority of the population, and that resistance could only lead to bloodshed. Shamte no doubt also had in mind the fact that East African governments were already showing clear signs of sympathy for the Revolution, and no support could be expected from Kenya or Tanganyika.

53. One of the reserve police officers, W.R.M. Belcher, took especial care — involving an evidently hazardous return journey to Malindi to bring out a rearguard — to ensure that no African policemen were left behind. Belcher to the author, 24 November 1976.

54. Some later returned to Zanzibar, where a few were imprisoned.

who had earlier been designated Deputy Commissioner of Police by the Shamte government. Sketi was later hacked to death by the mob. Okello gives figures of seventy killed, 173 wounded and 818 detained, with nine Freedom Fighters killed and 401 wounded; these figures, however, can only be seen as very rough approximations, being recalled some time later when Okello was in prison. But all organised opposition to the Revolution on Unguja was now over, although shooting and killings continued in the rural areas for some time, notably at Bumbwini in the north where Arabs armed with sporting weapons held out for several hours. Other groups of Arabs fought on at Nungwe and Bububu until they were overrun and massacred. Arab resistance was often ineffective because the distance between estates prevented any concentration of strength; also the ferocity of their attackers often paralysed resistance. One Arab survivor commented:

They rose and murdered all the Arabs they could catch, slitting their throats by night as they slept. Some of us escaped to dhows but my parents were chased along the beach by a crowd — though my mother was African. They ran into the sea to swim to the boats, but some of the crowd followed, caught hold of their hair and drowned them.[55]

The day was to end with Okello virtually in full command together with a few of the lesser A.S.P. leaders, but with the three major figures, Karume, Babu and Kassim Hanga, still away.

Now in power, Okello planned the next political moves while at the same time pursuing the second phase of the Revolution, the Terror. His own personal position, in any long term, was weak; he had hitherto been unknown, and his followers were the most recently-arrived mainlanders, a group trusted by neither the longer-established mainlanders nor the indigenous Shirazi. But he had no confidence in the former A.S.P. leadership; he had kept his plans secret from them. He was only linked with the youth league of the party, and it is possible that he took their views into account in preparing his next moves. He himself was determined to remain 'leader of the military forces' to secure the revolution and force the divided A.S.P. and *Umma* leaders to work together.[56] He therefore

55. R. Fiennes (Sir Ranulph Twistleton-Wykeham-Fiennes), *Where Soldiers Fear to Tread*, London, 1975, 95. An Italian photographer flew over Zanzibar photographing from the air some of the killings, also Arabs desperately trying to seek safety by swimming out to sea. The sequences appeared in an abusively racialist film entitled *Africa Addio*. Their authenticity has been challenged but the appearance of characteristic Zanzibari *sakafu*, or clove drying-floors, seems to confirm authenticity.
56. Okello, *op.cit.*, 147-9, recounts his calculations at the time. Babu was to

proclaimed a republic with himself as Minister of Defence and Broadcasting and as Leader of the Revolutionary Government, with Karume as President, Kassim Hanga as Vice President, and Babu and other A.S.P. leaders as ministers.[57] On the following day, 13 January, Okello developed his plans. He appointed further officials, mostly fairly recently-arrived mainlanders,[58] and gave some thought to the constitution of his proposed 'People's Republic', in which he sought to incorporate clauses for 'economic freedom'. These clauses were intended to provide for land distribution, the nationalisation of fishing, for transport and businesses to be made into co-operatives, free medicine and education, unemployment pay, and adult education schemes. From his position of unchallengeable strength he banned the Z.N.P. and Z.P.P.P., threatening with dire penalties anyone found still supporting them, and broadcast an invitation to Karume and Babu to return.

The next few days saw an intensification of the Terror to consolidate Okello's victory. His description of it reveals all too clearly his own satisfaction in the scenes of devastation, fire and bloodshed:

We combed the town conducting house to house inspections breaking in where we found locked doors. When one group finished in one quarter of the Arab section, it switched to another quarter and was replaced for second or third checks by new groups. Continuous reports were sent to Raha Leo HQ on the number of Arabs killed and detained in these searches. People rarely stopped to eat and the searches of the houses were exhaustive.[59]

be included in his plans so that 'we could keep an eye on him'. It seems that at this point too Okello decided to accept Kassim Hanga, who had earlier been on his execution list.

57. Jumbe was to be Minister for Health and Social Service, Othman Sharif Minister for Education, Hasnu Makame Minister for Agriculture, Idris Wakyl Minister for Commerce and Babu Minister for External Affairs. In another broadcast, Okello nominated Makame for Finance and Salah Sadalla for Agriculture.

58. He claims that he selected thirty-one people, some but not all A.S.P. members, to form a Revolutionary Council, and appointed E. Kissasi (see fn. 29) to be Commissioner of Police, Joel Kilonzo, another mainlander police officer, to be Commissioner of Prisons, and Adam Mwakanjuki, Secretary of the A.S.P.-linked Dockworkers and Stevedores Union and Secretary of the Z.P.F.L., to be Commissioner for Labour. Ingen and Mfarinyaki were appointed 'Provisional Commanding Officers of the Revolutionary Army'. He also deputed people to be responsible for those arrested and detained, casualties, confiscated property and weapons, and appointed a personal staff.

59. Okello, *op.cit.*, 154–5. Monuments commemorating revolutionary 'victories' were later erected on the sites of some of these fracas.

A number of witnesses later commented on the obvious fact that many victims had been pre-selected. The atmosphere of shootings and burnings — many Arab house, farm or store owners were burnt alive in their premises — was made more terrifying by the Field Marshal's broadcasts promising imprisonment, destruction and death to all who resisted him and encouraging a spy-mania.[60] Several observers commented that among the most ferocious and zealous of Okello's followers in this grisly work were Makonde, whose filed teeth and often unkempt appearance made them easily recognis able.[61] Zanzibar's hospital quickly became filled with casualties, women and children as well as men; the injuries ranged from matchet wounds to burns, mutilations, and other results of torture. A large number of women had been raped.[62] Many Asian Muslims, particularly Ismaili, locked themselves in mosques for sanctuary. Special attention was paid by the revolutionaries to the Mangas, broadcast orders by Okello singling them out for severe treatment; the more fortunate were rounded up for concentration in detainee camps. These, with others arrested, were transferred a little later to a small offshore island where many suffered severely from heat, thirst and hunger. Bodies were buried five to an average-sized grave in some graveyards or pushed down well-holes; special mass-graves had to be prepared and a doctor was sent from the mainland to supervise the mass-burials. Local vendettas were settled in blood; Asian houses and properties were pillaged, and many entire Arab families were murdered in the bush. In large areas of the Arab-settled western side of Unguja wrecked stores and burnt-out houses stretched along the roads, sometimes with white rags of surrender hanging from broken window frames. The communal hatreds bequeathed from the past and tuned to extremes by the communal politics of the previous ten years had finally erupted into communal slaughter; as the violence progressed it became a deed in which all

60. *East Africa and Rhodesia*, 30 January 1954, provides translations from BBC monitorings of a number of these broadcasts. As remarkable examples of their kind, four excerpts are included in an Appendix at the end of this volume.
61. Makonde had figured conspicuously among those attacking the Malindi police station, where two men were killed. The Makonde in Unguja were mainly from Mozambique rather than Tanganyika, but in both territories this people had had a long tradition of violent protest and revolt.
62. Okello's men entered the hospital and forcibly prevented any accurate documentation of the numbers of women and girls who had been raped. Interview Dr K. Patel, 27 July 1977.

felt themselves participants and to some extent linked by a common guilt. The massacres and the burnings bore the character of the pogroms of European history; the deaths ran into several thousands.[63] It should, however, be noted that the better-educated and more moderate A.S.P. leaders were appalled by the carnage — their falling-in with Okello's activities was a mixture of fear and a hope of reducing the bloodshed. Aboud Jumbe, for example, personally drove the wife and baby of Waring, the British commander of the P.M.F., to safety on 14 January.

After the evacuation of Malindi, Okello concluded his day of triumph by proclaiming a curfew and distributing looted food to his followers. He divided the City into zones, appointing one of his mainlander lieutenants to each with the exception of the port, which was given to the Secretary of the A.S.P.-linked Dockworkers and Stevedores Union, Adam Mwakanjuki. Hawker, as the senior British civil servant left in Unguja, offered the help of expatriates to the revolutionary leaders at Raha Leo, and followed up this offer with a visit there. His offer was gladly and gratefully accepted at the time but was later to be portrayed as a British attempt to retain power and influence.[64] Hawker was joined at his house in Zanzibar City by Crosthwait, the British High Commissioner who was living at a dangerous distance outside the city. Both realised that the siting of a diplomatic mission at the home and office of the senior public officer was anomalous, but felt it to be justifiable, particularly if a major problem was to be an evacuation of British people. It did however lead to the High Commissioner's Union Jack being riddled with bullets the following day; after a protest to Karume the Deputy Field Marshal arrived to apologise. Most of the remaining British civil servants felt their prime duty was to save life rather than attempt to restore a collapsed order; many in addition had sympathy with

63. There have been various estimates of the dead, ranging between 3,000 and 11,000. One difficulty with any assessment is the absence of any reliable information on the number of deaths in Pemba, and another is that a number of people only died much later, as a consequence either of wounds, privation in detainee camps or being killed when finally emerging from besieged houses. A. Ledger, the Zanzibar general manager of Smith Mackenzie, the large British trading concern, drove around Unguja after the violence and on the basis of counting burnt-out houses estimated a figure of 8,000. This figure may be slightly but not much above the true total. Further deaths occurred during the deportations.

64. Hawker had for many years known Karume, who valued his services, retaining him for three months. Hawker to the author, 19 October 1976, enclosing letter P127/C1/1 of 20 January 1964 from himself to Karume setting out the sequence of events.

African aspirations and past frustrations, though none approved of Okello's methods. Many were therefore prepared to maintain services for which they were responsible; the smooth running of these services — including broadcasting, telephones, water, the port, the airport, works and medical services — made the new government's task much easier. It also produced the curious transitional working alliance of revolutionaries and British civil servants, the latter supported in some measure by the Royal Navy, which was in turn to contain and check Okello.

The Struggle for Power

In Dar es Salaam Karume, Kassim Hanga and Babu duly heard of the Revolution and of Okello's plans for their inclusion in a revolutionary government. Babu was roused from sleep by the Cuban embassy to break the news; the embassy must have been perplexed that their 'favourite son' knew so little. At some time all three met and made arrangements to return, the transportation once again being effected by Feinsilber and Abramovich.[65] Zanzibar's 'Finland Station', where they landed on the morning of Monday 13 January, was the village of Fumba, some 12 miles south of Zanzibar City. They immediately went to Raha Leo, which was now surrounded by a crowd of two or three thousand excited Ng'ambo residents still armed with weapons ranging from rifles and machine carbines to swords and matchets.

The return of Karume had major significance. The Revolution now had an identifiable leader, a Zanzibari, known by all for many years, rather than a sinister and hitherto unknown mainlander. He was a leader with whom the outside world, the civil service and others could talk; among those who wanted to talk were the more moderate A.S.P. leaders and members who were intimidated by Okello. Ministers-designate and A.S.P. leaders gathered round Karume, and from 16 January the terms 'Cabinet' and Revolutionary Council were in use, although the precise membership was not announced. Karume's return, furthermore, opened a period of competition for power, the protagonists reflecting all the duality of Zanzibar's history — the young Arab *Umma* radicals representing the western Indian Ocean culture in its latest Nasser-influenced

65. Kyle, *Spectator*, 14 February; Smithyman to the author, 16 June 1977. The tidal system was such that it enabled all three to make the westward journey in a *mashua*, or canoe, with relative ease but eastward journeys needed a stouter craft. On his arrival Babu arranged for himself to be photographed, for propaganda purposes, paddling a canoe.

form, very similar to the Middle Eastern and Arab Socialist movements, while Okello represented the new mainland African dimension and Karume and the A.S.P. leadership the different indigenous fusions of past Arab and African cultures, Muslim and peasant. Sheer weight of popular support made a Karume victory probable; this was to be the result of the struggle, but for many weeks it was to remain in the balance.

Earlier visitors to Raha Leo that morning had been Hawker and Crosthwait, the latter's position strengthened by the arrival of the British naval vessel *Owen*.[66] Although *Owen*'s captain had to advise Crosthwait that he did not have sufficient men to cover an opposed evacuation, he was able to say that a frigate was on its way and would arrive later in the week. However, the ship was able to act as a secure signal system and to provide food for the British community. Crosthwait had at this time inevitably to spend much time in the preparation of evacuation plans. Aboard *Owen* already were one or two officials who had been particularly at risk, such as Special Branch policemen. Crosthwait had thought at first that almost all British people would have to be evacuated, but in the absence of any attacks on Europeans the plans were reduced to arrangements for women with small children.

At Raha Leo Hawker raised a number of pressing administrative matters and Crosthwait sought assurances for the safety of British subjects; both men were well received and the desired assurance in respect of British subjects was given. Hawker, who knew the whereabouts of the former ministers, also agreed to try to persuade Shamte to broadcast a formal resignation and an appeal to end the bloodshed in return for a promise of safe conduct. Shamte preferred that Muhsin should make the surrender, which was tape-recorded by telephone and broadcast. Shamte signed a formal letter of resignation. The ministers then surrendered, but in the general excitement Muhsin was struck in the face by a matchet and arrived bleeding at Raha Leo for a terrifying reception by Okello himself.[67] Okello however did ensure that neither he nor any other minister was further assaulted; they were all consigned to detention, to prove indefinite.

66. The ship was under orders not to intervene in internal Zanzibari affairs, as also was the frigate, *Rhyl*, when she arrived.

67. Okello, *op.cit.*, 152, describes the scene: 'When I heard he was being threatened, I ordered him to be brought up to my office. When he stepped inside, I pointed a pistol at his face and asked, "Do you want me to kill you or let you live?" He replied numbly, "Do as you like, Sir".' Okello had said in a broadcast that Muhsin was to be hanged.

The next few days saw the new leaders of Zanzibar competing for control and authority. Many of the more militant revolutionaries wished to see Karume as a ceremonial President only, with real power in the hands of Kassim Hanga. Karume threatened to resign in such circumstances, and Othman Sharif, despite his past differences with Karume, supported Karume's claim to leadership as he feared Kassim Hanga's Communist connections. Competition now took the form of gaining influence with Karume, whose Presidency no one challenged further; one feature of the competition was the lack of co-ordination in events in different parts of the territory, reflecting divided counsels. At this stage Karume had no particular quarrel with the British, and on the morning of Tuesday 14 January he and all the new ministers walked around the *Beit-el-Ajaib* shaking hands with staff, British, Asian and local, and asking them to continue to serve the new government, an appeal endorsed by Hawker. In Zanzibar City itself business life began cautiously to move again with a few shops opening and some food appearing in the markets. Whether of his own volition or under pressure from Karume, Okello broadcast on 14 January instructions to his followers to desist from burning, arresting and looting, under pain of severe penalties. These he listed as sixty-five years' imprisonment together with fifty strokes for looting, and hanging, burning alive or shooting by novice riflemen for the illegal possession of arms. He claimed that a secret camera had been installed in the houses of all Europeans to identify looters. Two days later he was again urging the return of captured firearms in similar threatening terms.[68] Although the first frenetic violence was over, the atmosphere remained menacing, with groups of unkempt armed men patrolling the streets, conducting frequent vehicle and personal searches and asking questions which revealed marked spy-mania. Occasionally bursts of firing and the smashing-in of doors of Arab houses were to be heard. It was a testing time for expatriates and Zanzibaris alike; all stood in equal fear of the Field Marshal. Okello himself, for reasons not entirely clear, seems to have decided that although he had originally planned the revolution for the benefit of the Zanzibari Africans and not himself, he wished to retain considerable power in his own hands. Two possible reasons for this change of view were a renewed lack of confidence in the A.S.P. leadership and, perhaps more probably, his personal exhilaration in the drama and violence of the revolution. The latter added to the already existing tensions.

The former policemen aboard *Salama*, at that time under surveil-

---

68. *East Africa and Rhodesia*, 30 January 1964, gives the text of this warning broadcast of 16 January.

lance from an armed habour launch manned by revolutionaries, faced Hawker with a problem. On his order the *Salama* was moved down the coast to avoid an incident, but later under British naval escort it was brought back to Zanzibar and all the policemen, except the British officers, were disembarked. All had been promised an amnesty, safe conduct and continued service; it is doubtful whether this was honoured in all cases.

The *Seyyid Khalifa* had meanwhile departed with the Sultan and his party; they were not allowed to land at Mombasa, the Kenyan government evidently fearing repercussions among its Coast Arab population; but permission was given for them to fly to Britain from Tanganyika. On arrival in Britain, the Sultan was met by a junior minister, the Duke of Devonshire, and provided with a pension based on interest on an investment of £100,000 on condition that he remained in the United Kingdom, or the £100,000 as a final payment if he left the country. The British government's view was that because of Britain's long association with the House of Seyyid Said, Jamshid should not be left in destitution; the arrangement of course led to criticism of Britain in Zanzibar.

Karume's presence increasingly provided a focus of loyalty for A.S.P. supporters who had not been involved with Okello. Several reasons contributed to Okello's loss of status over the next days and weeks. As already noted, his only real base of support was among the most recently-arrived mainlanders, few of whom had skills to offer the revolutionary government. Also, Okello was not a Muslim while Karume in a significant broadcast on 16 January reminded Zanzibaris that Ramadan began the next day and called for fasting and prayer, a simple reminder but one with obvious political implications.[69] The excesses of the Revolution precluded the possibility of any mainland government supporting Okello. Karume on the other hand was known and respected. When he asked for a force of police-men from Tanganyika, clearly to be used as a counterpoise to Okello's men, Nyerere willingly sent some 130 men,[70] whose value in fact proved less than expected since they were equipped with old-fashioned re-loading .303 rifles while Okello's men had automatic police carbines. The Tanganyika policemen tended to remain in their accommodation and avoid activities that might bring them into con-flict with Okello's men. In these conditions Okello could still inspire feelings of both nightmarish incredulity and terror among the A.S.P. leaders; on one occasion he forced Karume to go on his knees

69. *Ibid.*

70. Before their respective Army mutinies, both Kenya and Uganda had also said that they were willing to supply policemen.

and kiss his feet, and he inspired an equal fear among the Babu group.[71] The desirability of disposing of him was one matter on which they could all agree, a sentiment which gained strength after the mutinies of the mainland armies during the week-end after the Revolution. This type of anarchy and disorder which Okello seemed to epitomise was precisely what the A.S.P. leadership no longer wanted. Hawker, for example, was told to accept no orders from him. Lastly, Okello undermined his own position by absenting himself from Zanzibar.

Parallel with general resistance to Okello, the pattern of a second conflict among the revolutionary leaders was emerging, that of the militant pro-Communists and Arab radicals headed by Babu and to some extent by Kassim Hanga against the more moderate Western-oriented A.S.P. leaders such as Othman Sharif. In the middle was Karume, a rough figure with no formal education, a man not by temperament a revolutionary leader, but pleased to find himself one although often confused by the issues. His initial reaction was to hope for British advice and support but for the next eight weeks he was to fall increasingly under the influence of Babu, who turned many of the events to his political advantage. Using the simplistic Marxist ideological analysis of a first-stage bourgeois nationalism leading to independence being followed by a second-stage revolution of the masses of workers and peasants, he was able to flatter Karume's sensibilities. But Karume never succumbed wholly to Babu's pressures, and was not above appointing or using Okello's followers to check Babu.[72] What did, however, leave Karume with a sense of bitter injury and resentment against Britain and other Western nations was the failure of London to recognise the new government, although numerous Communist and African countries were doing so, and Western press reporting which was considered to be hostile. Babu, too, could mobilise expatriate Communist expertise to help run the country.

It is against this background that the events of the next few weeks need to be seen. Although the arrival of the Royal Navy frigate *Rhyl*

71. Okello's repeated statements that he had learned his military tactics from the Bible, and occasional boasts of his ability to interpret dreams and of having been a brigade leader of Mau Mau, must also have been alarming. (*The Times*, 17 January 1964). J. Rimmer, a British education officer in Zanzibar at the time, was an eye-witness to Karume's humiliation. J. Rimmer to the author, 25 July 1977.

72. Okello, *op.cit.*, 181; Petterson, a U.S. diplomat, also commented on Karume's use of Okello's followers to contain Babu in a despatch to the State Department, 14 February 1964.

during the night of 15–16 January, carrying on board a company of British Army infantry, served greatly to restore British confidence and morale, it was portrayed by militants as the beginning of British interference[73] despite a statement by *Rhyl*'s Captain, A.M. Power (later Vice-Admiral Sir Arthur Power), that he had no orders to disembark his troops.[74] Rumour and suspicion centred on *Rhyl*'s logistic support ship, the auxiliary vessel *Hebe* — a large ship with conspicuous derricks; in anticipation of misunderstanding, *Hebe* was moored some way from Zanzibar City but she was nevertheless believed by many Zanzibaris to be some form of commando assault vessel being kept in reserve. A group of revolutionaries appeared at Hawker's house, demanding that Crosthwait take them to see *Hebe*, but Crosthwait refused to deal with anyone other than Karume.

On arrival, Captain Power with other naval officers, Hawker and Crosthwait were summoned to a full meeting of the provisional Zanzibar government[75] to explain why *Rhyl* had arrived. The meeting looked impressive with Karume and senior A.S.P. members at one side of a long table, and the Deputy Field Marshal at one end. One Royal Navy officer, on being introduced to a minister as the Minister for Agriculture, distinctly heard another minister complain that that was what he thought he was. The administration was far from complete. Crosthwait gave his explanation, stressing anxiety over the safety of British subjects and property; and outlining arrangements for wives and children to be evacuated aboard *Hebe*;[76]

73. The B.B.C. had ill-advisedly broadcast news of the planned arrival of *Rhyl*, including the fact that she was carrying soldiers.

74. *Rhyl* had been ordered to Zanzibar from Aden when news of the Revolution reached Whitehall. She embarked a company of the 1st Bn The Staffordshire Regiment at Mombasa, and sailed into Zanzibar harbour at night without using lights or the harbour lights (in case these had been tampered with), a remarkable feat of radar navigation. Taking no chances, *Rhyl* was maintained in a state involving illumination of the hull and keel, anticipating boarding or other hostile action. Her crew and the soldiers provided blood for the Zanzibar hospital. Although under strict orders not to interfere in the local political scene, *Rhyl* would undoubtedly have landed the soldiers in the event of any assault on British residents.

I am grateful to Vice-Admiral Sir Arthur Power and two other officers of H.M.S. *Rhyl* for information on her arrival. The surmise in the previous sentence is, however, my own.

75. Hawker's Diary noted: 'It really was the most fantastic party. [. . .] I pointed out to Babu (who has a very lively sense of humour) that the sight of four British naval officers sitting round the table with three Men of War in the harbour could hardly be in keeping with the best tenets of Moscow or Peking. . . Babu was delighted with this. . .'

76. Karume and some of his ministers were opposed to any evacuation at

Hawker was also able at a second meeting to offer his solution to the problem of the *Salama*. He tried to obtain assurances in respect of the safety of the former ministers, but this was a matter of controversy among Karume's ministers and nothing could be arranged. Later in the day there occurred a fresh incident revealing personal ambitions not shared by all the A.S.P. leaders when Karume and Babu with an armed escort personally arrested the U.S. Consul Picard and his Vice Consul Petterson in an hotel and announced the closure of the U.S. Mission.[77] Picard had ill-advisedly exchanged theories and rumours about the Revolution, including stories of the killing of Europeans and the presence of Cubans, with a group of sensation-seeking American journalists who had arrived without permission by dhow — stories which could only serve to worsen misunderstandings. Picard had also tried to interfere with the airport communication system. The following morning Hawker managed to mediate and arguing that Picard's conduct was his own responsibility, saved the Mission although Picard and the journalists were expelled.[78]

The touchiness of the political scene was again made clear during an incident on 19 January when *Rhyl*'s signals officer, Lieutenant-Commander J. Fawssett, was arrested. Fawssett was manning the only secure signal link from the British High Commission to the outside world, which was now in the Smith Mackenzie Company's headquarters building.[79] He also supervised boat traffic. One of Okello's men was suspicious of the contents (washing powder and some wireless batteries) of a bag carried by Fawssett, who was then

this time, regarding it as a loss of prestige for their administration and a sign of British reluctance to continue to assist by the provision of expatriate officials.

77. In the hotel Babu had shouted 'Why waste time with these Americans? We have nothing to do with them.' When Crosthwait tried to raise the matter with Aziz Twala, one of Kassim Hanga's followers and a junior minister-designate, Twala replied: 'This country can do without American recognition', and walked out of the room.

78. The American reaction to the Revolution is discussed below, page 103. It would seem that Picard suffered a *crise de nerfs* at this time. A. Ledger, writing to his wife on 22 January, described a group of photographers faking bloodshed around a wrecked car and then photographing their work. The *New York Times* in particular disseminated reports of Cubans.

79. The High Commission had by now moved from Hawker's home to the Smith Mackenzie headquarters; Smith Mackenzie's senior official, Ledger, wrote proudly to his wife noting that the Union Jack once again flew over the building which had been the British consulate until 1874. Early in the Revolution the offices of Cable and Wireless had been occupied.

taken off to the former Sultan's Palace at gunpoint for interrogation. He was questioned first by two of Babu's men and then by
Okello's nominee as Commissioner for Police, Edgington Kissassi, a
mainlander ex-inspector. Kissassi alleged that the washing powder
was explosive and that the batteries were detonators, and reported
accordingly to Karume. Karume ordered his deportation, probably
as a compromise solution. After intervention by Crosthwait,
Fawssett was given a good meal and released to return to duty. But
the Soviet press made a feature story of the event alleging that a
British spy had been landed from a warship with the object of con-
tacting opponents of the Revolution. It was believed at the time that
the incident had been engineered by Babu to force a protest from
Crosthwait, so that Karume, yielding to his irritation, might order
the expulsion of all the remaining British and U.S. nationals.

Also on 19 January Okello, suffering from strain and a throat
infection, departed for Dar es Salaam,[80] but his visit was interrupted
by the Army Mutiny on the night of 19–20 January and he returned to
Zanzibar on the 21st, to depart again for Pemba on the 22nd. Pemba
had shown no enthusiasm for the Revolution. In December and early
January there had been an outbreak of violent crime, and a group of
Makonde had taken over an area in the extreme north-west of the
island, known locally as Kigomasha, as a 'no-go area',[81] but otherwise the atmosphere was very relaxed. The Arab district commissioner, Muhammed Abeid el Haj, was quite popular and the Pemba
general secretary of the A.S.P., Rawal, was an Asian. On the day of
the Revolution itself Sullivan on Unguja asked urgently for all the
police firearms on the island, but the aircraft transporting them
began to run out of fuel and, unable to land at Zanzibar airport,
which except for the control tower was in revolutionary hands, flew
on to Dar es Salaam where it was interned. Okello's broadcasts
transferred to Pemba something of the bitterness of Unguja, though
Abeid prevented serious outbreaks until Okello's arrival. Okello
landed from the *Seyyid Khalifa*, now renamed *Jamhuri*, with the
Police band; his assertion of his authority was a bizarre mixture of
lengthy orations,[82] British military music and public executions and

80. He claims that President Nyerere arranged the aircraft for him, and that
Karume saw him off; also that in Dar es Salaam he was welcomed by
Kambona and Kawawa. This is possible, out of a mixture of fear and a wish
to remove him from Unguja.

81. The local detachment of the police, which contained a high percentage
of Pemba men, believed that the Makonde had magical powers of defence
and refused to enter the area. Interview, T. Longland, the police commander, 9 February 1977.

82. One reason for Okello's vengeful style was that the authorities in

beatings. A number of people were killed, but in Pemba there was a noticeable preference for violent humiliation and public floggings, and for Asians and Arabs to be held to the ground while their beards were cut off and heads shaven, with of course raping of women and girls and lootings of Arab and Asian homes and stores. Once again the Makonde appeared to have been the most violent of Okello's followers. Ali Sultan Issa, a militant follower of Babu's, educated in Cuba, was installed as a new administrator[83] with a fellow-Ugandan of Okello's, Titus Mbau, one of the mainlander ex-policemen, as a link to Okello personally. Rawal's previous service to the A.S.P. proved no protection for him: his house was confiscated, his head was shaven, and he was made to sweep roads in the sun in the same way as other Asians.

Okello's two periods of absence however had affected his control and status in the capital, as had the fears of further disorder aroused by the mainland mutinies. Although following the Tanganyika army mutiny *Rhyl* and her soldiers had been ordered to proceed to Dar es Salaam, the Tanganyika policemen did provide some limited protection for Karume; and when Okello returned from Pemba he found a changed situation, with technical assistance promised from China and East Germany. He also started to received personal messages threatening his position; these noted that as a non-Muslim he could not satisfy the aspirations of the indigenes.[84] It appears that when Karume's ministers met, less important issues were discussed if Okello was present[85], and when on 24 January the composition of the supreme authority, the Zanzibar Revolutionary Council, was announced in numbered order, he himself was rated only as number twelve in a council of thirty — and outside the Cabinet which consisted of the first eleven names.

The lists noting two appointments were yet to be made, ran as follows:[86]

Pemba had offered to harbour the Sultan and a government-in-exile on 12 January. Okello's own account claims that he flew to Pemba, this is incorrect. He also claims to have taken with him a number of A.S.P. leaders, including Ali Sharif and seven others whose names he gives. But these latter appear to have been of no consequence — their names do not feature in any other context.

83. Ali Sultan Issa was the son of the works overseer in Pemba, a loyal servant of the government. He had spent most of the late 1950s in extended visits to China and other Communist countries.

84. Okello, *op.cit.*, 177–8, provides his recollection of the text of one of these. He says that at the time he thought it was sent by a Z.N.P. Arab.

85. *Ibid.*, 176, in which Okello notes in some detail the results of a discussion on salaries. He claims to have refused a salary of £500 per month.

86. *Zanzibar Gazette*, 25 January 1964.

 1. President Abeid Karume.
 2. Vice-President Abdulla Kassim Hanga.
 3. Hon. Abdulrahman Muhammed Babu, also appointed Minister for External Affairs and Trade.
 4. Hon. Hasnu Makame, also appointed Minister for Finance and Development.
 5. Hon. Aboud Jumbe, also appointed Minister for Health and Welfare.
 6. Hon. Saleh Saadalla, also appointed Minister for Agriculture.
 7. Hon. Idris Abdul Wakyl, also appointed Minister for Communication and Works.
 8. Hon. Othman Shariff, also appointed Minister for Education and National Culture.
 9. Hon. Abdul Aziz Twala, also appointed a Junior Minister in the President's office.
10. Hon. Hassan Nassor Moyo, also appointed Junior Minister for Communication and Works.
11. The Commissioner of Police — Mr Edington Kisassi.
12. Field Marshal John Okello.
13. Hon. Seif Bakari.
14. Hon. Yusuf Himid.
15. Hon. Ramadhan Haji.
16. Hon. A.S. Natepe.
17. Hon. Pili Khamis.
18. Hon. Khamis Hemedi.
19. Hon. Hamid Ameir Ali.
20. Hon. Said Idi Bavuai.
21. Hon. Said wa Shoto.
22. Hon. Muhammed Abdulla.
23. Hon. Abdulla Mfarinyaki.
24. Hon. Hafidh Suleiman.
25. Hon. Khamis Darwesh.
26. Hon. Khamis Abdulla Ameir.
27. Hon. Muhammed Mfaume Omar.
28. Hon. Muhsin bin Ali.
29. Hon. Muhammed Juma.
30. Hon. Daud Mahmoud.

Of these, excluding those already noted, Makame was one of the A.S.P. moderates, a former *mudir* and government Labour Officer who became an A.S.P. Member of the legislature and Party treasurer in 1961; Jumbe, a former teacher, had also been an A.S.P. moderate Member of the legislature; Saleh Sadalla was another A.S.P. moderate Member; Wakyl had been a teacher until his election to the legislature in 1963; Twala was one of the more militant revolutionary A.S.P. and Z.P.F.L. members; Moyo was Secretary-General of the Z.P.F.L.; Himid was an ex-Works Department lorry-driver and a member of the A.S.P. The 'Official Version' notes Himid, Bakari, Haji, Natepe, Khamis Hemedi, Ameir Ali,

Bavuai, Shoto, Abdulla, Suleiman and Darwesh all as A.S.P. members of the Committee of Fourteen. Ameir was a trade unionist follower of Babu's; Omar was an A.S.P. trade unionist and the last three had been A.S.P. legislature Members from at least 1961, Daud Mahmoud since 1957.[87] Only Mfarinyaki, apart from Okello, was a recently arrived mainlander and he was the only close associate of Okello on the Council; already the process of rejection foreseen by Okello had begun. The Deputy Field Marshal, Ingen, was not a member, nor were other of his principal lieutenants.[88] The Council met in the 'People's Palace', the former town palace of the Sultan; its Clerk, Salim Rashid, a product of the London School of Economics, was another *Umma* Communist sympathiser.

The formation of the Z.R.C. was followed by its natural political and industrial consequences. On the political side, Karume declared Zanzibar a one-party state on 30 January. *Umma*, which had been maintaining a low profile so as not to be accused of usurping power, was disbanded by Babu and ostensibly merged with the A.S.P. In practice, however, former *Umma* members tended to remain a party within a party, and this exercise in entryism served to strengthen Babu's position generally and in particular with Karume, as the former *Umma* group provided a certain measure of educational and administrative ability. On the industrial side the two trade union federations agreed to dissolve and a new Federation of Revolutionary Trade Unions (F.R.T.U.) was formed,[89] pledging loyalty to the Z.R.C. Here again Babu supporters were conspicuous.

87. Makame had studied administration for one year at Exeter University; Jumbe had at one time been Vice-Principal of the King George VI School; Wakyl held a Makerere diploma, had taught at a teachers training college and then been a primary school headmaster; Moyo started life as a carpenter with only primary level schooling, he studied in the Soviet Union at one stage; Natepe was Secretary of the Youth League and Bavuai had a brother who had been an A.S.P. member. Ameir had been Secretary of the Z.N.P.-linked Maritime and Allied Workers Union, Omar had been secretary of the A.S.P.-linked Boat Builders Union and President of the Z.P.F.L.; the last three were A.S.P. 'Old Guard' of very limited ability. Daud Mahmoud had been a headman and Koran teacher; Juma had once been secretary of the A.S.P. but his other political experience was limited to a small district council.

88. Other notable omissions were the amiable but ineffective A.S.P. General Secretary, Thabit Kombo, and Babu's other principal aides, Foum and Ali Mahfoudh. Mwakanjuki was retained as Labour Commissioner.

89. *East Africa and Rhodesia*, 30 January 1964. Its officials were: President, Mohamed Mfaume (Secretary of the Boat Builders Union, Z.P.F.L./A.S.P.); Vice Presidents Khamis Mansur Khamis and Ismail Salih

It was now clear that the Field Marshal's days were numbered. Karume told Keith Kyle, *The Times* special correspondent, that Okello was a member of the Z.R.C. and while he took part in decision-making he had also to abide by decisions made. Okello's resentment at certain decisions made on 28 January during his second trip to Pemba became very clear in a crisis on his return. The crisis was probably the result of some of the Tanganyika policemen being arrested by Okello's followers, so necessitating urgent action by Karume in the form of an attempt to order Okello's men off the streets. But this was a premature move for which Karume had not yet sufficient power. Back on Unguja, Okello marched into the broadcasting studio where angry voices raised in his support could be clearly heard by listeners, and made a bitter speech about his rejection. A notably dramatic meeting of the Z.R.C., at which Karume ordered Okello to lay down his pistols on the table and out of reach, occurred about this time.[90] Another crisis appears to have occurred between 5 and 7 February when for two nights Okello's men were not to be seen on the streets and then suddenly reappeared.

Okello himself quarrelled with Karume over land nationalisation, the latter being opposed to a complete take-over; he also became aware of more attacks on him, some disguised as attacks on recently-arrived mainlanders and non-Muslims. He found Karume increasingly hostile. After a third visit to Pemba and attendance at a rally of several hundred people on 19 February, when both he and Karume addressed the crowds, Okello left Zanzibar on 20 February, escorted to the airport by Karume. In his autobiography he claims that his decision to leave Zanzibar was based on his wish to explain his views to mainland political leaders, and that in this period he went first to Uganda, where he was welcomed by the Prime Minister, Milton Obote, and then on to Nairobi where he was welcomed by Kenyatta and the leading Kenyan ministers, and also by Nyerere.[91] According to his version of these meetings the mainland leaders promised to

Ismail; Secretary-General Khamis Abdulla Ameir (Secretary of the Maritime and Allied Workers Union, F.P.T.U./Z.N.P.); Deputy Secretary General Ahmed Diria Hassan (Secretary of the Zanzibar Government Workers Union, Z.P.F.L./A.S.P.); Treasurer Kadiria Mnyeji (Treasurer of the Agricultural and Allied Workers Union, F.P.T.U./Z.N.P. Mnyeji was also a founder member of *Umma*).

90. Professor T.M. Franck, who was in Zanzibar at the time, to the author, 13 October 1977.

91. Okello, *op.cit.*, 180–3. Before his departure Makame gave Karume £357.17 with which to pay off Okello. Hawker to the author, 11 November 1976.

appoint a mission to travel with him to Zanzibar to smooth out his differences with Karume. It was, he wrote, while waiting for this mission in Dar es Salaam that he read in a newspaper that he had been banned from Zanzibar; he added that several Tanganyikan ministers reassured him that the report was probably based on rumour only and advised him to remain in Dar es Salaam. Nyerere also asked him to stay in Dar es Salaam to await a visit from Karume. The behaviour of these leaders towards Okello suggests strongly that they had all been previously approached by Karume with a request to keep Okello out of Zanzibar, at any cost and on any pretext. It seems that Okello made one final attempt to return to Zanzibar early in March. At the airport he was confronted by Karume supported by a number of followers of Babu, all armed, and accompanied by other members of the Z.R.C. Karume advised Okello that a special aircraft was on its way to take them both to Dar es Salaam to see Nyerere. He was left with no option but to travel in it. On arrival in Dar es Salaam they were separated and after one abortive meeting in which Nyerere made it clear that he did not like Okello's methods, and some further waiting in the capital during which Nyerere sent messages that he was too busy to see him, Okello was taken by Kambona to Nairobi. He was almost immediately told he could not remain there and obliged to return to Uganda. His migrant revolutionary role in Zanzibar was ended, and an order formally banning his return was issued by Karume.

His name, however, continued to inspire dread. During his brief visit to Kenya with Kambona the armed forces were put on alert. In an attempt to recapture a position on the stage, Okello — by his own accounts — attempted to travel to the Congo (Zaire) to mount a revolution there. In Tanganyika he was detained and then expelled. He was later imprisoned in both Uganda and Kenya under circumstances far from clear, a sexual offence being alleged in Uganda and illegal entry in Kenya. After the 1971 coup in Uganda, General Amin visited Okello and the two men were photographed shaking hands. Nothing further was heard of Okello after that occasion. The Deputy Field Marshal, Ingen, also departed from Zanzibar at the end of February; he had slashed a fireman who had passed him on the stairs at the airport, an example of mindless violence that was too much for Karume, who ordered his deportation to Kenya.[92]

By the time of Okello's departure the conflicts between the other groups on the Z.R.C. were becoming sharper. These can be over-emphasised, since all shared a common belief in securing the Revolution and in a redistribution of economic assets and employment opportunities; but differences over method, extent and the sources for foreign help widened. Most important of all was the question of who was ultimately to emerge as the supreme leader. Babu had ambitions for personal power perhaps with Karume in some honorary and ceremonial Presidency; Kassim Hanga hoped for a partnership between himself in Zanzibar and Kambona on the mainland. Karume, for his part, found that he was enjoying power and became less and less inclined to share it or to accept figurehead status. At first, for example, Karume had hoped for some form of legal continuity. He told Judge Horsfall that he wanted the courts to function normally,[93] as he hoped that this would facilitate British recognition. With Okello dispensing summary sentences and the militants demanding a speedier procedure, Karume gave way and a system of decree legislation came into force — the President and the Z.R.C. becoming a joint legislative body.

The arrangements for this were drafted by T.M. Franck, Professor of Constitutional Law at the University of New York. Franck had been legal adviser to the A.S.P. in 1963 and immediately after the Revolution was invited by Karume to advise on legal matters. The issuing of the invitation was delayed, probably deliberately, by Kambona. On his arrival Franck attended meetings of the Z.R.C. in late January and early February 1964, advising it not to draft a constitution immediately, but to rule by decree. But he did urge the Cabinet to ensure that all decree legislation should be shaped with an eventual return to democratic government in mind, a piece of advice generally ignored, and to enact a decree defending personal and property rights. This latter issue of property rights met with strong opposition from Babu, and the question of any decree of individual rights was postponed.[94] An enabling Decree — the Legislative Powers Law, 1964, which simply stated the new source of legislation — was issued and formed the basis of all subsequent revolutionary decree legislation. The former courts virtually ceased to function, particularly prior to Okello's departure when prison sentences of from thirty to ninety years and beatings of up to forty-five strokes were being awarded to prisoners of the Field Marshal

93. Mr Justice Horsfall to the author, 17 November 1976. The Chief Justice of Zanzibar, Sir Gerald Mahon, was away on leave; he refused to return and Karume consequently considered Horsfall to be the senior justiciary.

94. Professor Franck to the author, 13 October 1977 and Petterson to the State Department, 11 February 1964. A Zanzibari who wishes to remain anonymous has also given me evidence on this point.

The Revolutionaries of Zanzibar II: the political leaders. *Left to right*: E. Kisassi (in uniform), Saleh Saadallah, Idris Wakyl, Kassim Hanga (in white), unknown, Abeid Karume (in dark suit), Othman Sharif (in spotted shirt), Ms Biubwa Amour Zahor, Abdulrahman Muhammad Babu.

charged with offences such as 'abuse of government'.[95] Major instruments of decree legislation began to appear in February and March. Among them were a Preventive Detention Decree, a Constitution Decree which promised a Constituent Assembly within a year, a decree giving the government powers to confiscate all immovable property, and in late March a decree providing for the death penalty for anyone organising a counter-revolution; this decree also gave the President power to expel such persons from the country. Another decree forbade any legal proceedings being instituted over any event that had taken place on 12 January.

The Preventive Detention Decree legalised the detention camps at Ziwani, Mazizini, Langani, Cooper's Institute, in several schools, and on Prison Island; the resources of the Works Department were needed to make these hygienic and secure for their 2,200 or so inmates. After an appalling few days, conditions in them became more tolerable.[96] One of the British judges, in his role as Prison Visitor, visited the Central Prison and in his report noted that the prisoners, among whom were former ministers, looked well-fed and showed no signs of ill-treatment. All pre-revolution prisoners had been released, and he found forty of Okello's prisoners together with 549 detainees. The local Kenya and Tanganyika branches of the Red Cross were allowed to help staff and look after the camps. Blankets, food, clothing and cooking pots were provided by various mainland Red Cross branches and distributed by local volunteers — mainly teachers and senior pupils. Clinics were set up, the government assisted with the provision of food, and additional Red Cross staff arrived from Britain. Some staff also went round built-up areas in which Arabs had congregated for safety with food and medical supplies. Each camp was inspected daily by a Red Cross official. The Commissioner of Prisons, a Kenyan named Kilonzo, was a notably humane official and often personally arranged minor comforts for prisoners and for enquiries in respect of missing relatives. The new Commissioner of Police, Kisassi, also arranged for Tanganyika

95. On 9 February, for example, Horsfall, as Prison Visitor inspected the Central Prison. He was commenting to Kilonzo, the revolutionary Prisons Commissioner on the severity of the sentences awarded to the Field Marshal's prisoners when Okello unexpectedly arrived. Okello said the Courts must confine themselves to petty crime and civil matters; all political issues were to remain with him. Horsfall to the author, 17 November 1976.
96. Horsfall to the author, 17 November 1976; the British Red Cross Society kindly sent me a copy of their National Headquarters Circular 27/A 64 of 13 February 1964; Mrs J. Adams of the Red Cross gave me further information on 20 July 1977 (interview).

police to guard those camps where incidents of beatings-up by guards were reported.

Okello appears to have decided who was to be detained, screening all Arabs on Unguja and interning all Z.N.P. members and many others.[97] But the Cabinet, and in particular Jumbe as Minister of Health, decided on the treatment of those detained which, perhaps as a sign of anxiety over the violence, was humane and correct. Jumbe himself, on at least one occasion in tears, broadcast appeals for humane conduct. Asians were not detained, but a large number left in the first month after the Revolution and many more following during the year; they were generally stripped and searched before their departure and allowed to take only some £10 in cash.[98]

At about this time the Z.R.C. took the decision that the best solution for a number of the Arabs, in particular the surviving Manga, was expulsion, to be arranged at once to take advantage of the trade wind. Karume appears initially to have hoped that the Royal Navy would transport the deportees, and flat rejection of this idea may have contributed to his growing annoyance with Britain. Dhows, some old and unseaworthy, were therefore requisitioned and captains or on occasions unqualified dhow crewmen were paid £9 for each Arab transported. It was said that in some dhows as many as 150 were carried.[99] The destination was to be the Arabian Gulf; the dhows were forbidden to call at any East African port. The conditions in the dhows were so bad that the British Port Officer refused to give clearance; one report says that Karume signed the orders personally. The Red Cross were not allowed to supervise. More than 450 people were packed into the first three dhows that sailed. The dhows were issued with 600 gallons of water for a trip that might last anything from three to six weeks; Western merchant ships were asked to keep a watch out for them and provide food and water if necessary, but not to intervene in any other way. It seems that Zanzibar's Arab population was reduced by at least a further

97. Among these was the kindly and sympathetic Salim Barwani, who had been the government's labour officer in the previous decade and was much liked by Africans. On a visit to one camp, Karume saw Barwani and instantly ordered his release. Karume also treated Sultan Khalifa's widow with kindness and respect.

98. The Indian government paid for the passage of a number of Asians at this time. Petterson to the State Department, 14 February 1964, gave a figure of 1,000 Asians departing in a month, but this figure seems somewhat exaggerated.

99. Information on the measures for this deportation was included in Mr Justice Horsfall to the author, 17 November 1976, and Belcher to the author, 24 November 1976.

5,000 in this way, and by previous or subsequent voluntary departure to exile in canoes referred to with grim humour as 'VC10s'. The
Arabs went to Dubai, Abu Dhabi, Kuwait and Egypt and some went
to Aden. They were not welcomed in Oman until the coup of 1970
when Sultan Qaboos allowed them to return to the true home of their
ancestors and relatives. Once in Oman, the Zanzibari Arabs,
although mostly speakers of Swahili rather than Arabic, quickly
became a community noted for their hard work and professional
skills even to the extent of arousing some local resentment. A
number received senior appointments in the paramilitary police
force,[100] and others served in the Royal Guard. It was estimated that
in the mid-1970s the Zanzibari community in Oman numbered some
8,000 to 10,000. This estimate may provide a clue to the total
numbers exiled or deported, though it should be borne in mind that
others went elsewhere.[101]

After this major exodus the lot of those Arabs, mostly of long residence, who chose to remain slowly improved, provided that they
accepted their loss of privileged status and the end of the old order. A
correspondent wrote of them in 1965: 'They have lost the arrogance
typical of their ruling days. Their shyness, their unobtrusive gait as
they shuffle along the narrow lanes. . .gives the centre of the town
the atmosphere of a ghetto.'[102] The factors that were to assist their
eventual partial re-integration were: first their religion, secondly the
fact that many were able to claim an ancestry that was part-African,
and thirdly a certain interest in their welfare that was shown by the
Egyptian embassy. But one further serious economic consequence of
the expulsions was the rapid decline and death of Zanzibar's Indian
Ocean dhow trade.

Pemba, too, underwent two further periods of upheaval. On his
second visit Okello took with him 200 of his followers to implement
the rooting-out of supporters of the old order, and the same
sequence of looted or burnt houses, pillage, beatings and rape was
repeated; all to be repeated again during the Field Marshal's third
and final visit. Rawal, the Asian Secretary of the Pemba branch of
the A.S.P., was again unable to help his fellows and was himself

100. J. Townsend, *Oman: the Making of the Modern State*, London, 1977,
53.
101. The Arab population of the two islands totalled approximately 50,000
in 1963. By death, deportation or departure, this total seems to have been
reduced by between 12,000 and 15,000 by the end of 1964.
102. *Analyst*, 1965, No. 3, article entitled 'Zanzibar After the Long Knives'
by Ephraim Roget.

among the 2,000 imprisoned.[103] After a period in gaol he was released and went to India.

February and March saw the first specific measures to secure and implement the Revolution.[104] Efforts to disarm revolutionary enthusiasts, by a mixture of exhortation and threats, were redoubled. Attempts were also made to recapture some of the criminal prisoners set free on 12 January. Longer-term measures fall into three distinct groups: the taking over of certain premises and properties; the replacement of British by other expatriates, mostly from Communist countries; and 'land reform'. The taking over of property began, obviously, with the Sultan's palaces, and was followed by the Tayabali Karimjee Club (which still tried to refuse admission to Africans) on 28 January. There followed the take-over in February and March of the town and country properties of many leading Arab and Asian individuals and families;[105] this was usually effected at gunpoint. The English Club was taken over in this way on 8 March, a contributory reason for its nationalisation being a visit earlier in the day by Duncan Sandys, the British Government's Secretary of State for Commonwealth Relations — a visit that had not led to official diplomatic recognition. Ground rents for housing in Ng'ambo and other areas were abolished at this time.

The future of land was evidently a matter of great controversy within the Z.R.C.; a little while after the formation of the Council the Minister for Agriculture had 'and Land Reform' added to his title. Babu and the Marxists sought a full land nationalisation with state management, but this was not Karume's preference, and apart

103. Although it was proclaimed a 'prohibited area' shortly after the Revolution, Horsfall succeeded in obtaining permission from Kassim Hanga to fly there. He received reports of Asians, given permission to emigrate, being robbed on the journey and of those who protested being beaten. He also learned that the new Commissioner had taken at gun-point all monies paid into the local court as a result of litigation. Horsfall protested to Kassim Hanga, who supported the Commissioner saying 'All successful litigants were bad people, usually landlords, money-lenders or capitalists. They are all people who have no existence in the Zanzibar Peoples Republic.'
104. *The Times*, 4 February 1964, report by K. Kyle, notes that he was told the Z.R.C.'s aims at this time were mass literacy, political education and the dignity of labour. Village co-operative stores were to replace Arab traders, and urban housing construction and land reform were to be the major legislative priorities.
105. These included the properties of Suleiman Lemke and Ali Muhsin, Tayabali Karimjee's private buildings, the properties of A. Jevanjee, and many others. Gazette notices listing the properties appeared some time after the actual take-over.

from the 'taking-over' — in this context an ill-organised occupation by peasants, mainly Hadimu — of the larger Arab estates, and a vague statement on 3 March that all land was nationalised but without details of any further arrangements, no legislative changes were made for some time.

The civil service was an easier target. The non-European Permanent Secretary for Communications and Works was removed to prison at gun-point on 22 January; it may be surmised that his inability, in the confusion of that time, to construct detainee camps was the cause.[106] The future of the British staff was in Karume's hands, Babu and Kassim Hanga having plans for their replacement by new staff from Communist countries. Karume was becoming progressively disillusioned with Britain over the recognition issue: although recognition came, it was granted too late. Personal harassment occurred from time to time; British officials were not allowed to move about, and on occasions were ordered to vacate their houses.[107] The Z.R.C. issued an instruction on 26 March that all of them were to leave by the end of April. The following day this instruction was countermanded (in some cases at gun-point) in respect of a short list of key officials, the 'Forbidden Twelve' — engineers, doctors, a dentist and officers of the government steamers — who were ordered to be prepared to remain. But even these were ordered out by May. The process of change was often very dramatic. The Z.R.C. appointed a 'research committee' of followers of Babu and Kassim Hanga to look at various departments; on 10 March the committee arrived at the Works Department, where it met in one of the building's corridors for five minutes, ignoring the senior British officials. New and unskilled men were promoted on the spot and those Asians they replaced were taken away in a waiting vehicle.[108] The new Z.R.C. government repudiated pension liabilities, a catastrophe for the vast majority of the non-Europeans dismissed.[109] The

106. The Works Department was seen by the Z.R.C., particularly the Babu groups, as of especial importance. Among the tasks given to British officials were the construction of a wire and machine-gun post fence around the former Residency, now as 'State House' Karume's abode, and the preparation of towers for gun-mountings.

107. One British official was detained for being in possession of crested writing paper of the former government. Officials who had left in the confusion of 12 January were, however, allowed to return to pack up their property — in most cases intact.

108. W.D. Scott, Zanzibar Works Department at the time, to the author, 10 November 1976.

109. Almost all the British and a small number of the senior Arab officials

replacement of the dismissed professional staff by new men became a matter of controversy, since it was related to future foreign policy.

Foreign Reaction to the Revolution

The first reactions to the Revolution were very mixed. African states watched with some sympathy while anxiety and horror spread throughout almost all the Arab Muslim world, with the exception of President Nasser's Egypt, where the initial reaction was to view the Revolution as a British-Israeli plot.[110] Above all, Muslims in East Africa, for whom the Sultanate had been a revered institution, were profoundly disturbed. The unease in East Africa increased after the subsequent events in Dar es Salaam and further attacks on Arabs.

The crucial reaction, however, was that of Britain. Britain alone had local forces adequate to intervene; and, at a later stage, recognition by Western countries awaited a British lead.[111] The initial British reactions were based on fears for the safety of the British community; for this reason a unit of British troops was moved to the R.A.F. base at Eastleigh Airport, Nairobi, in readiness to fly to Zanzibar.[112] No consideration was given at any time to political intervention.[113] However, the Kenya government was unwilling for troops to be used even for this limited task, and it quickly became clear that the revolutionaries intended no harm to British lives or property.[114] It also became clear that they enjoyed — at least on

enjoyed a British government guarantee as members of the Oversea Civil Service.

110. In Iraq the newspaper *Al-Jumburiyah*, quoted by Radio Baghdad, spoke of a human catastrophe comparable to Palestine.

111. The only Western nation tempted to pursue a more forward policy was West Germany. An official from the West German Embassy in Dar es Salaam visited Karume early in February, and Bonn even announced its intention to recognise Karume. It was then realised that this attempt to pre-empt the G.D.R. had failed, and Bonn refused to proceed any further. Slowest of all was France, a delay leading to the expulsion of the French Consul.

112. Intervention to rescue lives of nationals in acute danger is permitted under international law provided that the intervening power limits action to the safety of its own subjects and does not interfere with internal political developments.

113. The first plans envisaged an air-landing of the 2nd Bn. Scots Guards, supported by the 1st Bn. The Staffordshire Regiment. The plans were scaled down, and eventually only one company of infantry actually reached Eastleigh. The ambitious initial plans reflect the confusion and apprehension aroused by Okello's broadcasts.

114. It is noteworthy, in this context, to record the consequent continuity of

Unguja — considerable popular support, and that there was no prospect of the Sultan mustering sufficient support for a restoration, even from Pemba. The troops were therefore stood down and, as already noted, those who later arrived on board *Rhyl* never disembarked.

There remained the more serious problem of who were the competent persons with whom to negotiate in the new government, and of recognition. In Zanzibar the confusion was obvious; two messages arrived in London seeking recognition, the first on 12 January signed 'John Okello, Leader of Freedom Fighters', and the second on the 13th from Karume as President of the Republic.[115] There had been, further, American reports of the killings of Europeans and the presence of Cubans to make calm consideration difficult, and Zanzibar was one of the matters discussed by the British Prime Minister, Sir Alec Douglas-Home, during his visit to President Johnson. Even when an authority did appear and the British High Commissioner on the spot strongly urged recognition, it seems that there were other impediments, which in the context of British politics at the time must have played their part in determining policies.[116]

The year 1963 had been a difficult one in the process of British decolonisation. The Cyprus question had reappeared and was acute, necessitating troop reinforcements in January 1964; the situations in Aden and Malaysia were disquieting. In Africa the Federation of Rhodesia and Nyasaland had collapsed, and Kenya had attained independence. The Conservative government was under sharp right-wing criticism for proceeding too fast with decolonisation. No Conservative cabinet minister could be expected to welcome a radical and bloody republican revolution, least of all Duncan

British business interests for several months. Although the port of Zanzibar was briefly closed, British-India and Union Castle ships began calling again on 23 January, and the port was handling shipping much as usual by the end of the month. Any political intervention would, of course, have ended all trade abruptly and for many years to come.

115. President Nkrumah of Ghana replied to Okello promising early recognition. A comedy turn was provided in London, where one D. Phombeah convened a press conference and announced that he was a public relations officer for the new government. Phombeah was accompanied by Omar Zahran, the First Secretary of the High Commission, appointed before the Revolution but in sympathy with it. Press questioning led Phombeah to admit that he was a Tanganyikan student.

116. In the section suggesting these impediments which follows, the author's reconstruction is his own; he neither received nor sought any official apologia.

Sandys, the Minister in the recently amalgamated Commonwealth and Colonial Office, who had presided over the final stage of Zanzibar's transition to independence. Furthermore, no precedent existed at this time in the Commonwealth's history for a violent revolutionary development of this type; in the view of contemporary British preconceptions of East Africa, there might be special dangers in the immediate recognition of a revolutionary régime. Press reports of the time suggest, not surprisingly, that all Britain's apprehensions were increased after the various army mutinies, unexpected and ominous as these were. The views of other Commonwealth countries, particularly at first Tanganyika, were far from clear. And lastly, the Prime Minister of Southern Rhodesia, Winston Field, was in London in January 1964 seeking independence on the basis of the 1961 Constitution; it was not within the limits of practical politics to grant an immediate recognition to the revolutionary regime in Zanzibar while stalling on a Rhodesian demand for independence. All these factors seemed to point to caution, as did the reactions and parliamentary remarks of right-wing Conservative M.P.s.[117] It may be conjectured that such considerations lay behind London's delay in recognising Karume and the Z.R.C.; the delay led, however, to a steady weakening of the British position in Zanzibar to the advantage of Babu and the radicals. In despair, Karume asked Professor Franck to plead his cause in London but Franck was unable to make any headway. Ministers in a number of African governments, including in Dar es Salaam Kambona and, after his own decision for recognition, President Nyerere, all urged British recognition for Karume in order to strengthen his position against Okello. From Zanzibar, Babu protested at the delay to *The Times* correspondent on 1 February, arguing that the British High Commission should be closed. The correspondent was left in no doubt over Karume's mounting resentment. Finally, despite a last-minute personal plea from Sandys, on 19 February the full Cabinet of Zanzibar, headed by Karume himself, ordered the British High Commissioner and the senior remaining U.S. diplomat to leave the country.[118] Obviously embarrassed, Sandys told the House of Commons that consultations

117. For example, in the House of Lords, Lord Colyton, a respected former junior minister in the Colonial Office, suggested that the whole Revolution had been planned in Peking.

118. On the following day the diplomats departed. A week later, a Union Jack was the subject of a humiliating incident in a Zanzibar City square for which an apology was subsequently offered. On 21 February the British business community in Zanzibar City presented a memorial to Karume regretting the departure of the High Commissioner, expressing the hope that Whitehall would soon grant recognition, and affirming loyalty to Karume

with the Commonwealth were taking a long time,[119] but Karume's pressure won the day with the granting of British recognition on 23 February. With British recognition came that of Australia, New Zealand and Pakistan. Ceylon followed a few days later. The mission staff returned, and a visit by Sandys personally followed on 8 March. But by this time, Karume had made new friends, and many features of these new friends' views were to last long after the friendships themselves had soured. Karume's disillusion went with Britain extended even to the British Red Cross, despite his earlier very real gratitude for their work in the camps.[120] The situation must have been bewildering in the extreme for Karume. He was, for example, fed with stories of British military aircraft flying regularly over Zanzibar, stories carefully orchestrated by Babu and his followers.[121]

The other country that played a crucial part in the matter of recognition was Tanganyika[122]. Here also were considerable complexities. No one, not even the Zanzibari leaders in Dar es Salaam, had known previously of Okello; Kambona at least had been expecting a later revolution led by Kassim Hanga. No one knew what might be the reaction of the British and, equally important, of those British officers and soldiers who were serving on secondment to the Tanganyikan Army should there be attacks on British people. Nyerere disliked violence, and he had a profound distrust of the Soviet Union. The rivalry between Nyerere and Kambona was worsening. There was generally an atmosphere of rising militancy in the

and his government (but not to the Z.R.C.). Karume was very pleased with this memorial, which accepted his claim to office.
119. Some Opposition (Labour) M.P.s objected, alleging U.S. influence and arguing that the Commonwealth's African members had already recognised Karume. *Parliamentary Debates, Commons,* 20 February 1964. There is, however, some reason to think that the U.S. was by this time frustrated by British delays and was urging recognition on London. Franck to the author, 13 October 1977.
120. A newly-arrived Red Cross official had unwisely permitted photographs to be taken in the camps; these, with misleading captions, appeared in the U.S. press, and Red Cross officials on Unguja were accused by Kassim Hanga of subversion. Interview, Mrs J. Adams, 1977. This led to the ending of all Red Cross, British and International assistance at the end of June 1964.
121. Franck to the author, 13 October 1977. Franck was at the time living with Karume in State House, and he describes Karume scanning an empty sky through binoculars.
122. The material which follows is based on interviews and correspondence with British officers serving with the Tanganyika Army at the time.

country; Algerians had arrived to establish camps for Frelimo, and Israeli military training staff were seeking to replace the British. On hearing the news of the revolution, Kambona, as Minister for Defence, ordered the British commander of the Tanganyika Army, Brigadier P.S. Douglas, to fly with him to Zanzibar. After waiting several hours at the airport, however, they flew to Nairobi for a meeting with Kenya ministers. The meeting discussed the events in Zanzibar; its main purpose, however, may well have been to remove from the British brigadier any temptation to intervene.[123] Nyerere was out of the capital, and the Vice-President, R. Kawawa, refused to allow any despatch to Zanzibar of the 1st Tanganyika Rifles, which had also been sent to the airport[124] by Kambona. Kawawa had been informed of the nature of the violence,[125] and was clearly both worried and baffled by it. Despite the return to Zanzibar of Karume, his obvious difficulties with Okello led Nyerere on 15 January to order the preparation of a plan for an assault landing from the sea. Whether Nyerere would have sent any forces beyond the policemen already noted to help Karume will never be known, for on the week-end of 18–19 January the Tanganyika Army mutinied. Although this event had been likely for some time, its violent manifestations and even more violent consequences represented a spreading of the Zanzibar anarchy. The presence of this anarchy in Dar es Salaam was one reason why Nyerere delayed further in deciding on recognition of the Karume regime; another reason was a passing preference to wait until the February O.A.U. Foreign Ministers Conference. But in the event recognition was granted on 23 January.

The United States reaction to the Revolution was also a complex one. In general, much U.S. policy at this time, particularly regarding smaller anglophone territories, was that of following the British lead. In Zanzibar's case there were additional special features. As

123. Other theories advanced for this trip have suggested that Nyerere ordered Kambona to Nairobi so that he should be away; that Kambona wanted to be out of Dar es Salaam in case it was the scene of a premature uprising or collapse of authority; or that it might need the combined representations of all three governments to restrain Britain from intervention. No firm evidence for any of these theories exists.
124. At the airport the British battalion commander, Lieut.-Col. (later Major-General) R.S.N. Mans formed a small key group of British personnel with the battalion's machine-guns in order to fly with this group alone to Zanzibar in the event of attacks on Europeans. Crosthwait advised that this was unnecessary.
125. The operators at Zanzibar Airport were in touch with Dar es Salaam until the afternoon of the 12th; as the day wore on the operators in Dar es Salaam could hear the firing when Zanzibar transmitted.

already noted, the mission was in the hands of a junior diplomat of uncertain judgement, and there existed in Zanzibar a satellite tracking-station which was staffed by U.S. nationals; the latter had for some time been a target for radical criticism.[126] The United States in general attracted far more hostility from the militants than Britain, the former imperial power. Posters appeared; one portrayed an African girl, a baby wrapped on to her back, a rifle in one hand and an expression of militancy, with the caption 'U.S. Imperialism, Get Out of Africa' in English, French — and, as an indication of their probable origin — Spanish. An American destroyer, the *Manley*, was sent from Mombasa to evacuate the families of the tracking station staff. The evacuation was panicky and led the Z.R.C. to be critical of any parallel British evacuation. Reports from the sensation-seeking American journalists, fed by the U.S. mission with inaccurate rumours of the presence of Cubans and the murder of Europeans, also coincided with acute U.S. apprehensions over Cuban subversion in Latin America. A sudden Cuban world conspiracy was perceived,[127] with Zanzibar as perhaps more dangerous than even the British believed. The expulsion of Picard, the U.S. charge d'affaires, and the later closure of the mission have already been mentioned. The U.S. government finally conceded recognition at the same time as Britain, and an experienced career diplomat, F. Carlucci,[128] was appointed to succeed Picard. Bitter anti-American articles appeared continually in the revolutionary press,[129] and major demonstrations against the United States took place on 9 and 11 April, being organised respectively by A.S.Y.L. and F.R.T.U. The closure of the tracking station was ordered on 9 April, to the advantage of the Chinese who secured some of the equipment. On 16 April, the Zanzibar delegate to the United Nations alleged that an Anglo-American invasion was being planned.

In contrast to the Western powers and Tanzania, Communist countries and many African states gave speedy recognition — and

126. Babu persistently misrepresented the station as a 'rocket base'.
127. The U.S. State Secretary, Dean Rusk, had expressed concern over Cuban agents in Panama. The Army Secretary, Cyrus Vance, claimed that the Panama government had arrested ten people for subversion, and that the U.S. government had identified these as having been trained in Cuba.
128. Carlucci's previous experience may have included Central Intelligence Agency work; he was to become a senior C.I.A. official in the late 1970s.
129. 'America will not hesitate to bring more disorder to Zanzibar as it has done in many parts of the world' was the headline in the government newspaper of 29 January 1964. The Zanzibar Students' Union demanded the removal of the tracking station on the same day. Petterson to the State Department, 29 January 1964.

reaped the benefits in influence.[130] China was particularly well-placed to help since a Chinese ambassador for Zanzibar had been selected before the Revolution; he merely arrived with his staff, among whom were some Swahili-speakers, and the embassy formally opened on 15 February. East Germany, in pursuit of its national policy of winning recognition and friends, was also quick to offer help. For the Soviet Union, the Revolution necessitated a hurried reversal of its previous analysis, which had portrayed the Z.N.P. as a mass popular anti-imperialist movement, and the A.S.P. as the agents of the British.[131] It also signalled the need for some attempt to work in harmony with the Chinese for the sake of appearances, and a need to overcome Tanganyika hostility and suspicion.

East German officials and staff began to arrive for the Treasury, the hospital and general medical services,[132] the broadcasting service, the government steamers and the Education Department. They were the hardest-working and most efficient of the new expatriates, and gained influence even among the former *Umma* group whose ideology was in some respects nearer to Peking. The Chinese predominated in the Works Department[133] and in work of various types in the rural areas. They lived in a building in Stone Town, departing early and returning late each day.[134] They would only say of their activities that they were 'digging', but political education with an anti-Soviet and anti-East German flavour was reported. 'Digging'

130. Kenya, Uganda, Ghana and Ethiopia were the first states to recognise the new regime, followed a week after the Revolution by the Soviet Union, Cuba, Czechoslovakia and North Korea. By the end of the month China, East Germany, North Vietnam, Israel, Egypt, Yugoslavia and most other Communist countries had all given their recognition.
131. D. Morison. *The U.S.S.R. and Africa*, London, 1964, 123–4, quoting from Soviet writers, notes the pre-Revolution view that the Z.N.P., although perhaps dominated by its right wing, was a broad alliance of all sections of the populace while the A.S.P. was a pro-British party through which the British hoped to retain control. Almost overnight the A.S.P. became the party of workers and peasants, and the Z.N.P. simply the bourgeois leadership of a first-stage bourgeois independence.
132. The East German hospital staff included some notably efficient nurses, and medical specialists such as plastic surgeons and dieticians. Miss S. Murphy to the author, 15 December 1976.
133. The Chinese Adviser to the D.P.W. arrived on 9 April. The P.W.D. had been 'nationalised', a meaningless gesture since it was already a state department, on 7 March.
134. Both the Chinese and the East Germans protected the residence area of their nationals with barbed wire and a steel gate.

may have been a reference to a trench defence system that was prepared around the coast of Unguja at the time. Outwardly, though, they appeared willing to work with the Russians. A few Ghanaian teachers arrived a little later. Finally, on 17 March, ostensibly to collect a cargo of cloves, a Soviet ship arrived at the port, which had been declared a forbidden area and was being taken over by Russians. Lorries moved a cargo by night from the ship to a site near Mazizini where, later, military training was observed. The Soviet vessel had in fact unloaded a cargo of weapons — rifles, light machine-guns, three light anti-aircraft guns and T40 protected personnel-carrier/scout cars — part of a consignment almost certainly originally destined for Somalia.[135] A few Soviet instructors also seem to have arrived at this time, to be followed by Chinese, again in small numbers, for a rival training centre on Pemba. But on Unguja most of the weapons were earmarked for a new political police force, the former conventional police force, still recovering from the confusion of events, being reduced to minor crime and traffic work. The arrival of these weapons from the two major Communist powers so alarmed Emperor Haile Selassie of Ethiopia that he offered President Nyerere the services of the Imperial Air Force.

Union to Preserve Autonomy

The supply of weapons was a major factor in the gaining of influence by Communist countries. They were also a major development in the rivalry between the various factions in the Z.R.C. Not only did their arrival indicate that Zanzibar was becoming a pawn in the great power rivalries in the Indian Ocean, but some of the weaponry appears to have fallen into the hands of both the major factions competing for power and influence. Karume — who, if rough and poorly educated, was also shrewd — seems at this point to have become seriously alarmed at the course of events. One group of Arabs had been removed, but it seemed that a new group and a new hierarchy of revolutionaries were replacing them. Many of these were former *Umma* party figures[136] of which the most vocal were

---

135. The scout cars had special low-pressure tyre fittings, easily discernible in photographs, of a type used by desert vehicles. It is possible that a few Chinese weapons also arrived at this time.

136. Among these were Khamis Musein Abeid, a former Z.N.P. member educated in China and North Korea, who joined *Umma* and was in this period Area Commissioner for Donge; Ahmed Abubakar Quallatein, a former customs officer and P.W.D. official who had become an F.P.T.U. official in 1960 and joined *Umma*, and was at this time an administrator; and

Arabs. This represented a threat to Karume's personal position and beliefs. These concerns were to lead Karume in March and early April to consider the idea of a union with Tanganyika.

The atmosphere in Zanzibar City in February, March and April had remained tense. Expatriates were harassed, road blocks were set up, and there were some shooting incidents. A total dock strike, which ended as suddenly as it began, took place on 27 February. 'Nationalisations' were liable to take place at the point of Freedom Fighters' guns, or at a wave of Karume's walking stick, and then as quickly be rescinded.[137] Most of the Asian civil servants, and many Arabs also, continued to be ejected summarily from the government service, and their special schools were closed. Many hundreds emigrated or prepared to emigrate. In some cases money and jewellery were smuggled out, but mostly such goods were abandoned or discovered in thorough physical searches before departure was allowed. The state and grant-aided schools were all renamed,[138] the latter being taken over entirely; non-African pupils were ejected, to be replaced by African pupils after a hurried re-scrutiny of past preliminary examination papers.

A vast triumphal parade took place on 15 February, the day of the ending of Ramadan, known as *Id ul Fitr*; thousands of people paraded past Karume, who was closely guarded by Tanganyika police. Many of the women, observers noted, had abandoned their veils, but this mark of liberation was not to be repeated at other rallies in 1964. As the British expatriate officials departed,[139] plans for a new economic order were discussed endlessly by the different groups in the Z.R.C. with the Soviet, Chinese and East German experts hurriedly flown in, against the background of the anti-American demonstrations already noted. On 11 April all British and U.S. residents, private and professional as well as official, were ordered to leave by the end of the month. Expatriates found especial

---

S.A.-R.M. Kwacha, an ex-teacher, Z.N.P. member and general secretary of *Umma* who was at this time Area Commissioner for Zanzibar City. Ali Sultan Issa and Salim Rashid, both already noted, also fall into this group.

137. Three cinemas were nationalised by the 'Freedom Fighters' on 26 February, a measure rescinded later the same day by Karume.

138. The new school names were Lumumba (formerly King George VI) College, Nkrumah (formerly Seyyid Khalifa) College, Obote (formerly Seyyida Nunu) School, Ben Bella (formerly Seyyida Matuka) Girls Secondary School, Gamal Nasser (formerly Seyyid Khalifa) School, and Fidel Castro (formerly Seyyid Abdulla) Secondary School.

139. The final departure was apparently without rancour; several members of the Z.R.C. came to the airport to wish Hawker well and thank him for his help. Hawker to the author, 19 October 1976.

difficulties in making arrangements for their departure.

A number of factors and incidents made clear, as had the affair of Lieutenant-Commander Fawssett, the rivalries between the Karume and Babu groups. One of these was the negative nature of much of the revolutionary political rhetoric, which was almost entirely concentrated on abuse of the past regime; this concentration did not reflect any lack of aims for the future[140] but rather the number of confused and irreconcilable aims held by the different revolutionary groups. For example, Karume was pleased with the news of British recognition on 23 February, but the left-wing radicals were annoyed. In his turn Karume was annoyed when petitions and pleas were addressed to Babu and not to him. On 28 February, Mdungi Usi, the Assistant Director of Information, was arrested following an earlier transfer, itself significant, of his office from the Ministry held by Othman Sharif to that of the President; the reason for his arrest appears to have been that he attempted to publish a speech, given by Karume at a youth rally, in which Karume had urged his audience not to become involved in cold war matters.[141] Karume was prepared to show profound concern for the detainees, particularly women and children, when alone with Red Cross officials, but on being joined by other members of the Z.R.C. he would loudly proclaim his indifference.[142] Similar confusion and usurping of authority was to be seen in the appointment of a senior East German Finance Ministry official, Gentsch. In Berlin before his departure, Gentsch saw a telegram from Zanzibar requesting the help of a senior official; in this telegram it was stated that Hawker was a reactionary who must be replaced as he had too much influence on Karume.[143] Nor, despite their leader's departure, were Okello's followers yet in line; some

---

140. Kassim Hanga, for example, told Carlucci of his goals of housing, road construction and rural electrification. Carlucci to State Department, 27 February 1964.

141. Karume evidently appeared somewhat unexpectedly at the rally, which was being addressed in anti-Western terms by militants and Communist diplomats. Carlucci attributed Mdungi Usi's arrest to an 'order [by] middle-level Commie sympathisers in GOZ'. Carlucci to State Department, 29 February 1964. Mdungi Usi, a founder member of the A.S.P., was later killed in prison.

142. Mrs J. Adams to the author, 20 July 1977.

143. Hawker, Final Report, 4 April 1964. Gentsch also left Berlin in the belief that he was to be an Executive Permanent Secretary, but on arrival he learned that he was to be only an adviser. Hawker found in the hand-over period that they had many ideas in common, so much so that Gentsch asked him not to pass his ideas on to Twala, who had become the Minister, as Twala would attempt the opposite to anything proposed by Hawker.

Z.R.C. members admitted firing upon the Freedom Fighters in early March.[144] The replacement and removal of moderate officials and ministers continued throughout February and March, culminating in April in the removal of Othman Sharif, then nominated as High Commissioner in London. Sharif protested publicly at the leftward trend of the government, which he saw simply as caused by the hostility of the Western press. But there is no doubt that Karume himself was attracted by a number of features in the new Marxist ideologies offered to him, and saw some of them, if not all, as suitable for Zanzibar.[145]

The arrival of the weapons, a substantial quantity of which fell into the hands of one of Babu's principal lieutenants, the Arab Ali Mafoudh, made the friction worse. Karume's nominees for command of his proposed people's militia were Yusuf Himid and Seif Bakari, rather than Mafoudh and other adherents of Babu. To a fuller support of Karume also returned the more 'African' of the militant revolutionaries, Kassim Hanga and Twala. But on both sides of the Zanzibar Channel, doubts as to whether the islands could survive as an independent state were growing. The past friendship between T.A.N.U. and the A.S.P., and the military support given by Nyerere to Karume in January, once again drew the leaders together. Karume, fearful of being a pawn in east-west or Sino-Soviet Indian Ocean rivalries,[146] and anxious for protection, came to accept that a union with Tanganyika would be the most effective means of preserving autonomy. His concept of the Union was not that of Kassim Hanga and Kambona, who saw a revolutionary African partnership and fusion.[147] Karume's concept of the union

144. Ledger to Mrs Ledger, 4 March 1964.
145. Hawker, who knew Karume well, wrote of him at this time: 'At the time of the Revolution I think that Karume was undoubtedly pro-British. But I think that his new friends from China, Russia and East Germany have weaned him away from that position and I feel sure that he now quite genuinely believes that they are the countries which have to offer the sort of conditions he wants.' Hawker, Final Report. In the author's opinion, however, this assessment omits Karume's emerging apprehensions.
146. United States naval activity in the Indian Ocean at this time appears to have alarmed both Karume and the mainland.
147. Roget, *op.cit.*, quotes Kambona as saying to him: 'All is not lost in Zanzibar. Of course we need a bold economic and social policy. . . The problem for us is not a choice between the Eastern and Western blocs. Our choice is between international Communism and African socialism. Now Karume is an African, Hanga is a Communist but he is also, and very deeply so, an African. I know him well; he is my best friend. With these two men

was the striking of a new balance for Zanzibar between its two historic cultures, not absorption by either one of them. Still less, then, was Karume's concept of the union the same as that of Nyerere, who saw it as an African regaining of an area that had been lost, and who spoke in terms of a marriage which would in time and by sharing lead to a full and complete merger. Nyerere, along with his ideals for the future, was in addition strongly motivated by his distrust of the growing influence of foreign Communists in Zanzibar, and saw a non-aligned union as a means by which this development could be controlled. British, and also possibly American, advice may also have contributed to Nyerere's decision, these events all occurring before the relations between Tanzania and Britain became soured over Rhodesia.

In terms wider than the immediate crises, the proposed union was logical. Zanzibar was too small and isolated to survive alone fully independent, at least by the standards of 1964; Tanganyika could offer a pooling of resources to the benefit of both parties, and the A.S.P. from its earliest days had had close links with T.A.N.U. A flurry of exchange visits followed, these taking full advantage of the absence of Babu in Indonesia. Early in April, Karume visited Dar es Salaam, Kambona made several trips to Zanzibar, Kassim Hanga and Twala visited Dar es Salaam on 21 April ostensibly 'to discuss May Day celebrations', and on 22 April Nyerere, Kambona and a third Tanganyikan cabinet minister, Lusinde, all visited Zanzibar.[148] Nyerere urged speed, and at one point it was reported that he had used a threat to withdraw his police as a pressure to hasten the negotiations. In preparation for the formal announcement the Tanganyika police force in Zanzibar was in the event strengthened by a further 100 men, and both these and the force already in Zanzibar were given new semi-automatic rifles.[149] And with no further consultation with any other East African government (to the subsequent annoyance of Uganda), the Union of Tanganyika and Zanzibar was brought into effect on 26 April following the hasty passage of an Act of Union through the Tanganyika National Assembly. Nyerere became President, with Karume and Kawawa as, respectively, First and Second Vice-Presidents of the Union. Kambona became the new United Republic's Foreign Minister,

Zanzibar may yet be saved for Africa.'
148. *Africa Confidential*, 9 May 1964.
149. The source of these rifles is far from clear. Reports at the time suggested a major Western government, probably West Germany or Britain, but possibly the United States. Policemen went back to the mainland in batches of fifty to learn to fire the new weapon. *Africa Confidential*, 9 May 1964.

thus in theory supplanting Babu.

The announcements were made in Dar es Salaam. In Zanzibar the publicity was on a much reduced scale; for example, the first reference to the union only appeared in the Zanzibar Official Gazette on 19 September, and continued use was made of the title of 'President of Zanzibar' for Karume in preference to that of Vice-President of the new republic. But an added benefit for Karume was the departure of so many of his political rivals — Babu, Kassim Hanga, and others — to serve the new union government either because of its wider political or career opportunities or out of frustration at the confusions and rivalries in Zanzibar.

This consociational union left Zanzibar the institutional autonomy which Karume desired; Zanzibar retained its own budget and own economic policy — though enjoying the protection of mainland backing for the currency. All the Zanzibar ministries and departments remained intact to pursue their own agricultural, trade, banking, medical, educational and other policies. Zanzibar's militia were not amalgamated more than in name with the forces of the mainland; they retained their own camps, weaponry, training facilities, promotion structure, Soviet advisers and political training. The union also excluded the administration of justice.

The local East German and Soviet reaction was one of disappointment and some bitterness, and such few indications that the Chinese revealed also conveyed disapproval. The group of former *Umma* members was equally confused, and would not discuss the union with foreign correspondents.[150] One or two supported it, the majority seeing it at first as likely to strangle the Revolution and suspecting involvement by Britain or the United States; these criticisms, however, were not to last. Nevertheless, Babu found on his return that the union had dealt a blow to his prestige, and that some of his followers had switched their allegiance to Karume. He prevented his remaining militants from criticising the union, simply urging them to preserve Zanzibar's local autonomy and no doubt believing that the considerable hold his former *Umma* followers had on middle-level posts in Zanzibar would secure his position. He himself became one of the five Zanzibar ministers[151] in the new twenty-two-strong United Republic cabinet, in the relatively minor

150. These reactions are described by Roget, *op.cit.* Roget was in Zanzibar at the time. Ledger to Mrs Ledger, 28 April, perceived some Chinese reaction.
151. The others were Karume, Kassim Hanga (Minister of State), Makame (Minister of State in Kambona's Ministry of External Affairs), Moyo (Justice Minister) and Wakyl (Information and Tourism).

role of Minister of State (one of three) concerned with Economic Planning. He did, however, on occasions use his pre-union title of Foreign Minister of Zanzibar to pursue certain foreign policy aims of his own, thus adding to the confusion. In May 1964, for example, he accompanied Vice-President Kawawa on a visit to Peking — a visit during which the construction of the Tanzam railway was officially discussed for the first time.

The union was not to end the differences in ideology between the various Zanzibari revolutionary groups. It did, however, limit first the scale of direct Communist power in the islands, since Dar es Salaam was a more attractive stage. Secondly, it reduced the factionalism occasioned by the presence of the personalities of rival leaders; these had now by choice or perforce to spend their time in Dar es Salaam. The local stage had been cleared for a slow but steady assumption of personal power by Abeid Karume, who wished to use that power both to preserve in Zanzibar its traditional cultures and to prevent total absorption by either.

The Revolution should not be viewed solely in either class or race terms as an African rising against an Arab establishment. It also manifested a striving for a new identity, neither wholly Arab nor wholly African. In this quest for a Zanzibari identity there is a thread of continuity from Sultan Khalifa to Abeid Karume and in some measure even Ali Muhsin. All had very different concepts of what that Zanzibari identity should be, but all can lay some claim to patriotism.

IV. THE ZANZIBAR OF ABEID KARUME

A Populist Autocrat

Almost all contacts between Zanzibar and Britain were broken with the expulsion of British and U.S. citizens in April and May 1964. Only two or three British people were to remain. For this and other reasons, notably the impossibility of conducting fieldwork or research in Zanzibar itself, present knowledge of the Zanzibar of Abeid Karume is bound to be far from complete. From a limited range of sources,[1] however, it is possible to trace the outline of the main developments, though not always to check on the accuracy of detail. There are also inevitably many omissions which, it is to be hoped, will eventually be made good.

Power was to pass increasingly into the hands of the President of Zanzibar, either by the absence of other leading figures in Dar es Salaam, or by deliberate and shrewd political manoeuvring. Although, for the whole period of his Presidency, Karume's effective power-base never extended much beyond the Hadimu and the mainlanders who had arrived in the first half of the century, this majority provided a great measure of support on Unguja. A key figure was the Party Secretary, Thabit Kombo, an Unguja Hadimu. In the Tumbatu areas and on Pemba Karume was in time able to reinforce his position by securing his own grasp exclusively on an increasingly thorough security system, on the one hand, and on the other by a certain number of specific economic and social achievements. These buttressed him against the fear and resentment aroused by several oppressive measures and arrangements, and secured for him acquiescence and in time a grudging respect even on Pemba.

In his sixtieth year and lacking any formal political education, Karume had no ideological political solutions to offer. He was not without shrewdness, and he was a rousing orator on occasions such as party rallies. He suffered in some measure from a sense of inferiority, particularly regarding his command of English, which was better than he himself would allow. This made him subject to outbursts of irritation, but it also exposed him to flattery. He could at

1. Sources that have been generally used in this section include *Africa Confidential*, *Africa Report*, *Africa*, *African Contemporary Record* and interviews and correspondence with Zanzibaris who wish to remain anonymous, in respect both of their names and of the particular material that they gave me. Other sources are noted as they appear.

times be both stubborn and stupid. His sense of inferiority may also have been responsible for a deterioration, over the next few years, in certain aspects of his personal character and behaviour. His sole pre-revolutionary experience of ministerial office had been a brief one as Minister for Health in the caretaker government between the two 1961 elections. This had left him with little idea of ministerial responsibility or accountability, an attitude strengthened by his disillusionment with parliamentary democracy and his dislike of experts. In office he never travelled further than the mainland coastal area.

His style of rule became increasingly personal and despotic, like that of a Sultan of old; his aims, never clearly articulated despite his Castro-like preference for long rambling speeches, were those of populism[2] rather than socialism. We see a figure who had more in common with, for example, a post-1918 East European populist leader such as Bulgaria's Stambuliisky than with any form of African or non-African socialism. This pattern of politics tends to emphasise a leader at the expense of a party or a movement, and the authority of both the Z.R.C. and the A.S.P. (the latter having lost almost all internal consultative processes) became more and more subservient to Karume's will. Karume generally distrusted the well-educated, and many in this category sought employment on the mainland. One exception was Wolfgang Dourado, a London-trained barrister of Goan origin who became Attorney-General and in whom Karume placed considerable trust. The other important

2. Populism is a term notoriously difficult to define, it being an emotion or a syndrome rather than a clearly stated ideology or programme. P. Wiles, in *Populism its Meanings and National Characteristics*, edited by G. Ionescu and E. Gellner, 1961, 166–71, notes the following attributes of populism; attitudes may be judged more important than achievement (i), and leaders must represent this attitude in their style (ii); populist leaders claim a special bond with the masses (iii); the movement may be loosely organised (iv), loosely defined (v), anti-intellectual (vi), and both anti-establishment and counter-establishment (vii); conspiracy fixations may lead it to mindless violence (viii) but it is opposed to class conflict (ix); leaders may become corrupted by success (x); the economic aims are small co-operatives (xi) of people with little capital (xii), foreign finance is opposed (xiii) but small local capitalists may be permissible (xiv); populism can be urban, especially among artisans and recent immigrants (xv); populists do not object to either a strong state (xvi) or economic inequalities (xvii), so long as they serve populist interests; it is isolationist (xviii), religious (xix), opposed to science and technology (xx), often nostalgic for a vision of a lost past (xxi), and on occasions mildly racial if facing an oligarchy of a different ethnicity (xxii). Karume's Zanzibar contains all these attributes except possibly (xiv) and (xx). Karume himself was quite content that he should be referred to as '*mwana haramu*' (literally 'the old bastard') in common speech.

exception was Aboud Jumbe. Many of the old guard on the Z.R.C., farmers and low-level artisans, had no ambition other than to enjoy the fruits of success. The A.S.P. offices and branches often became an additional arm of the administration rather than a political organisation, as one visitor wrote:

When one visits the A.S.P. office, on the first floor of an unfinished building, the entrance is crowded with people, particularly with women. It is more like a market than the head office of a political party. Wrapped in shawls of many colours, the women crouch on the floor and wait for the moment when the Party Secretary will receive them, listen to their complaints or give them his instructions. The Secretary, a happy vigorous old man, very paternal and very popular with the Africans, behaves with them exactly like a tribal chief. There is certainly a link between him and the African masses, but it is more a spiritual than an organisational or structural one.[3]

The party's officials were appointed by Karume. As a party, it had always suffered from being more a loose and divided association of Africans — mainlanders and indigenous — from different areas rather than a body with an agreed specific programme. This defect under a leader who was a strong man but with little coherent policy produced a government that was authoritarian, often very crude, and generally also mindless and inefficient. Dramatic posters and slogans were constantly used in efforts to mobilise in the public. But only a few measures suggested any coherence in policy. The inefficiency was worsened by the fall in educational standards and the magnetic effect of the Union with Tanganyika in attracting some of the very small number of the trained indigenes away from the islands.

An early but instructive example of the new directions was seen in the 1964 May Day celebrations and their aftermath. These had been planned by the militant radicals as a show of strength, and they were determined not to let the Union spoil the occasion.[4] Karume too was content that the union theme should receive little mention. So the Union's Second Vice-President, Kawawa, was snubbed, with the Soviet and Chinese delegations receiving the places of honour. All, including Kawawa and the visiting diplomats, were greeted by displays of the Z.R.C.'s Zanzibar flag and the Zanzibar national anthem. Mahfoudh's military men with their Russian guns and vehicles, named the People's Liberation Army (P.L.A.) to mark the occasion, provided the military display. But by the end of the year

3. Roget, *op.cit.*
4. Roget noticed how quite senior officials deferred to juniors, young former *Umma* Arabs who happened to be influential in the party hierarchy.

Himid was securely in command of the force, and Ali Mahfoudh, although nominally second-in-command and recently elected to the Z.R.C., was on his way with a body of men and equipment to Mtwara on the mainland. There they began assisting Frelimo, with whom Mahfoudh was to become very popular; this re-arrangement, admirable for Karume, was probably effected by the Soviet military advisers who would not have wanted the pro-Chinese Mahfoudh. Although, in other spheres of Zanzibar life, the influence of the *Umma* militants was to last longer and, by virtue of the skills they could offer, constitute some measure of revolutionary socialist dialogue with Karume, these men had passed the peak of their strength. Babu himself made a permanent home on the mainland, never returning to Zanzibar for fear of arrest.

One major foundation of Karume's power over the next eight years, particularly the early formative ones, was to be the development of the People's Liberation Army, (P.L.A.) with the help of a Soviet mission of between forty and sixty persons. Another foundation, perhaps more important, was the security service; its members were referred to as *panya* (rats). They arrested mild critics and those who grumbled capriciously over food and other shortages, merely stating that the critics were 'enemies of the revolution'. In the first eighteen months after the Revolution, they could arrest, torture and imprison without trial. Foreigners from Western countries were closely watched[5] and a surveillance system over foreign mail was in operation. The security staff was trained, efficiently, in East Germany; a large percentage of the students — sent there supposedly to study academic disciplines (over 200 were sent in 1966) — were in fact receiving security service training. Although both the torture and the numbers arrested were reduced by the end of 1965, these abuses continued on a smaller scale throughout the whole of the Karume era.

A somewhat random system of national service was introduced, for which the military was one option. Despite the Union, Zanzibar retained almost complete control over the local military units and their training. The exact size of the P.L.A. is far from clear, but a strength of some 2,000 to 3,000, very large for the size of the state, seems likely. One of Karume's most trusted lieutenants, Seif Bakari, became the second-ranking officer. Not the least of the bizarre

5. One of the few British specialists left in Zanzibar after May 1964 was told on one occasion by a senior minister that over 200 checks had been carried out to ascertain whether he, the specialist, was engaged in espionage. The senior security official in 1965-6 appears to have been one Ibrahim Makaungu.

features of this force, one of whose main covert tasks was to preserve Zanzibar's complete internal self-government, was that it was paid for out of the Union government's budget, although leading personnel also received local perquisites as well, an important factor in preserving their loyalty to Karume. The announcement in March 1966 that the Zanzibar units were to be part of the Tanzanian Peoples' Defence Forces was almost entirely meaningless. A very few joint exercises were held on the mainland. A few island detachments were occasionally posted to the mainland, but mainland detachments were only allowed on Pemba, and even then only in small numbers. No mainland units were posted at the Unguja military centres at Migombwani or Chukwani. A small number of personnel, including in 1965 Himid himself, went to the Soviet Union for help over the training of their forces, and others went elsewhere in Eastern Europe. The only concession the Union government appears to have obtained was the replacement of the Soviet advisers by Chinese ones in the late 1960s, a concession that in any case reflected Karume's developing preference for the Chinese and dislike of the Russians.[6]

A process began of enforced alignment of all aspects of the national life with the Z.R.C. In May 1965 the Z.R.C. voted that its affiliated organisations — the A.S.Y.L., Women's Union, the F.R.T.U. and others — should all be dissolved and replaced by A.S.P. departments for youth, workers, women and peasants; this measure does not seem to have been carried through fully in terms of the institutions. The desired effect, however, was obtained by the President's nomination of office-holders for these organisations, and by a system of supervisory political officers appointed to departments and institutions. Their title was linked to the concept of *siasa*, political activism and direction. A more ruthless application of the process was to be seen in the reorganisation of the courts system. In October 1966, in an order that was made retroactive to May, the President was empowered to appoint a special court of a maximum of fourteen[7] members to have exclusive jurisdiction over political offences, offences against the preventive detention legislation, and offences of theft or damage involving government or state corporation property. The court's procedure was not to be bound to any previous procedures; it was to meet in secret, and defendants were not allowed legal representation.[8] The court had power to award the

6. By the end of 1970, only four Soviet advisers were reported to be in Zanzibar, and these had departed by the following year.
7. In practice, the usual number appears to have been three.
8. While the state often used legally-trained prosecutors, the exclusion of

death sentence, and appeal lay only to the President. Only in 1966, however, did the Zanzibar government officially announce that it had ended the right of appeal to the East African Appeal Court, a right that had ended in practice with the Revolution. Although nominally the posts of Chief Justice and those of magistrates in District Courts and Muslim customary law Kathis' Courts remained until 1969 (the former mudirial courts being abolished), their range of activities extended only over minor matters, and defending counsel were again not allowed. Although theoretically appeal could be made from the District Courts to the Chief Justice's Court and thence to a 'Supreme Council' appointed by the Z.R.C. or even to the Z.R.C. itself, in practice justice was more commonly summary. This practice became the new law in 1970 when a system of local three-man people's courts was instituted.[9] The new magistrates appointed by Karume were generally A.S.P. officials, and they were not always literate. Again, defending counsel were not permitted, although witnesses could be called. Below these courts, village *masheha* or headmen continued as of old to hear cases in Primary Courts and Juvenile Courts. At both these levels, the justice dispensed was quick and could be somewhat rough. For minor offences punishment was by the end of the decade usually a period of road work or other construction work, with residence in an open prison.[10] Earlier in the decade sentences had at times been very severe, and the death penalty had been prescribed for a wide variety of offences, which included clove-smuggling, and the illegal performing of abortions and tonsillectomies.[11] Some evidence suggests that such sentences may have been carried out in cases of clove-smuggling.

In 1969 the government announced that anyone marrying a Zanzibari girl and moving with her to the mainland would have to repay the cost of the medical and educational services estimated to have been spent by the state on her upbringing, i.e. Shs 56,000. Permits were always required for travel to the mainland. In 1970 the government ruled that a deposit for the same sum of money might be required from people applying for a permit — a measure applied capriciously and apparently with the twin objectives of preventing

special defending counsel was justified on the grounds that their expensive training and fees were exploitative, and the state prosecutor could also summarise the defence arguments.

9. *Africa Report*, December 1970; also *Gazeti Rasmi la Serikali ya Tanzania — Zanzibar* (Official Gazette), 31 December 1969, Presidential Decree No. 11 of 1969.

10. See below, p. 125, for details of this system.

11. *Africa Report*, March-April 1974.

Asians from leaving with money or moveable property and stopping the annually increasing exodus of the more enterprising school-leavers. Relatives of people who fled, of any race, were often imprisoned arbitrarily.

Equally severe and authoritarian was the alignment of the media with the wishes of the Z.R.C. No criticism of the Z.R.C. could appear in the press, and in some areas loudspeakers were installed (transistor radios being actively discouraged) to ensure that only Zanzibar Radio broadcasts could be heard. The cinema showed imported Communist films.

Hence a strong overall control and surveillance in matters large and small, with periodic outbursts of oppression in certain areas and on certain communities, characterised the years 1964–72, particularly the earlier years. But the oppression was never total or deliberately designed to decimate whole populations; it was capricious in matters both large and small. The possession of contraceptives was declared illegal; Karume's objections were neither moral nor theological: he simply wanted the population to increase. Attempts — which failed — were made in 1964 and 1965 to force people to 'volunteer' for week-end agricultural work; only in the final Karume years, when the administration of projects such as rural housing schemes had greatly improved, was there any pride in communal self-help projects — it came to be a very real pride.[12] In the early years, the weight of oppression was felt particularly in Pemba. In 1964, communal labour obligations of three nights and Sunday morning work per week were imposed on all Arabs and Asians in that island; the order emanated from Issa's successor as Commissioner, Ahmed Diria Hassan — secretary, before the Revolution, of the A.S.P.-linked Government Workers' Union. Humiliations and public floggings of Asians for minor offences continued, sometimes prefaced by long compulsory political harangues. In September 1964, Mfarinyaki, the last Okello-group Z.R.C. member, together with one or two others of the group, burst into the Ithnasheri mosque in Zanzibar City, opening fire and killing two men and a boy, Mfarinyaki was arrested,[13] but later released — he was one of the Z.R.C. members who greeted Nyerere at the airport when he made a visit later in the year.

12. 'They talk about self-help on the mainland, we practise it here' was said to several visitors to Zanzibar at this time. This pride and communal spirit has developed greatly since 1972.
13. Karume apparently ordered an enquiry of which nothing further was heard, but Mfarinyaki himself is not heard of after the end of 1964. He was believed to have been deported to the mainland.

Arbitrary deportations of Asians[14] continued in 1964 and 1965. A final series of anti-Asian measures was introduced in 1971. At a meeting on 16 March, Karume told a mass rally that all non-citizen Asians must leave within a year. He claimed that there were still a large number in Zanzibar attempting to control the economy. The final ending of private businesses and trading which followed later in 1971 was also directed against the Asian community, with 234 heads of families specifically being named as prohibited immigrants. These measures together appear to have removed a large percentage of the remaining Zanzibari Asians.

In January 1965, the seventy-nine-year-old Abdalla Suleiman el Harthy, who although he had been President of the Zanzibar Arab Association for forty years was also an A.S.P. member and a former friend of Karume's, was abruptly deported.[15] Other Arab deportations followed. Capricious victimisation of other minority communities remained a feature of Zanzibar throughout the period. But in the field of religion, most faiths were not seriously discouraged, although all religious teaching was discontinued in schools. Otherwise, Islam generally was encouraged, the Anglican cathedral was left alone, and only the Roman Catholic Church (because of its heavy Goan membership) was subjected to harassment. In April 1968, however, Karume briefly perceived himself as threatened by conspiracies planned in places of worship, and a decree was issued threatening people with imprisonment for such practice.[16]

The notorious forced marriages of young Asian girls, including two under sixteen years of age, to elderly members of the Z.R.C. in 1970 represents another example of oppression, one personally authorised and approved by Karume, who appeared to want an Asian girl for himself. Four girls, of whom at least one was only fifteen, were seized and compulsorily married in this way; the ceremonies were conducted by a member of the Z.R.C., Hamid Ameir Ali,

14. Sometimes the deportations took the form of a refusal to readmit people who had left Zanzibar for personal or business reasons. In the case of seventeen Asians refused readmission in this way in 1964, the Indian government protested, in vain.

15. El Harthy was deported at twenty-four hours' notice, allowed to take only £20 with him, and obliged to leave his wife and family behind.

The el Harthy family held a special status among Unguja Arabs because the family had been and still is an important dynasty in Oman.

16. The suspicion arose from prayers that were evidently not considered respectful to the new regime. A group, said to have been former Z.N.P. members, were arrested, their later release as an act of clemency was promised. The E.A. Muslim Welfare Association also came under severe criticism from Karume.

whose qualifications as a *kadi* were apparently open to question. At a meeting Karume declared: 'In colonial times the Arabs took African concubines without bothering to marry them. Now that we are in power, the shoe is on the other foot'.[17] Members of the girls' families who protested were imprisoned and beaten, and a number of Asian Shi'a families were ordered to leave, an order later rescinded. Western press reports of the time suggested that the girls in question were 'Persians', but no Iranians lived in Zanzibar. A Pakistani origin is more probable. There were also rumours of other Asian girls being earmarked for a similar fate, and cases of girls committing suicide and of unsuccessful attempts at flight by families with young daughters.

To Karume and others in Zanzibar there was another dimension to this unsavoury incident. Colonial Zanzibar had been stratified racially, and Karume and elderly Z.R.C. members were not alone in wishing to destroy this stratification. Breeding immigrants out had always been a Zanzibar method of ending such distinctions. In 1966 a Presidential decree, the purpose of which was explicitly to encourage inter-racial marriage, had forbidden any attempt to oppose an intended marriage except on medical grounds or because of a party having a criminal record. In a crude and confused way, Karume believed he was moving towards an ethnic reconciliation. As part of this ideal he himself took, as what can best be described as custom-law wives, girls from several communities, including one Arab, reported to be a Manga.

Other equally crude gestures followed. Detainees were released from mid-1964 onwards. According to Karume's claims, 1,000 were released on 1 May 1964, another thirty in November, 106 in December 1965 and a further twenty-four in January 1967. Others were quietly released without publicity. It would seem that by the end of 1966, the detainees still in detention at the time of the Union (about 2,000) had almost all been released, although capricious arrests and reports of conspiracies, real or imagined, provided a

17. *Africa Report*, December 1970. There was considerable world reaction and strong criticism in the mainland press. Arab and Asian protests were made at the United Nations. Nyerere was disgusted and prevailed on Karume to ensure there were no further cases.

The Anti-Slavery Society also pursued the cases of the girls, at least one of whom was told that her parents were departing from Zanzibar and leaving her behind, which was not true. The girls were kept under continous guard and no one was allowed to interview them. After the death of Karume three of them were allowed to leave, while the fourth was said at the time to have become reconciled to her position. In 1979, however, she arrived in Dubai and stated emphatically that she had been forced to stay against her will.

limited but steady supply of new ones. The fate of those released in May 1964 was not always fortunate. A number decided to return to their former homes in the rural areas, which led to some resumption of the killings and a renewed Arab exodus.[18] Reconciliation was never extended to the former Z.N.P. and Z.P.P. ministers. Most of these were removed to the mainland after the Union for their own safety, and spent long terms in prison there.[19] A decree of February 1966 expressly forbade the return of all those who had left Zanzibar between 12 January and 31 May 1964. But by the end of the decade conditions had settled, the number in formal detention on the islands was certainly small and Karume's 1972 announcement that Zanzibar had no need of prisons and had closed them in favour of periods of reformative labour on state projects was meant to demonstrate this improvement. According to Karume, men sentenced to corrective labour of this type were to receive Shs 150 per month and the right to grow food, if the site so permitted. But the announcement was so phrased as to suggest that some would spend long periods in this manner.

These limited gestures of reconciliation were interspersed with plots and rumours of plots to overthrow Karume. That these took place is scarcely surprising in view of the oppressive nature of some of his actions, the fact that the large majority of the inhabitants of Pemba and many Tumbatu had not wanted a revolution, and also that the former Z.N.P. had attracted support from a significant minority of Africans. The most notorious of these alleged conspiracies was one in 1968–9, which became a question of the survival of the Union, involving as it did, and to the chagrin of President Nyerere, the execution of Kassim Hanga and Othman Sharif (it is examined later in the context of Zanzibar's relations with Dar es Salaam). Among the others, the most serious in the early years of Karume's government occurred in November 1964. Some 300 people, including many who had only recently been released, were arrested and made to stand with their hands above their heads in

18. Mrs J. Adams to the author, 27 July 1977.
19. The mainland government remained under great pressure from Zanzibar to keep them in detention, one reason for this again being concern for their safety. Various welfare organisations tried intermittently to intercede for their release. Ibuni Saleh died in prison in 1968, and Baalawy, Khatib and Saleh, retained on the islands, were released in 1968 and then re-arrested. It is probable they were eventually set free. Muhsin, Juma Aley and Mshangama were released, Muhsin in 1974 and the other two probably at the same time. Shamte remained in Dar es Salaam in reduced circumstances with his movements limited and under surveillance. Ali Muhsin has published a bitter account of his experiences in mainland prisons.

open compounds for long periods of time. Sixteen leading plotters were named, and five of these, not named, were executed;[20] The whole conspiracy was said to have been one of former Z.N.P. supporters grouped together as the 'Peace Fighters Union'.[21] Two documents, obvious forgeries, were produced purporting to show how Arab political parties were forming in both Mombasa and London with the aim of returning to the old regime. In 1966 riots broke out in Pemba, of which food shortages were evidently the cause. A detachment of the P.L.A. was sent to restore order, which was only done after some bloodshed.

In 1968, two more events suggestive of suspicion and unrest occurred. At a full meeting of the Z.R.C. with the press present, Karume declared that all Comorians, known as the *Wangazija*, would have to renounce their country of origin, and officials of Comorian ancestry would have to resign at once and repay their earnings.[22] A military exercise, said to be normal training, took place at the same time, on 20 November, and gunfire was heard. The Zanzibar government claimed that the exercise had been designed to prevent a 'Mali-type' coup. A number of Comorians lost their jobs in the following month. A little later it was announced that people of Portuguese colonial origin were ineligible for government employment. Rumours of a left-wing conspiracy were rife at the time of the action against the Comorians, and it is possible to see a common thread, that of suspicion of Babu. Babu was in part-Comorian, but curiously was not affected by the measure since his father had been a minor Portuguese colonial functionary, with Portuguese and not French nationality — hence the need for the second measure. The latter overlooked the Makonde, who, on being instructed to pay a

20. Terror and torture in the investigations and in the camps were reported. A well-founded eye-witness report stated that some detainees under interrogation were buried in sand up to their necks and then left to die. Mr Justice Horsfall, quoting from a witness known personally to him, to the author, 17 November 1976.
21. Some form of magical belief appears to have motivated some of the conspirators; a witch doctor had stated that if a cow was burnt for five minutes and still lived, the Sultan would return. Unfortunately for the conspirators, the burnt cow lasted the prescribed time. *Africa Digest*, 5 November 1964.
22. In answer to an evidently pre-arranged question from Kissasi as to why Comorians were so reactionary, Karume replied 'They are not Africans.' In amplification, he took nationality in the period of the 1914–18 war as the criterion; the Comorians, in order to avoid conscription as porters, had insisted on their rights as French subjects. Also the Comorians had earlier tended to support the Z.N.P.

sum of money to acquire Zanzibar nationality or 'face the consequences', reacted with anger. The measure was then rescinded. The next group to fall under suspicion were Shirazi, especially in non-Hadimu areas. It is in the context of this spread of suspicion that the last alleged conspiracy, in 1971, against Karume must be seen. At a spectacular mass rally which Karume addressed, nineteen Arab and Shirazi conspirators, every one already sentenced to death, were all put on show.[23] Karume later commuted the sentences to labour on a state farm, but none of the accused was ever heard of again. Following this affair, Karume announced that only a person with at least one African parent could be a citizen of Zanzibar, a definition of nationality that was contrary to the provisions of the Union's interim constitution.

These conspiracies, contained by Karume's security apparatus, should not be over-estimated in their significance. Thabit Kombo's claim, when doubts on the stability of the regime were put to him in 1964 — : 'Oh, you know, Karume and I have only to show ourselves in the streets to rally the masses behind us'[24] — remained true for some time. By the end of the decade, however, acquiescence had been replaced by fear. This was manifested by the virtual absence of common crime in the later years of Karume's rule.

The Zanzibar Revolutionary Council

In the eight years 1964–72, the Z.R.C. steadily declined in power and influence, becoming more and more a ratificatory body for the execution of the President's wishes. In return for this, its members were secured in office and privilege, although it appears that Karume often treated them roughly in private council. Its members were to be seen from time to time, with guns and female companions, and with some members often doubtfully sober. The more extreme and the old guard continued for some time to seize property, usually large

23. The conspirators included five Arabs who said they had come from Mombasa, but were in fact Zanzibaris. S.A. Seifu, M.H. Salum, M. Salum, M.S. Hemed and S.H. Alei and fourteen more Zanzibaris accepted as such. The five were said to have been trained in Dubai and claimed British, U.S. and Kenyan support, which claim Karume rejected. They were alleged to have had Z.N.P. insignia and automatic weapons. Their undoing was claimed to have been an unsuccessful attempt to subvert three army officers. These confessions were likely to have been obtained under duress for show purposes, and therefore need to be viewed with scepticism.
24. Roget, *op. cit.* One later observer commented that Jumbe appeared to be trying to stand somewhat aside from Karume's more crude exercises of power in these years.

houses or country estates, and women, and to order floggings of those who stood in their way. Nothing resembling the T.A.N.U. leadership code requirements in respect of property ownership applied in Karume's Zanzibar. The Z.R.C. was in no way elected; it occasionally appointed new members to vacancies, and members out of line would be sent to the mainland. Zanzibar's pre-Revolution experience of parliamentary democracy was always, — and, as has been seen, not entirely without reason — advanced to justify its procedures. Severe penalties, of between seven and ten years' imprisonment, were established for any attempt to form a new political party. The only election permitted was that for President of Tanzania (Nyerere) in July 1965, for which Karume urged all to register as voters, with the warning that failure to do so would be regarded as 'eccentric' and would be dealt with. In April 1967, Karume made a speech, publicised more widely than accurately in the West, in which he forecast that it would be some fifty years before Zanzibar could separate the executive from the legislative bodies, and allow the latter elected members to control the government.

In May 1965, changes were announced in the Zanzibar internal constitutional arrangements. In theory these stressed the predominance of the A.S.P.; ministers were to serve the party rather than the government and have offices at the headquarters of the A.S.P. Because the A.S.P. officials and hierarchy were presidential nominees, the result in practice was a strengthening of Karume's power and influence. The new machinery provided for a Central Committee, of which Karume, as President of the A.S.P., would be chairman with a membership of A.S.P. officials (including the reformed youth and women's organizations), police and army leaders, and four members nominated by the President. Below this was to be a 'National Committee', composed of those members of the Z.R.C. who were not appointed to the Central Committee, together with the members of the latter body, who were of course Z.R.C. members. This 'National Committee' was thus in fact the Z.R.C., and continued to use its name and methods. The new arrangements were also to provide for a meeting of the A.S.P. in Congress once every three years, an event which never actually occurred in Karume's lifetime. In 1970, in a change which was largely semantic, ministers of the government became re-styled as 'chairmen', Karume altering his title to Chairman of Zanzibar the following year. The nomenclature was Chinese, and the change reflected the respect in which the Chinese were held by Karume. But it also contained a linguistic assertion of autonomy. The term *Mwenye Kiti* (lit. 'the holder of the chair') was adopted at the time that this title was being discarded on the mainland in favour of *Kinara* (lit. a small lighthouse). *Kinara* would not have accorded with Zanzibari Swahili. The practice, however, was not that of Peking, where at that time a committee advised a minister on the policy to be followed by his department, this committee consisting of party members with a chairman who was not always the minister. In Zanzibar the chairman and minister were the same individual, the Z.R.C. member responsible for the subject portfolio. After Karume's death, the term 'minister' returned.

Changes in portfolio responsibility also occurred from time to time. In September 1964, Saleh Saadalla became Minister for Works (in place of Wakyl, who was moved to Dar es Salaam) with Moyo as his successor in Agriculture and Land Reform. Moyo had briefly been a Union government Minister of Justice, but the post was abolished. In December 1964 Ali Sultan Issa was moved to Education. In July 1968 Moyo was moved to Education and Issa to Health, and Rashid Abdulla, who had earlier been a junior minister, was advanced to Agriculture. In 1970, at the time of the change of title, the major ministries were held by Moyo (Education), Thabit Kombo (Trade), Jumbe (Workers Security), Issa (Health), Rashid Abdulla (Agriculture) and Hamdau Muhidin (Works).[25] A final series of changes in February 1972 moved Abdulla to Health and Muhsin Ali (an original Z.R.C. member) to Agriculture.[26] Issa, the last Babu follower on the Central Committee, was given no portfolio — a fact which was to prove significant.

Legislation appeared in the name of the Z.R.C., with a presidential assent to each decree. Decrees remained in English, but rules and notices made under them came increasingly to be issued in Swahili.

Zanzibar and the Union

Full internal self-government, with no interference from Dar es Salaam, was a subject on which all members of the Z.R.C. were

25. The 'Vice-Chairman' and 'Assistant-Chairman' for the ministries were respectively: Ali Muhsin and H. Salehe (Education); Khamis Ali Khamis and Salimin Amour (Trade); A.B. Qualletein and Mohammed Sheikh (Works); Mohammed Mahmoud and Musa Othman (Agriculture) and Muhsin Ali and Feruzi Balozi (Health).
26. Other moves were Khamis Ali (a former Vice-Chairman for Works and Commissioner for Pemba) to Vice-Chairman for Internal Trade with Ali Karume, a relative of the President, to Vice-Chairman for External Trade. Qualletein, the most notable follower of Babu at this lower level, was similarly discarded.

agreed, even those militants with diminishing influence. Nyerere's January 1965 visit to the islands was probably the first intimation to many Zanzibaris of the existence of the Union, so little had it been publicised. Karume firmly stated in 1968 that the Union had been carried forward as far as was necessary and that he planned no further unifying measures. Nyerere tried several methods of exerting influence and authority over Zanzibar; it seems that at one stage he hoped to be able to buy the Z.R.C. members out by cash payments. He also hoped that his patronage, in offering Union appointments to leading Zanzibaris and providing generously for the islands in the Union parliament, would extend his influence. But in the end he was reduced to acquiescence in the hope of eventual change, the only alternatives — the use of force or dissolution of the Union — being by his perspectives out of the question. His policy of patience, extending even to open support for Karume's attitude over elections,[27] was made more difficult in a number of ways. In 1968 the Union government's Minister for Home Affairs, Sijaona, had hinted that once enemies of the Revolution had finally disappeared, it would be possible for Zanzibar to have elections. He gave this hint in answer to parliamentary questions about Zanzibar from mainland members, but it drew an angry riposte from Karume, who accused mainland members of being 'imperialist stooges'.[28] In July 1969 Karume criticised those who afforded shelter to refugees from Zanzibar, an implicit attack on Nyerere; also in 1969, he re-arrested in Zanzibar some of the former government's ministers who had been released on the mainland, which was a further irritant. But Karume had the advantage of considerable support on the mainland, partly arising from revolutionary prestige and partly from visits and speeches — and generous donations of Zanzibar money to local football clubs.[29] Many mainlanders in private voiced sharp criticism

27. As late as April 1971, in an address to the National Assembly, Nyerere warned that in his opinion elections in Zanzibar would lead to attempts to subvert the regime and minority rule.
28. Karume developed his theme by claiming the colonial power had introduced the electoral system only to prolong its rule, not to listen to the voice of the people. True democracy, he claimed, could exist without elections; if a man was first a true representative of the people of his area, he could perhaps later be selected for parliament.
29. It will be recalled that the 'official version' of the Revolution had recorded the whole sequence of events as being the result of careful master-planning by Karume. When Karume was asked, at the University of Dar es Salaam, about the role of Okello, he simply replied that since at the time of the Revolution Zanzibar had no army, there could have been no Field Marshal.

of events in Zanzibar, and mainland military commanders were scathing over the performance of the islands' units. Officially, however, little or no criticism was allowed either in the press or in public speeches.

The arrangements of the 'second interim' constitution of Tanzania gave the Union government, in theory, strong powers over foreign affairs, defence, police, banking, external trade and borrowing, taxation and customs;[30] in practice, Zanzibar continued to follow its own path in every field. The Tanzanian parliament included a vastly disproportionate number of members from Zanzibar, between thirty-five and thirty-nine in 1965, increasing to over forty-five and on occasions over fifty in the next two years. The precise number varied. In 1965 Zanzibar was given thirty-two seats — nominated in practice by the Z.R.C. — together with the three regional commissioners from the two islands and four of the ten 'Presidential Choice' members. By 1966 the number of the latter had been increased to sixty-two, an increase incorporating the Z.R.C.'s thirty-two but also permitting an increase in other Zanzibari nominees to a maximum of twenty. At this time then the Union legislature comprised 107 elected seats, seventeen regional commissioners, and a small number, usually less than ten. Presidential Choice members from the mainland. From Zanzibar came the thirty-two Z.R.C. nominess, three regional commissioners, and a varying number, usually between twelve and twenty, of other Presidential Choice members, a few of whom were Union ministers of Zanzibari origin. Zanzibar might then have some forty-five to fifty-five seats out of about 180 in the legislature[31]. But in practice this seemingly powerful group contributed little to parliamentary proceedings, the Presidential nominess only occasionally contributing, while the Z.R.C. nominess were mostly absent. Their membership, on full salaries paid by the Union government, often aroused resentment.

Although in theory Tanzania was one state, visitors from the mainland were required to produce passports or other official travel documents before being given permission to land, and Zanzibar customs officials generally raised charges on would-be importers of mainland Tanzanian products. By the end of the decade, people and goods from the Tanzanian mainland were reported to be often

---

30. The list also included constitutional revision, emergency powers, currency, posts and telegraphs, harbours, aviation, exchange control and movement of citizens.

31. In 1967 Tanzania's total population was 11,000,000, of which Zanzibar's figure was approximately 325,000.

subject to more rigorous checks than those from elsewhere. The Union government always appointed a generous proportion of Zanzibaris to Union (i.e. non-mainland) posts such as diplomatic missions, thus seeking to re-inforce the Union. No reciprocal gesture was made from Zanzibar.

From the mainland's point of view, the worst experience of the Union was the fate of Kassim Hanga and Othman Sharif, which became a major source of embarrassment to Nyerere at home and abroad. After a brief period as a Minister of State, Kassim Hanga had first become the Union government's Minister for Industries, Mineral Resources and Power — from which base he proclaimed the need for a heavy industries policy of Stalinist severity,[32] and then again a Minister of State with special responsibility for the union. Othman Sharif was sent as the Union government's ambassador to Washington, to be recalled almost immediately following a diplomatic quarrel.[33] On his return, the Z.R.C. decided that he had fallen under Western influence, and on a charge of treason he was sentenced to death in his absence in April 1965. This sentence was immediately commuted to a ten-year prison sentence by Nyerere who, again almost immediately, secured his release from prison. But he was not given another Union government post. In the period 1964–6, Kassim Hanga's friendship with Kambona developed and he was to find himself caught up in the latter's quarrel with Nyerere, a quarrel itself made worse by Kambona's European Communist contacts and views on Zanzibar.

It appeared that an alliance between the Z.R.C. and the mainland radicals was emerging, a challenge that Nyerere had to withstand in order to survive. He had earlier been sympathetic to Kambona, arranging special facilities for him in the Netherlands in the belief that Kambona's condition needed medical treatment. But in 1967 he was faced with what he saw as proof of disloyalty, and Kambona, stripped of office, left Tanzania hurriedly to pursue his vendetta from exile. Kassim Hanga lost his post in a Union ministerial reshuffle at the same time[34] and was arrested in December 1967, and was

---

32. H. Bienen, *Tanzania, Party Transformation and Economic Development*, 1967, 221–3 notes a remarkable speech of Kassim Hanga, in presenting a five year industrial plan in 1964. He admitted the enormous cost, but judged heavy industry could be achieved by sacrifice. He talked of a coal and steel industrial base supporting a machine-building industry, which would produce tens of thousands of tractors for an agricultural industry to be reorganised into large state farms.
33. See below, p. 148, for the details of this issue.
34. Babu was also apparently anxious to resign in protest at the lack of

accused, together with his bodyguard, of attempting to subvert military personnel. In an interview which he was permitted to give in prison, Kassim Hanga denied the charge that he was involved in any conspiracy with military officers, and insisted that he was merely trying to reconcile Nyerere and Kambona.[35] In early 1969 he was released, and went to live in a house owned by Kambona. But later in the year he and Othman Sharif, by this time a director of International Gems (Tanzania), were arrested on the mainland, apparently at the insistence of Karume. For a while Nyerere refused to send them to the islands, but in September they were flown to Zanzibar and there they were executed, probably by a firing party, although one report alleged that their execution was by drowning. In a speech in October, Karume announced that four men who were leading a conspiracy of fourteen to overthrow the government had been executed by a firing squad.[36]

It is almost certain that both Othman Sharif and Kassim Hanga wished, for different reasons, to end Karume's rule, but a formal conspiracy seems very unlikely. Each, however, was a serious potential rival to Karume; Othman Sharif was a friend of Nyerere, and both he and Kassim Hanga had considerable following in the A.S.P. Both, too, aroused all Karume's inherent distrust of the educated. It seems that Nyerere's decision to return them to Zanzibar was made following assurances that they would receive a fair trial, for which he trusted Karume. Equally, there is little doubt that Karume saw the disposal of his rivals as essential, and threatened the break-up of the Union if they were not returned. Their fate was a matter of the greatest private distress to Nyerere. John Hatch, a personal friend of both Sharif and Nyerere, wrote of the latter at this time: 'I know that

revolutionary fervour at this stage. In February 1967 Makame became a Minister of State in the President's office, but in the June reshuffle, when Kassim Hanga was excluded, Wakyl was moved to the President's office and Makame was sent to Information and Tourism. Babu was moved to Lands, Settlements and Water Resources, a key post in the months after the Arusha Declaration and one more satisfying for a man of his views. This reshuffle reduced the proportion of Zanzibari ministers and junior ministers from one-third to about one-quarter, a reflection as much of the criticism they often invited as of population realities.

35. *Africa Confidential*, 1968. He was reported as appearing gaunt and nervous.

36. A third was almost certainly Ali Mainy Tambwe, one of Babu's followers and a former junior minister in Babu's ministry. Tambwe, Sharif and Kassim Hanga were all named by Karume as being among the plotters, but the fact that they were among the four executed was not announced. All were said to have been trying to subvert the military units.

Nyerere acted in good faith and will always remain profoundly distressed over his mistakes.'[37]

Autarky and Nationalisation

One of the clearer and more consistent themes of policy in Karume's period of rule was his quest for economic self-sufficiency for Zanzibar. His vision was of his state freed from any dependence upon anyone, and in particular free from the fluctuations of world prices for such vital commodities as rice and sugar. For this vision the islands' inhabitants were to be severely restricted in their imports, at times to a point of hunger; all agricultural aid programmes were to be linked to self-sufficiency, and rural land and education policies were to be subordinated to this aim. The importing of non-essentials such as Coca-Cola was stopped early, and reductions in other imported foodstuffs were made whenever possible, shortages being thereby created. But many foodstuffs that were imported as a result of particular trade and aid agreements with East European countries were of very poor quality. Determined to save the Shs 3 million that were spent every month on importing rice, flour and sugar, Karume announced a drastic control system for imported foods in June 1971. This system provided for a weekly ration of 1 ½ lb. of flour, 1 lb. of sugar and 1 lb. of rice by means of vouchers administered by the Chairman of the Department of People's Equality and Workers Rights, all to be supported by a propaganda campaign on the theme 'grow more rice to eat', and by the opening of an agricultural camp at Bambi in central Unguja, where young volunteers were to be paid Shs 150 per month, with preferential treatment in a nearby new rural housing development. But food shortages worsened in Karume's last months, and long queues became a regular feature of life. Land reform, to be examined later, was based on Karume's view that an independent rural cultivator system was more likely to produce efficiently for the overall aim than any imposed collective or commune system.

Much foreign aid accepted was related to self-sufficiency. This included the gift of six small coastal fishing boats from East

---

37. J. Hatch, *Two African Statesmen, Kaunda of Zambia and Nyerere of Tanzania*, 1976, 253. It is perhaps also relevant to note that among the followers of Kambona who were later arrested in 1970 were some described by a defecting K.G.B. officer as having 'close ties' with Moscow. These, according to the defector, did not include Kambona; but the group might earlier have included Kassim Hanga. *The Times*, 27 May 1980, report of interview with I. Dzhirkvelov.

Germany in 1965 and the subsequent purchase of thirty-six rather larger boats and ten deep-sea vessels in 1966, the arrival of twenty-two Chinese water engineers to advise on irrigation projects in 1965, considerable Chinese help with rice and sugar production schemes from 1966 onwards, the importance (second only to security) attached to the choice of courses in food production and fishing for which young Zanzibari students were sent to East Germany and elsewhere, the gift of tractors and the provision of a tractor and a farm implements repair shop from China, and the Chinese construction of a shoe factory and a cigarette factory.[38] Not all the schemes were successful. The East Germans' diary project at Mtoni was a serious disappointment, and their projects for fishing and fruit-canning processing plants were apparently abandoned. Poor planning by Soviet advisers at the outset was responsible for failures in the tuna fishing project. But on balance the policy has, in a harsh way, served to benefit the islands.

Overall economic strategy was set out in two development plans, the first for three years in 1965 and the second for four years in 1967. The first, although subsequent to the Union, bore no relation to economic planning on the mainland, and the second bore only token relation to the Union's plans. Both plans were said to have been 'approved by the Z.R.C.', and were in all probability laid before it. Their aim was in each case economic self-sufficiency. The first plan, foreshadowed by Karume in July 1964 and announced by Twala as Minister for Finance in January 1965, envisaged the spending of some Shs 33,600,000 on agriculture, social services and urban rehousing. Agriculture was to concentrate on rice-growing and sugar cane, and process plants were envisaged for fruit-canning, shoes, coir, lime and sugar. Chinese advice and aid were sought for both growing and processing projects.

The social service improvements were to concentrate on medicine and education. For the latter twenty primary and three secondary schools were planned, but these targets were not reached. Also envisaged was a university, which remained a cherished hope to Karume's death. In July 1965 Twala announced a sharp increase of 10 per cent on the price of petrol and an even more severe increase in the duty on unprocessed tobacco from Shs 6 to Shs 25 per 100 lb.; these measures were intended to assist financing the plan. Even more important for the financing of Zanzibar's development was relief

38. The shoe factory was begun in 1965 and finished in 1967, but it soon experienced difficulties over leather supply. The cigarette factory was something of an unnecessary duplication, as one was also being built on the mainland.

from the severe cost of such services as defence, air services, posts, overseas representation and police; these were now mostly paid by the Union government. The 1967 plan, to cost Shs 84m., reiterated the shoe factory and other processing plants for fruit, fish and coconut, added two dairy plants, one for each island, and plans for rural bus services. In this rather more carefully prepared plan, it was announced that the emphasis of school education would be scientific and a call for volunteers was made for public works, in particular housing for which specific projects were set out. The call was phrased in terms suggesting that reluctance to respond to it would be imprudent. This somewhat authoritarian call does nevertheless, appear to have been, the start of the increasingly successful Zanzibar communal self-help programmes; perhaps one reason for this was another measure announced at the same time — the formation of a body to investigate the illegal sequestration of property. Society was beginning to stabilise, and work for oneself and the community was beginning to become worthwhile again.

The major factor for Zanzibar's overall post-Revolution economic recovery, however, lay outside the parameters of plans or mainland subventions: it was the swing of the pendulum of clove prices to record levels, and the resumption of purchase by Indonesia. This began late in 1965 following a trade agreement.[39] The Soviet Union too became a substantial purchaser of cloves at this time. Despite the upheavals on Unguja and Pemba, Zanzibar was well placed for a return of trade because the Clove Growers' Association had at the time of the Revolution between 270,000–300,000 bags of cloves stored in godowns awaiting a return of trade.[40] In 1967–8, clove prices almost trebled from about $550 per ton to over $1,500, which in turn was nearly doubled in 1969.[41] Production, too, recovered; a record of 18,000 tons was claimed for 1968.[42] In April 1971, Karume was able to boast of Zanzibar foreign reserves of £14,000,000.

Ever-growing reserves made a great appeal to Karume's unsophisticated populist thinking. Almost as if they were a tin box of money

39. In November 1964, agreement was reached with Indonesia on the resumption of trade relations, a specific agreement for 3,000 tons of cloves worth $2,100,000 was reached in September 1965.
40. C.D. Knight, Acting General Manager of the C.G.A., to the author, 12 January 1977. *Africa Confidential*, October 1971, estimated stocks of 32,000 tons, but this seems a little high.
41. *Africa Report*, March-April 1974.
42. The Economist Intelligence Unit's *Quarterly Economic Review of Tanzania, Mauritius* (Annual Supplement, 1976) contains a useful note on Zanzibar's clove production, on which this section is based.

buried under the bed, reserves were to be kept against any misfortune rather than be spent on development needs or remedying food shortages. His last years seem to have seen a fall in clove production, although export momentum and growth of reserves were maintained by sale of stock. No crop figures were published after 1968, but totals of between 2,000 and 7,500 tons seem likely. One reason for the fall in production was that a good year was often followed by a medium one and then a poor one. A second reason may well have been neglect of planting and tending in the immediate Revolution period, and a third the poor prices that were paid to the actual clove-grower, sometimes less than 10 per cent of the overseas purchase price. Other practical difficulties were clove-bush disease, labour shortages and careless cutting by unskilled pickers. One consequence of the poor price was illicit nocturnal smuggling of cloves by coastal dhows, for which a penalty of ten years' imprisonment was at first laid down, soon to be changed to the death penalty together with confiscation of boats[43] — a measure of the serious harm done to the economy by this practice. Nevertheless the overall increase in prosperity appears to have had another consequence, namely an increase in the wages paid in Zanzibar City and the other towns to a level far above that of the mainland, seemingly as much as Shs 500–600 per month or more even for unskilled workers.

Although Twala, as one of the militant Marxists, was able, within the parameters of Karume's overall search for self-sufficiency, to inject a number of his own more radical ideas, the arrangements for land redistribution bear the clearest hallmark of Karume's own populist thinking prevailing over socialist doctrinal theory. Supposedly a revolutionary regime and, after 1967, one united in a state committed to *ujamaa* village communes, Zanzibar's land policy was almost the reverse. Individual peasant producers were to be the basis of the new land order after redistribution, a basis that achieved a considerable measure of success and might have achieved even more if the peasant grower had received a better price for his produce.

---

43. According to *Africa Confidential*, October 1971, flotillas of coastal dhows were engaged in this picturesque moonlight ocean smuggling. The Zanzibar government at the time was paying a grower Shs 1.5 per lb; on the mainland between Shs 8 and Shs 10 per lb could be obtained. The government was able to sell to Indonesia at Shs 14 per lb, and in smaller quantities to India at Shs 21 per lb. The demand, and therefore the market, for cloves was extending to Singapore and Hong Kong.

The State Corporation for External Trade received confirmation of its monopoly at this time.

The land redistribution was implemented by Moyo, as the Minister for Agriculture and Land Reform, with Taher Adnan, a product of Makerere and Oxford and a follower of Babu, as Land Reform Officer; the major instrument of legislation was the Land (Distribution) Decree, No. 5 of 1966. Apart from the seizure of certain properties for the use of Z.R.C. members, the method was the division of estates into three-acre plots, 'title deeds' for which were handed out to peasants at periodic ceremonies. The principal beneficiaries appear to have been the Hadimu and the mainlander arrivals of the first half of the century; the reasons for this were largely geographic, in that they lived nearest to the former Arab estates, but they were also the communities most committed to Karume and the Z.R.C. Many in fact only received a new title to land which they had previously share-cropped, and in other respects the legislation was a recognition of what in practice had already happened. A steady succession of plantations were taken over on both Unguja and Pemba in the next years.[44] By February 1972 it was claimed that 71,145 acres of land, property of former 'feudalists', had been given to 23,715 families.[45] The plots were not freehold in any Anglo-Saxon legal sense of the term, but were owned on a period (usually life) lease system more nearly related to Middle Eastern Islamic usage; ultimate legal ownership of all land remained vested in the state. The peasant could grow and sell to his profit, although in some village areas profit was shared. The legislation provided that a peasant could generally pass his plot on to his son, and apparently plots could even be sold, although the decree did not technically permit this. But a village committee or a government officer ensured that proper use was made of the land, which might otherwise be confiscated, and purchase of two or three plots by one wealthy farmer to form an estate was forbidden. The government also retained the right to direct, either in part or in total, what the peasant could grow. The village communities in some areas owned tractors. By 1972, some 180 were said to be in operation, let out to farmers at a hire charge of Shs 28 per acre.[46] A Rural Settlement and Village

44. For example in June 1965 the expropriation of thirty-four farms was announced, followed by fourteen more in the next month and 236 more in December.

45. The earliest publicised steps in the programme were at a ceremony at the People's Palace (the former Sultan's palace) on 28 June 1965, when Karume gave out title deeds and a cash grant of Shs 500 each to the first thirty of an initial group of 900 selected peasants. By February 1966, Adnan was claiming that 280 peasants had received plots following the confiscation of 650 plantations.

46. Information on land arrangements appears occasionally in the press and

Development Fund was set up in 1967, to which workers in rural areas were directed to pay 3 per cent of their monthly earnings, and traders were directed to pay a sum equivalent to 10 per cent of their trade tax. The fund was however used to benefit Unguja farmers more than those of Pemba, again a reflection of the base of Karume's power.

This system of leased plots formed the main structure of agriculture. The second set of institutions were a small number of state farms, generally farmed by squatters rather than wage-paid labour, and intended to produce crops of especial importance. One such farm existed ready-made at the time of the Revolution, the colonial government's agricultural research farm at Kizimbani, which continued to give away seedling plants. With Chinese help two more, one of 1,300 acres being at Upenja, were opened in 1966 for rice-growing. A fourteen-acre state poultry farm was also opened at Mtoni, and at the time of Karume's death plans for a 3,000-acre government sugar plantation at Mahonda were being finalised; 1,000 acres of palm were being cleared for the scheme, which was to be linked to a newly completed sugar refinery.[47] The disappointing dairy farm project at Mtoni (assisted by the East Germans), for which eighty Jersey cows and bulls were imported, was another of these state projects.

There are numerous theoretical arguments in favour of a mixture of supervised peasant plots with state farms as a basis for agriculture in emergent territories. Individual incentive remains; with tactful supervision, the most suitable crops can be grown; resources and implements can be shared voluntarily, and the negative effects of coercion are reduced to the minimum. Much of the Zanzibar practice appears to have been sound, at times successful, and where faults occurred these were administrative rather than structural. It may perhaps be claimed as Karume's major achievement in the field of development.

Profits from clove sales were paid into the newly-formed People's Bank of Zanzibar, *Benki ya Wananchi ya Zanzibar*, which by the

Tanzanian government statements. I am grateful for some notes on this and other subjects from Professor R.H. Green of the Institute of Development Studies at Sussex University. Islam's second Caliph, Umar I (634-44), ordained that a true Muslim should own no more land than he could farm himself, and if he failed to use it the land should be forfeited. Both these ideas are present here.

47. This factory was also situated at Mahonda. It was built with Chinese help, and it was hoped that when in full operation it would produce the balance of 25 per cent of Zanzibar's sugar needs that still had to be imported.

end of the decade had become effectively the only bank to operate in the islands. The expatriate banks had been closed down, and even the mainland state banks were only permitted very small offices for certain specific functions. A Public Finance Control Commission, with Gentsch as Chairman, was set up in August 1964; and in October 1965 a special commission to study the setting up of a State Bank, to work with but not be a subsidiary of the Central Bank of Tanzania, was appointed.[48] The State Bank was formally founded on 1 January 1966, and profits from the increasing clove sales of the next years paid into it, for onward holding jointly by the London National and Grindlay's Bank and the Moscow Narodny Bank, the former having the larger share.[49] Foreign currency reserves for Zanzibar, then, started to rise spectacularly in a Union that had a desperate overall short of foreign exchange.[50] Karume's concept of autonomy and hoarding produced a situation in which Zanzibar obtained the best of both worlds. The Tanzanian shilling was used, protected by the East Africa Currency Board and later by the Central Bank of Tanzania; currency cost Zanzibar nothing in terms of administration or note-printing, but all local profits and foreign reserves were kept locally. Zanzibar, of course, paid a subvention to the Union government in respect of services supposedly common, but, as has been shown, the actual operation of those services in the islands reflected Karume's prejudices rather than the policies of the mainland, and in any case the subvention (even if it was always paid in full) was both below the cost of the services provided and far below the amount Zanzibar could have contributed, in the good clove years, to overall Tanzanian development.

The remaining commercial and industrial sections of Zanzibar's economic life were all acquired in the four years after the Revolution. At first, and mainly in respect of smaller Arab or Asian-owned plants and small stores or businesses, these were often taken over by force, the owner being prevented from re-entering the premises.[51] In

48. Its chairman was another East German, Ebert, and other terms of reference directed special attention to staff training and the transfer of all accounts to the newly-formed Bank.
49. Persistent rumours alleged that the account was in Karume's own name and that even the Chairman for Finance was not allowed to draw on it. After Karume's murder, Wakati, the Governor of the People's Bank, vigorously denied the accusation. It may well have been, however, that Karume so arranged the account that his signature was necessary for the release of funds.
50. The total was generally believed to be £25,000,000 at the time of Karume's death.
51. A typical example of this was the acquisition of nineteen coir, fibre and

respect of larger European trading concerns, the method followed was that set by the Bank; the relevant legislation, Decree No. 1 of 1966, giving the President powers to create public corporations. A state institution with a legal monopoly would then be set up; as soon as its staff considered themselves capable of acquiring a sector, the monopoly was applied, and expatriate firms were thereby obliged to cease trading and close. Only the petroleum firms escaped this process of acquisition. A few of the formal 'nationalisations' appeared to be more political rhetoric than effective policy, as for example the Zanzibar Electricity Board and the Clove Growers Association, the former an autonomous para-statal corporation that merely received a new name and some loss of autonomy,[52] and the latter a local growers' association taken over and later incorporated into the State Corporation for External Trade, *Biashara ya Zanzibar ya Nje*, or *Bizanje*, which continued its monopoly of clove-handling.[53] *Bizanje* was given to the Director of Economic Planning, an extremely able former official of the Veterinary Department named Dr Ahmed Rashid, to run; Rashid was of a Comorian Arab family and a follower of Babu. Other leading state corporations formed in the early years of the Revolution included the Zanzibar Wharfage Corporation, the State Building Corporation, a State Industries Corporation, a State Rice Mill Corporation and a State Import Trade Corporation. All were formed primarily to meet Zanzibar's own interests, with in most cases few or no links with their mainland equivalents.

Many of the goods which were allowed to arrive appear to have been badly made and inessential, while more urgently-needed items such as clothing were invariably in short supply. News of the arrival of cloth would lead to queues of hopeful purchasers. Confusion was on occasions increased by somewhat arbitrary allocations of functions to particular corporations on the basis of the competence of their administration rather than any more logical planning. The whole process was rounded off by a decree in May 1971 when the

coconut oil factories in April 1965, followed soon afterwards by the taking over of six soft-drink plants. A further decree in the following month nationalised more Asian-owned premises and garages.
52. The take-over was nevertheless dramatic, troops surrounding the plant and offices, and British technicians being summarily deported. The new name of this Corporation was 'State Fuel and Power Corporation'.
53. The C.G.A., the world's largest clove industry, was the last of the pre-Revolution economic institutions to be taken over, late in 1966. The handover lasted one day, the outgoing British general manager giving up his position to an indigenous headman who spoke no English and had had no commercial training.

final extinction of all private business was announced for the next month, penalties of heavy fines or imprisonment being attached to breaches of the decree; as already noted, this measure was principally directed against Asian businesses. A system of family co-operatives operating through state-owned premises, held in the name of the A.S.P. for the retail and distributive trade, had been attempted for some time before the announcement, but these appear in practice to have operated more as small private family businesses,[54] particularly after failures in a number of more formal co-operatives. Where small 'family business' co-operatives were non-Asian, these appear to have continued unmolested and a few Asians even survived by means of judicious payments. A limited encouragement to the return of tourists, initially on day trips only and throughout the Karume period in controlled packaged parties, was permitted as a small-scale foreign exchange source. These tourists were subject to surveillance and checks at road-blocks, they were not allowed to depart from their tour programme, and Zanzibaris were not allowed to entertain them without permission. An annual total of 1,500 tourists was announced as the aim in 1971, and early in 1972[55] construction of the badly-sited and badly-planned Bwawani Hotel was begun. It was intended that this should be a major luxury hotel for foreign visitors, with 120 rooms. Plans for other hotels, both on Unguja and Pemba, were drawn up, although construction only began after Karume's death.

Another traditional livelihood, fishing, suffered from the inefficiency and mismanagement of the Karume era. The price offered by the government was some way below that offered on the mainland, and this reduced the incentive to fish. The government's hopes that larger and more efficient fishing boats would produce larger catches met with the initial difficulty of the absence of any cold storage. The failures in planning for a serious commercial expansion have already been noted.

54. In state-controlled distributive systems, it can often in practice be more profitable to be the village branch of the state trading corporation, with some discretion over sales and prices, than to be an entirely independent small trader with no such discretion. In Zanzibar two A.S.P.-linked bodies, the Office of Peoples Equality and the women's organisation *Umoja Wa Wanawake* were to be responsible for the system of co-operatives.
55. A large hotel for tourists had been one of Karume's earliest aims, announced in November 1964. The long delay seems explicable only in terms of the general inefficiency of the regime. When it was eventually completed, the hotel was placed under Indian management.

Social Services

All too little of Zanzibar's returning prosperity was spent on the social services. A major aim of the Karume regime was an expansion of educational opportunities for Africans. The immediate post-Revolution reallocation of places has already been noted; in March 1965 guidelines for secondary school admission — based on calculations of the racial proportions of the population of 80 per cent African, 5 per cent Arab, 4 per cent Asian and 1 per cent Comorian — were announced[56] This ratio system was to prove unfortunate. In despair, many Arabs took their children to the mainland or abroad, and young Africans saw little need to work because places could be obtained with such ease. By the end of the decade, after the provision of free primary education to some 80 per cent of the islands' population, figures of 41,000 in primary and 3,200 in secondary schools were claimed, with school classrooms crowded and teachers working double shifts. Primary school standards had improved, and by the death of Karume primary education was almost universal. Secondary school teaching remained uneven in quality, and was far from universal. Political education, in particular the obligatory reading of Karume's speeches and some military instruction, was added to the curriculum in addition to the revised emphasis on science subjects.[57]

At the end of the decade, the East European system of a ten-year free compulsory school course (from six to sixteen) in one 'First-cycle' school, adopted as an aim of policy on the mainland, began to be introduced on the island. Under this system, the existing major secondary institutions began to accept pupils after a compulsory national Form IV examination, an arrangement not without new difficulties. From 1964 onwards, the education service had to face enormous staffing problems. Many of the best teachers, British and Zanzibari of all races, had fled or were expelled after the Revolution. East German, Ghanaian, Egyptian and other foreigners who were

56. The remaining 10 per cent were left unexplained. In practice, it was said that in this year 1965, 380 Africans, seventy-five Arabs, twenty Asians and five Comorians were admitted. In the following year, 1,111 Africans were in secondary education. The ratio system was abolished in 1977.
57. *Africa Report*, December 1970. Volumes of Karume's speeches were provided for political education. It was claimed that there were ninety-eight primary schools compared with the pre-revolution total of sixty-two. These new schools were partly the work of the local community, who had to build the building; the government then provided the teacher, who could be retained so long as the school remained efficient.

brought in [58] met with very varied levels of success,[59] particularly because their arrival coincided with the adoption of Swahili as both the national and official language. In a policy statement in 1971, Moyo reiterated the cherished ambition of opening a university, and announced that the examination system would in future be more closely co-ordinated with that of the mainland. He also urged more academic work, together with agricultural work so that school children and teachers should became involved in practical problems. All this was to be at the expense of sport and dancing in the schools. In practice, however, Zanzibar's school children did not receive the range of agricultural self-reliance activities that were so marked a feature on the mainland. The reason appears to have been the preference of the education officials to emphasise pride in and care of Zanzibar's particular national property and heritage. Students were sent to the mainland, where a certain number of university places were reserved for Zanzibaris, and to certain selected countries abroad, mostly Communist ones, for tertiary education. None were sent to Western countries. The East Germans promised to open a technical college and a 'school of economics', but in the event this seems to have taken the form of providing teaching staff for facilities in existing premises. The school of economics became in practice an administration institute, training officials for service in government and state corporations. The courses included book-keeping, typing and low-level management, and the best students went on to the mainland for further studies.[60]

Until 1969, in common with the mainland secondary school system, school examinations were conducted in co-operation with the Cambridge University Overseas Examinations Syndicate. This was allowed to private candidates up to 1970, after which, it was announced, purely local arrangements would be made, including the use of undergraduates for marking papers. One reason for this was to ensure that products of the Zanzibari system would have no qualifications that would be recognised elsewhere; another was to conceal the poor performance of the Zanzibar schools. But the difficulties and the opposition evidently proved too great, and in 1971 the Tanzanian national examination system was adopted for the islands. It was also said that a common abuse of authority in the early post-Revolution years had been the withholding of certificates

58. By 1971 Cuba, Czechoslovakia, China, Pakistan, Egypt and Sweden all appear to have contributed small numbers of teachers.
59. The East Germans in particular were criticised for poor English and out-of-date teaching methods. *Africa Report*, May 1972. Initially ten arrived in 1964, and the number had increased to some twenty by 1968.
60. Five East German lecturers were at the school of economics in 1967.

for examinations passed until communal or national service obligations had been discharged; Arab pupils who wrote their examinations in December 1963 suffered particularly in this respect. Another sure sign of the frustration felt by many school pupils and school-leavers was the 1970 decree imposing heavy payments and even prison sentences on parents whose children left the islands.

Most immediately visible among the legacies of the Karume era were the large blocks of flats, mostly built by the East Germans, in areas of the former Ng'ambo cleared for the purpose and named Michenazi. On occasions, the clearings were unnecessarily large, and people found themselves homeless. The design of the flats, which included open coal stoves, was generally unsuitable for a very hot tropical city with serious ventilation problems, and this was only remedied at considerable cost.[61] The flats were not popular among the ordinary people,[62] although they were offered at very low rents on long-term tenancies, which could be passed on to a next generation.[63] Many Zanzibaris still hoped for a home on land of their own for cultivation or stock; the narrow balconies on each floor of the blocks provided no room for people to sit and talk.[64] Labour used for their construction appears to have been provided through the civil offenders rehabilitation centres or communal or national service obligations, the latter being described as 'voluntary'. By 1972, 1,000 families had been rehoused in flats, mostly in the Michenazi blocks, but some also in one or two ambitious country town projects. Young A.S.P. officials, state officials and military officers who were A.S.P. members were selected as occupiers, furniture was provided and they were not required to pay rent.[65] Pre-Revolution housing in Zanzibar City was all taken over by the government without compensation; the houses were listed, and each was labelled with an A.S.P. number. Some of these were rented by A.S.P. leaders, they lived in some style in them; many others remained empty and deteriorated. Old Zanzibar City's Stone Town

61. The Ng'ambo flats were in blocks of 130 and cost some £200,000 per block at the time of construction. Owners of demolished mud huts were given a sum of money, said to have been £1,600, as compensation.
62. A number were apprently empty at the time of Karume's death. *Africa Report*, March-April 1974.
63. The average monthly rent, including water and electricity, was Shs. 36, claimed to be the lowest for state housing in Africa.
64. Some East Germans have apparently blamed Karume for the flats' shortcomings on account of his close personal interest in the project, an interest which led him to make frequent visits to the sites where he demanded changes of plan. The Zanzibaris refer to the area as 'Berlin'.
65. *Tanzania News Review*, February 1972.

developed a deserted appearance, particularly as almost all the small shops and stores in the narrow streets had closed.

Rural housing built in the period varied from blocks of flats, inappropriately extravagant like their urban counterparts and unpopular, to less ambitious but more practical conventional rural architecture. Karume envisaged eleven new country towns, five on Unguja and six on Pemba.[66] Blocks of flats were again intended to form the main feature of the towns, and these were begun at Wete, Chake Chake and Mkoani on Pemba, and at Makunduchi on Unguja. More successful, however, was the less ambitious brick rural housing built in some of the other towns and in certain villages. This was of a high standard, producing neat plans complete with administrative and party offices, dispensary and community centre.

Medical services appear to have been another victim of Karume's often sudden prejudices. World Health Organisation staff were expelled, Karume claiming that Zanzibaris were naturally healthy and had no need of them, but initially the East German staff of doctors and nurses were indispensable. At the 1964 May Day parade, the East Germans announced gifts of a clinic, and both a medical and a nursing training school. In the event, this seems to have amounted to the opening, late in 1964, of only a small medical auxi- liary and nursing training centre at the former Bohra Gymkhana Club, where a director and three instructors, all East Germans, taught some eighty trainees, mostly girls. Zanzibar City's main hospital was renamed the V.I. Lenin Hospital and enlarged. The East Germans fell out of favour and were replaced by Chinese, who added to the hospital a small manufacturing unit for simple drugs. They also built one small new hospital. But the Chinese in their turn became unpopular, one reason apparently being their increasing use of their own poor quality staff. In the country areas an attempt was made to set up a chain of small free rural medical centres, one for every six square miles, but staff was not always available for them. One consequence of the expulsion of the World Health Organisation staff was a great increase in malaria. Most serious of all was a chronic shortage of drugs, Karume being unwilling to release the necessary foreign exchange. In 1970, private medical practice was prohibited, thus lengthening the queues outside government dispensaries.

66. *Tanzania News Review*, February 1972. On Unguja the new towns were to be at Kisima Jongoo, Kilimani, Bambi, Makunduchi, Chaani and Michenazi. On Pemba, Chake Chake, Mkoani, Wete, Mtemani, Madungui and Jumbaimbwe were selected as sites.

Foreign Relations

The Union in theory meant the end of Zanzibar's existence as a state with its own foreign policy, but in practice this was to lead to a number of difficulties.[67] While many of these difficulties were of local origin, others were not. Underlying many was the way both the two super-powers saw — and encouraged others to see — Zanzibar in simplistic black-and-white terms and failed to appreciate that neither of their own forms of government was well suited to the territory.[68]

The first and most serious, one which nearly broke up the Union, was the question of the two Germanies. The Federal Republic was recognised by Dar es Salaam, and East Germany by Zanzibar, but Bonn at this time maintained the 'Hallstein doctrine' under which she would break off relations with any country seeking to recognise East Germany. A compromise, whereby the East German embassy in Zanzibar became a 'trade mission', was unacceptable to Karume, who demanded that the new united state should recognise East Germany.[69] The West urged Nyerere to curb the growing East German pretensions, but the Soviet Union urged Karume in the opposite direction, the East Germans advising Karume that the break-up of the Union would be preferable. Nyerere remained very cautious of wooing by either of the two German states, but in the summer of 1964 he offered East Germany one consulate-general, either in Dar es Salaam or Zanzibar. This was unacceptable to East

67. Much useful material on this subject appears in T.C Niblock, 'Aid and Foreign Policy in Tanzania', unpublished Ph.D. thesis, University of Sussex, 1971.

68. United States reactions have already been noted. *The Times* interviewed I. Dzhirkvelov, a defecting former K.G.B. officer and Tass correspondent, who served in Zanzibar at this time. In the interview, reported on 27 May 1980, Dzhirkvelov commented: 'Soviet strategy in Africa has failed, largely due to Moscow's inability to comprehend African conditions and the African cast of mind. . . . The Soviet strategy was to take advantage of anti-colonial sentiment and gain political influence over African countries by tying them to the Soviet Union economically.' Much of Dzhirkvelov's interview develops the theme of the difficulties he and others working in Africa faced in trying to convince Moscow of the real nature of African problems, and their frustrations over Moscow's assumption that Soviet socialism was suitable and inevitable.

69. East Germany increased its help in Zanzibar immediately after the Union to preserve its position; fresh parties of East German aid officials, one including Scholz, a Deputy Chairman of the Council of Ministers, arrived and with one group of these Karume, signing himself as Vice-President of Tanzania, concluded a Treaty of Friendship on 18 May 1964.

Germany, one of whose Deputy Prime Ministers, Kiesewetter, visited Zanzibar early in 1965, clearly anxious to force an issue. Nyerere was obliged to give way, allowing two East German consulates-general. Bonn had been prepared to concede one consulate-general in Zanzibar, but saw itself as having been tricked by the establishment of one on the mainland,[70] and refused to accept Nyerere's argument that the situation had to be resolved in a manner acceptable to the Zanzibaris. Bonn thereupon withdrew all military aid and threatened to cut off economic aid as well. Calmer counsels eventually prevailed, but no new aid schemes were offered to Tanzania for several years.

East Germany was at this time vital for Zanzibar, being its second largest aid donor in 1965–6, and replacing China as the largest in 1966–7.[71] Equally important, in internal Zanzibar political terms, was East Germany's training of Karume's security service. In addition to the educational, housing and agricultural and medical aid already noted, East Germany took over the operation of the Zanzibar broadcasting service, installing a new 10-Kw. transmitter in 1965, and East German staff also operated some of the technical telephone services. In late 1969 and early 1970, more than 100 East Germans were at work on their various projects, but Karume and the Z.R.C. then quarrelled with the East German consul, Buthner, and expelled him. By the end of the year most if not all of the East Germans were reported to be on their way home.[72] The precise and inflexible methods of the East Germans, who were unaccustomed to less sophisticated styles of administration, and the failure of some of their projects, seem to have been the main causes of the rift, although heavy loan charges may have contributed.

Zanzibar's relations with the United States were also a cause of embarrassment in Dar es Salaam. A crisis arose in January 1965 when the Z.R.C. claimed that two U.S. diplomats, Carlucci in Zanzibar and Gordon in the United States Embassy at Dar es Salaam, had been involved in a plot to overthrow the Z.R.C.[73] There is an element of the contrived misunderstanding about the incident, based on the misrepresentation of monitored telephone calls,

70. Bonn was prepared to accept a trade mission, this implying no recognition of the East German regime as such.
71. Different narratives provide differing precise amounts of money. *Africa Contemporary Record*, 1968, notes a Shs 35m. loan in 1965–66 and a contribution of Shs 13.52m. for 1966–7; Niblock records a grant of £500,000. When to these differences is added or subtracted the covert security service training costs, the precise amount becomes even more difficult to assess.
72. *Africa Record*, December 1970.
73. The incident is described in Niblock, *op.cit., passim.*

although it is impossible to say whether the misrepresentation was the work of Zanzibaris or East Germans. Carlucci asked Gordon to arrange for the State Department to send a goodwill message for the 'second twelfth', the first anniversary of the Revolution. Gordon asked for 'ammunition', i.e. arguments to convince the State Department, and for a specific date. All this was represented as evidence of a conspiracy. Nyerere, whether he believed the story or not, ordered the expulsion of both diplomats, and tried to mollify the American government by saying that he believed the diplomats were acting individually, which made any inter-government rift unnecessary. The American government, however, threatened to expel the Tanzanian counsellor in Washington, at which point Nyerere, still protesting, withdrew Othman Sharif. The Americans followed suit almost immediately with the withdrawal of their ambassador. Thereafter United States aid was limited to the funding of a small craft institute.

China began her relations with Revolutionary Zanzibar as the major aid donor, temporarily to be eclipsed by East Germany in 1966–7, but thereafter to make continued progress and steadily gain influence until the death of Karume. In contrast to the loans from other countries, notably East Germany, the Chinese ones were free of interest. China's initial move, in swift response to the Revolution, was a promise made to Babu as early as 19 February of aid worth £175,000;[74] this was followed by a series of loans, reportedly amounting to $12,000,000 by the end of 1970.[75] The schemes involved a large number of Chinese instructors and officials.[76] The Zanzibaris also benefited from some of the Chinese mainland aid projects; for example, Zanzibaris could purchase products of the Chinese-built textile plant in Dar es Salaam. Zanzibar also benefited from the China-Tanzania Shipping Line: Zanzibari crew were recruited for one of the latter's ships, and for shore-based staff. But the Chinese also benefited considerably in trade terms from many of these arrangements, both in the trade that resulted, and politically. Considerable quantities of rice were sold to Zanzibar. Bicycles, some medical supplies, tractor parts, and possibly the tobacco for the cigarette factory and other minor consumer goods could also be sold in Zanzibar and on the mainland. Sometimes the money received in

74. Minor matters not noted earlier covered by this and subsequent loans included omnibuses, a printing press, a major sports stadium (named after Mao Tse-tung), and irrigating projects.
75. *Africa Record*, December 1970.
76. The number is difficult to establish. It was certainly over 100 at the end of 1970, and figures as high as 400 have been suggested.

payment for these goods could be converted into Western currencies or otherwise used for Chinese purchases of Western technological products. Nevertheless, Karume had good reason in his last years to describe the Chinese as his best friends and not, as in 1964, the Russians. The relationship, however, came to be identified in the eyes of many Zanzibaris with Karume's policies and severe style of rule. They began to fear too great a dependence on China.

Zanzibar's contacts with China were, of course, acceptable on the mainland. One other minor but notable relationship, much less acceptable across the Zanzibar Channel but carefully rebuilt by Karume after an unpromising start, was with the United Kingdom. This rebuilding began and continued at a time of much tension between Tanzania and London over Rhodesia, the NATO link with Portugal, and certain other issues; it was viewed with disapproval in Dar es Salaam, that was heightened by the evident relish with which Karume appeared to regard the disapproval. It was essentially a non-political trading relationship, but one which was profitable to both sides, the most noteworthy transaction being the construction of Zanzibar's colour television station by the British electronics company, Pye. The main motive of the project appears to have been Karume's belief that by television he could communicate effectively to ordinary people. Provision was made for the erection of screens in public places, and colour television was decided upon in 1972.[77] Other agreements with Britain provided for Zanzibar's continued use of the Crown Agents' facilities, and for a British construction company to extend the airports at Zanzibar City and on Pemba.

Throughout the period 1964–72, Karume tended to act on his own if he wished or if the mood took him; for example in 1966 A.S.P. delegates went to Moscow for the Soviet Communist Party Congress. Most illustrative perhaps was Karume's studied indifference to President Nyerere when the latter took President Tubman of Liberia on a tour of Zanzibar in 1964, an indication of his true and unchanging view of the Union.

The Assassination of Abeid Karume

In 1971 there was no easing of the problems facing Karume, partic-

---

77. British films, varying from major productions to football matches, began to appear on Zanzibar's television. *Africa Report*, December 1970, notes that Karume had the words of a popular revolutionary song changed from 'We are not afraid of Americans and British' to the more general 'We are not afraid of capitalists and exploiters'. British firms were sometimes paid their entire account in cash.

ularly those problems of his own making. Dissatisfaction was spreading. Poor prices paid to the clove-growers caused discontent, and the plans to complete self-sufficiency in staple commodities and the actual existence of a rationing system for rice, flour and sugar were very unpopular.[78] The early popularity of Karume had soured into awe and fear, even on Unguja; fear was also behind the allegiance of his lieutenants and the Z.R.C. A new generation of young men who had been boys in 1964 was growing up to be critical of the regime, seeking a return to some form of consultation within the A.S.P. The censorship of media and communication was resented, and younger educated men were no longer willing to accept the authority of the ageing and corrupted Z.R.C. old guard. Many of these young men, too, were interested in developments on the mainland and did not wish to be so cut off from them as they were. Life in the islands had become dull and regimented. Karume and the Z.R.C., on the other hand, were apprehensive of this trend and became even less enthusiastic over the Union and contacts with the wider world. They were apparently once more thinking of secession.

The ceremonies to commemorate the eighth anniversary of the Revolution, once again held in February on account of Ramadan, were especially elaborate, probably with the intention of countering the dissatisfaction. A great parade, taking more than an hour to pass Karume, included the military, the uniformed youth movement, teachers and students, and a small detachment of mainland peoples' militia brought over for the occasion. At what was to prove the last of his great mass rallies, Karume called for more intensive political supervision and political education of youth, this training to include periods of work in agricultural camps to develop interest in and enthusiasm for agricultural self-sufficiency.

On 7 April 1972, Karume was murdered. At the time, he was on the ground floor of the headquarters building of the A.S.P., drinking coffee and playing *bao* (a Swahili game akin to draughts) with Thabit Kombo, the party treasurer Shah Kombo and other elderly A.S.P. members.[79] The sun was setting, and in the fading light two vehicles arrived outside the building, in one of which was a

---

78. A common saying in Zanzibar at the time was reported to be: 'We have reserves of money but no rations; on the mainland they have no reserves but no rations.'

79. This account is based on the prosecution's opening statement at the trial of a number of people accused of complicity in the murder, as reported in the *Daily News* of 16 May 1973. Earlier 1972 versions had offered slightly different accounts, in particular in respect of the number of people who actually entered the building.

Lieutenant Hamoud, recently returned from training in Eastern Europe. Hamoud was the son of Mohamed Hamoud, who had been the murderer of Mugheiry in 1955, and who had apparently been killed in detention in the early months of the Revolution. The son was determined to avenged on Karume, who he believed to have ordered the killing. Hamoud had often proclaimed his intention to kill Karume whom, like other *Umma*-influenced army officers, he believed to have betrayed the cause of the Revolution. Karume was aware of his views and was said to have remarked, when Hamoud was promoted, 'One day he will kill me'.

His military uniform gaining him automatic entry, and armed with a sub-machine gun, Hamoud walked into the building. Karume appears to have immediately understood Hamoud's intention and to have made some last remark, probably a prayer, before Hamoud opened fire.[80] Karume died almost instantly and Thabit Kombo was seriously wounded. The others present appear to have dived for cover under a table. Karume's guards rushed to the room on hearing the shots, and it has never been clear whether they killed Hamoud or whether he committed suicide, either on the spot or later. Equally unclear is the role of the other occupants of the two cars. They included Captain Ahmada Mohammed, a Comorian; Lieutenant Sindano, and African; and Ali Khatib Chwaya, an Arab civilian. It is possible that the two officers entered the building with Hamoud, but Chwaya (who had had links earlier in his life with *Umma*) did not do so.

After the killing, the two cars drove rapidly away to the Youth League headquarters, apparently looking for Colonel Seif Bakari, who however was not present. Bakari was known to be Karume's own choice as his successor. The cars then drove off to the north of Unguja, where two of Hamoud's associates tried to go to ground in a house, but were later shot dead while resisting arrest.

The murder of Karume threw the Zanzibar government into confusion and disarray. Himid, the P.L.A. commander, had only recently returned from East Germany and was ill. Effective power lay with Colonel Ali Mahfoudh who restored a sense of direction and assisted Aboud Jumbe in the preparation of and arrangements for the speech in which he announced his succession to Karume. But once the succession had been announced, there followed a large number of arrests, mostly in the islands but including some on the mainland. Those detained were largely former members of *Umma*

---

80. Accounts vary as to Karume's last words. It is suggested that he tried in vain to reason with Hamoud, and, more certainly, that his last word was a cry to the Prophet Mohammed.

including Babu himself who was arrested on the mainland. Others arrested were Colonel Mafoudh, despite his orderly control of the succession, Khamis Abdulla Ameir of the original Z.R.C., Ali Sultan Issa, S.A.-R.M. Kwacha, Tahir Adnan and Ahmed Badawi Qullatein. But although the former *Umma* group was blamed, it does seem that Hamoud acted alone except for two or three friends.

At the funeral the large crowds were noticeably quiet. One or two journalists believed that they detected suppressed relief, but while fear of Karume was without doubt one ingredient of popular feeling, respect, pride and some measure of veneration were also present. The mixture of awe and relief was such as had been experienced after the death of Stalin.

Conclusion

The death of Karume marks the end of the first post-Revolution era in Zanzibar, an era of upheaval, confusion and bloodshed. But despite many alarmist reports published in the Western press during the Karume period, the islands did not become another Cuba in the Indian Ocean. At no time was there a massive Communist military concentration or base, and there were no rocket installations of any kind, Soviet or Chinese. No Soviet or Chinese military units were ever based on the islands, and even at the respective peaks of their influence it is doubtful whether the total number of Soviet or Chinese military instructors ever exceeded a hundred from each nation. Although he was impressed by some aspects of Communism, Karume never became a Communist. Typical of his attitude towards ideologies was his simultaneous closure in April 1966 of the libraries of both the United States and East Germany, and the prohibition of films from either country. The Soviets became disillusioned by him and he is accorded only a passing mention, in the context of his murder, in the Great Soviet Encyclopaedia. On the other hand, Zanzibar became a very influential base for radical revolutionary — frequently Marxist-Leninist — ideas. These ideas could take a limited military form: Russian- and Chinese-trained Zanzibaris were in their turn to train Frelimo and other Southern African insurgency groups; many Frelimo men were themselves trained by Chinese instructors at a special centre on Pemba. From Pemba too was launched the revolutionary coup which overthrew the Mancham government in the Seychelles. Zanzibar developed a revolutionary style and tradition of which it was proud.

But the greatest impact of these ideas, with the widest significance for Africa and the world, was on mainland Tanzania. The impact was threefold. First, President Nyerere was left with what he saw as a warning; if social change were not accelerated and if necessary brought in by an imposed discipline, disorder and bloodshed would result. Secondly, the balance of mainland politics was altered after the Union by the addition of the Zanzibaris, led in particular by Babu but also by Kassim Hanga, most of whom formed a powerful reinforcement for the smaller group of mainland radicals. The Chinese dimension in Tanzanian affairs originated in Zanzibar with Babu and the *Umma* group. It could be said, metaphorically, that the foundations of the Tan-Zam Railway, between the Zambian Copperbelt and Dar es Salaam, were laid in the streets of Zanzibar City early in 1964. In Tanzania's internal policies, then, the Arusha Declaration of 1967 and its subsequent implementation should be seen not so much as a radical move to the left, but as an attempt by Nyerere, in an entirely new political environment with entirely new forces at work, still to plot some form of middle course. Lastly, in Tanzania's foreign policy, the inclusion of the islands within the Union has left Tanzania with an interventionist interest in the affairs of the Indian Ocean — in particular over questions such as those of the Seychelles and the Comores — in some contrast to the attitudes of Kenya.

The major failures of the Karume regime were only too obvious, and the new Zanzibar administration under Aboud Jumbe, appointed as First Vice President of the Union by President Nyerere, proceeded quickly to try and ameliorate some of the rigours of Karume's policies. Certain food imports were permitted and foreign exchange was released to allow the purchase of materials needed for development work, of medicines and of other urgent requirements.

A more liberal political atmosphere soon became evident. The A.S.P. returned to internal consultation and democratic processes, friction with the mainland was carefully reduced, and political and military links were strengthened. The culmination of this turning back towards Africa trend was to lie in the formal merger of the islands' A.S.P. with the mainland's T.A.N.U. party in 1977, to form the new Party of the Revolution, *Chama cha Mapinduzi*, and in subsequent elections at which voters could choose between two or more C.C.M. candidates.

But despite the *rapprochement* with Dar es Salaam, the individuality of Zanzibar remained. Islamic studies in Koran schools and in the state's schools, an Islamic Institute for the training of teachers and, perhaps most remarkable of all in view of the past, the teaching of Arabic in schools all came to distinguish the islands from the mainland. This marked revival of interest in Islam, some lingering remnants of the Nasserite tradition, and ideas complementary to the 'Indian Ocean Socialism' of the Seychelles and the new Mauritian radicalism, were to represent the non-African strands of Zanzibar's cultures and roots in the 1970s. This trend saw expression in the 1979 constitution for the islands, in which full local autonomy was entrenched.

The islands of Zanzibar and Pemba, then, have an importance in East Africa out of proportion to their size or population. The islands are the meeting-place in the Indian Ocean of the Arab and the African worlds. In this role of entry-port they have attracted the interest and intervention of other countries on several occasions, of which the Revolution in 1964 is unlikely to prove the last. But the interventions and immigrations have left their different marks on the islands' politics; these in turn can produce internal eruptions with implications for the internal politics of the neighbouring mainland. Abeid Karume was the product of such an upheaval. By his limited perceptions and with his equally limited abilities, the storm could be ridden out only by exercises of authority in an almost Stalinist style. Although born of two mainland African parents, he may be given the credit for a patriotism, often grim, generally misguided in practice, but always Zanzibari. The quest for a Zanzibar identity, embracing all the islands' inhabitants and cultures, remains for succeeding generations to resolve.

BROADCASTS BY JOHN OKELLO,
13 AND 14 JANUARY 1964

13 January

The Government is now run by us, the Army. It is up to every citizen, black, brown or white, to obey orders. Should you be stubborn and disobey orders, I will take measures 88 times stronger than at present.

Everyone must lay down his weapons, come out and stand by the side of the road, hands up, and as soon as he sees a military vehicle, stop it; he will be picked up by the Army to whom he will tell where his weapon is. If anyone fails to comply with this order and locks himself in a house, as others have already done — there are 200 or 400 of these — I have no alternative but to use heavy arms. We, the Army, have the strength of 99,099,000 [metaphor for boundless strength]. The Government which was brought to an end the day before yesterday was a Government of hypocrites and robbers, cursed and wicked people who do not respect humanity. We are a people who protect God's human beings, animals and other creatures.

14 January

(i) Vagabonds in the house of Hilali Kihanga in Dole are trying to harm innocent people with their firearms. I want Hilali to hang himself. He must first kill all his children by slashing them. I have no mercy. I, the Field Marshal, want to destroy that place completely. I am coming with my heavy arms.

I have arms which can completely destroy Zanzibar and Pemba. I can use these arms without regret. I do not want any captives. I have no alternative but to use my forces against any person who fails to comply with my previous orders.

(ii) Here is the Field Marshal of Zanzibar and Pemba. When I say anything I neither intend it as a threat; nor do I hesitate to take action. I am thinking of going to Mtendeni to destroy it if the people there do not obey orders. After 40 minutes I am coming to finish you off, especially the Comorians. I will pass through the place in my car flying my own pennant. I want to see all the men, women and children bow their heads to the ground with their arms folded. If they fail to do this at Mtendeni, I will destroy all the houses.

To all Arab youths living in Malindi; I will pass through Malindi armed with weapons of which I alone know. I want to see everyone stripped to his underpants and lying down. I want to hear them singing: 'Mr Abeid Karume, father of the Africans. God bless him in his task and that of the Field Marshal.'

(iii) The M.P. of Pemba of the hypocritical party which formed the Government that I did not recognize whose name is Umari Hamadi must go to the police by himself and his sentence will be execution — just as the sentence on Rashid Hamadi in Dole will be execution with no right of appeal. Salim of Kengeja will also be executed. If he likes he can execute himself. I will execute him in public by a firing squad or burn him with oil. The acts these persons committed have been discovered and we have C.I.D. evidence against them. Before Rashid Hamadi is arrested and before the time for his death he should expose all Ali Muhsin's lies. In any case he will die.

The broadcasts invariably contained and repeated strict instructions that Europeans were not to be attacked.

BIBLIOGRAPHICAL NOTE

The three volumes of the *Oxford History of East Africa*, of which the last volume was completed in 1973 and contains material published to that year, offer an almost complete bibliography of material in the English language; some Swahili material is also included. Since 1973 only three books in English have been published. The most important of these is Norman R. Bennett's scholarly *A History of the Arab State of Zanzibar* (Studies in African History 16, London, 1978), but E.B. Martin's *Zanzibar Tradition and Revolution*, (London, 1978) and *A Small Book on Zanzibar* by a Swedish-based group, Abdulaziz Y. Lodhi, Annette Rydstrom, Gunnar Rydstrom and Benkt Oberg (Stockholm, 1979), both make interesting descriptive reading. The paucity of books, in comparison with the numbers published about politics and development on the mainland, is an indication of the difficulties encountered by scholars.

The Library of Congress in Washington has published a small documentary bibliographical booklet, *Zanzibar's Afro-Shirazi Party 1957–1977* (Maktaba Afrikana Series, 1978), which lists A.S.P. policy statements, speeches by leading figures and party pamphlets; also listed are a number of articles in periodicals and scholarly journals that refer to the A.S.P. This booklet notes the language in which the material is written, and where copies may be found. Included in this booklet, and perhaps of particular interest, are the following:

Afro-Shirazi, chama cha ukombozi, Zanzibar, 1974. *The Afro-Shirazi Party Revolution, 1964–74*. Zanzibar, 1974. Allison B. Herrick, *Area Handbook for Tanzania*, Washington, 1968. R. Lemarchand, 'Revolutionary Phenomena in Stratified Societies: Rwanda and Zanzibar', *Civilisations*, v, no.1, 1968. Mosare, Johannes, 'Background to the revolution in Zanzibar', in I.N. Kimambo and A.J. Temu, *A History of Tanzania*, Nairobi, 1969. Mwanjisi, R.K., *Abeid Amani Karume*, Nairobi, 1976. G.W. Triplett, 'Zanzibar: The Politics of Revolutionary Inequality', *The Journal of Modern African Studies*, ix, no. 4, 1971.

The student of Zanzibar history will, however, quickly become aware of the narrow limitations of documents, either colonial or post-Revolution. Documents — at least any papers to which an historian is likely to have access for some considerable time — are unlikely to contain either full or accurate information on most of the major events and questions in a territory such as Zanzibar in the period 1964–72, in which politics and political rhetoric exclude almost all else. Further serious research must take the form of interviewing and analysis.

INDEX

Abdulla, Muhammed, Z.R.C. member, 54n. 91-2
Abdulla, Rashid, Minister, 129
Abdulla, Sultan Seyyid, 43, 46
Abeid el Haj, Muhammed, government officer, 89
Adnan, Tahir, government officer, 138, 153
African Association, formation, 16-18; during 1948 General Strike, 32
African nationalism, birth of, 6; early forms, 16-18; post-1945, 22; in 1961, 44; in 1963, 47-9
African Wharfage Company (Zanzibar), in 1948 General Strike, 27-34
Afro-Shirazi Party, 42; in 1961 elections, 44-5; in 1963 election, 47-9; Okello's membership, 52-8; position at independence, 58-62, 65-8; in the Revolution's early days, 71, 75, 78, 83-6; to departure of Okello, 86-94; further rivalries within, 94-102; in events prior to Union, 111-5; in Karume era, 118, 120, 121, 128-9, 142-5; at death of Karume, 151-5
Afro-Shirazi Party Youth League, 54, 55, 78, 92n, 107, 120, 152
Afro-Shirazi Party Women's Union (*Umoja wa Wanawake*), 120, 142
Afro-Shirazi Union, 41
Agricultural and Allied Workers Union, 42, 92n
agriculture, 2, 3; in colonial period, 7, 9, 18, 20, 21, 42; at independence, 58-9, 66; Z.R.C. proposals for, 79, 100-1; in Karume era, 134-42; *see also* cloves and clovegrowing; copra
Alawi, Yahya, government officer, 22

Aley, Juma, Minister, 62n, 63, 75, 125n
Algeria, 70
Ali, Muhsin bin, Z.R.C. member, 91, 129
All Zanzibar Journalists Organisation, 60
Ameir, Hamid Ali, Z.R.C. member, 54n, 91, 123-4
Ameir, Khamis Abdulla, Z.R.C. member, 59, 91-2, 153
Anton, police inspector, 73
Arab Association, in 1948 General Strike, 32; post-1945, 38-9; exile of president, 123
Arab nationalism, post-1945, 22; in 1950s, 38-40; in 1961, 44; radical form in *Umma* Party, 46; *see also* Zanzibar National Party
Argwings-Kodhek, C., Kenya politician, 50
Arusha Declaration, 133n, 154
Asian community, 2; in colonial era, 5, 7, 15-16, 18, 23, 48; attacks on during Revolution, 74, 80-1, 110; in Karume era, 121-4, 140-2, 143

Babu, Abdulrahman Muhammad, Z.R.C. member, early career 45-6; at independence 59-62, 66; in the Revolution, 75, 77-9; on return to Zanzibar, 82-94; rivalries with other Z.R.C. members, 94-102; during quest for recognition, 102-9; immediately prior to Union, 111-5; in Karume era, 132n, 133n, 138, 141, 152
Bakari, Seif, later Col., Z.R.C. member 54, 72, 77, 91, 112, 119, 152
Barnabas, Herbert, 32, 41
Barwani, Ali Muhsin, *see* Muhsin, Ali